ENTERTAINMENT NATION

ENTERTAINMENT NATION

HOW MUSIC, TELEVISION, FILM, SPORTS, AND THEATER SHAPED THE UNITED STATES

Edited by
KENNETH COHEN AND JOHN W. TROUTMAN

Foreword by
KAREEM ABDUL-JABBAR

Director's Note by
ANTHEA M. HARTIG

Principal Photography by
JACLYN NASH

In Association with the National Museum of American History

Smithsonian Books
Washington, DC

CONTENTS

WHAT WE TALK ABOUT WHEN WE TALK ABOUT POP CULTURE

KAREEM ABDUL-JABBAR

"Nobody puts Baby in a corner."
"It ain't over till it's over."
"You're gonna need a bigger boat."

These quotes originated in the delicious ether of popular culture, but they have since evolved into familiar phrases used to express common struggles in our daily lives. Younger people using these phrases may not even know where they came from, but they intuitively know what they mean.

"Nobody puts Baby in a corner" started with *Dirty Dancing*, but now it's used anytime someone feels they are being trapped by people in authority. Baseball manager Yogi Berra coined the phrase "It ain't over till it's over," and today anyone facing a tough challenge quotes it to conjure up the grit they need to keep going. "You're gonna need a bigger boat," from *Jaws*, is uttered whenever someone confronts a formidable obstacle for which they feel ill-equipped—even though it is rarely a murderous great white shark.

Pop culture isn't just a simple entertainment to distract us from the daily dark of existence; it's a vibrant language that articulates our shared hopes, shared joys, and shared pain. Its effectiveness is that it expresses these thoughts and emotions through images, stories, music, athletics, and dance—languages of sound, sight,

and movement that transcend mere words. The edgy joke on *The Conners* about the perils of struggling to pay a house mortgage can be understood by billions. John Coltrane blowing sax on "Giant Steps" lifts the spirits whether you're from Harlem or Hong Kong. Watching the battle-ravaged thirty-two-year-old 4–1 underdog Muhammad Ali defeat the undefeated twenty-five-year-old behemoth George Foreman had the world on its feet cheering for the unrealistic hope in underdogs everywhere.

Sometimes the power of pop culture comes not just from the work itself, but from the communal, tribal rite of sharing the experience with others. We are moved not just by the performance but by watching it with others who are also being moved. The crowd amplifies our emotion, and as a result we feel more than we would alone. Sitting in a crowded theater as others gasp, laugh, and cry imprints the art more indelibly on our beings. These experiences emphasize that we are not alone in our struggles or successes.

Even when we experience pop culture alone, our response is heightened by the knowledge that others are also experiencing it. There's a palpable excitement in anticipating talking to others about the game, the show, the song. Water-cooler conversations about basketball or the Real Housewives or Batman aren't just idle chatter—they're people bonding, sharing opinions and passions in

a nonjudgmental situation where arguments are as quickly forgiven and forgotten as last year's *People*'s Sexiest Man issue.

For decades the world population has shared international megahit movies (*Avatar*), musicals (*Cats*), books (*Harry Potter*), and music (*Thriller*). This has given the world a communal culture that exists alongside our unique ethnic or national cultures. This communal culture tears down the Babel tower of language because a person can travel around the world and find pop culture they have in common with people who don't dress, eat, talk, or look like them. The world has been Netflixed—sharing shows from multiple countries—and as a result we are all closer without having compromised our precious individual heritages.

The pop-culture works that engage us are many and varied, flowing swiftly through society like floodwaters carrying the flotsam of a submerged city: album covers, pictures on the wall, books, video games. Eventually what doesn't resound becomes waterlogged and sinks to the bottom, while what remains afloat are the works of substance, the works that resonate with what it means to be human.

Like reading scattered runes, the future of a society can often be foreseen by examining what its members embrace as part of their culture. It reflects their values, their fears, their strengths, and their weaknesses. Pop culture doesn't just reveal the campy

zeitgeist of instant gratification, the fluff of cotton candy that disappears the moment it enters the mouth and leaves nothing behind but useless calories and a sweet chemical aftertaste. Instead, pop culture is also a motivator for social and political change. Graffiti, street art, memes, TikTok skits, comic books, YouTube performances, and more have the ability to instantaneously reach millions to highlight social injustices and mobilize those millions to act for change. Outrage ignites change when it is fueled by the art of pop culture.

Pop culture gives a voice to those whom traditional gatekeepers have silenced. When we see more of the marginalized—experience their art, hear their songs, see them on stage—we are quicker to welcome them into society and merge their culture with ours. Pop culture sets society's course by proclaiming what kind of people we want to be—and legislators and politicians scramble to catch up.

What is it we see when we look at Captain America's shield or Mia Hamm's Olympic jersey or John Coltrane's saxophone or Mister Rogers's sweater? We see icons of one person's accomplishment but also of humanity's achievement. More important, we see the striving of people to express their common need in a language anyone can understand.

We see "the stuff that dreams are made of." (Look it up.)

LET US ENTERTAIN YOU

ANTHEA M. HARTIG

It could be a song. One that strikes something in you, compelling you to listen repeatedly, memorizing the words so you can sing along and hear it fully realized inside your head. Takes me back to Simon and Garfunkel's *Bridge over Troubled Water*, that seminal album my older cousins dug and thus I did too.

Or a certain movie or episode of your favorite television show, in which you see yourself or your people, learn history, or see the future. For me it was watching *Little House on the Prairie*, after reading a book a day in fourth grade from the boxed set I had received for Christmas. Or as a college senior devouring the dark dystopia of Margaret Atwood's *The Handmaid's Tale*.

Recall the first time you saw a live performance and felt the energy of combined athleticism and artistry—maybe your first basketball or baseball game or soccer match. I remember the excitement of seeing on television, along with 90 million other viewers worldwide, Billie Jean King defeat the chauvinist Bobby Riggs in the so-called Battle of the Sexes tennis match.

The soundtracks of our lives, images of our shared past, cringeworthy celebrations of expansionism or upholding of racist and sexist stereotypes, moments of unparalleled human creativity, virtuosity, and athletic achievement—all of these roll up into the power and complexity of American cultural production and the global reach of US entertainment.

Now, over a decade in the making, we are thrilled to present *Entertainment Nation / Nación del Espectáculo*—one of the most ambitious projects the Smithsonian's National Museum of American History has ever planned and delivered. We have never built a major exhibition dedicated to entertainment, a dynamic installation that will run for twenty years with objects continually rotated into display. The reach of *Entertainment Nation / Nación del Espectáculo* will extend poignantly here in this volume and beyond the museum's walls to digital and live programming, educational curriculum, a full online exhibition available to all—and moreover into more conversations. I am eternally grateful to the curatorial, editorial, design, production, education, communications, operations, and fundraising teams at the museum and to our donors and supporters who made this project possible.

With its remarkable collections, revealing entertainment's embeddedness in virtually every corner of American life, the National Museum of American History can share the multifaceted narratives of this weave of cultural production and related evolving technologies like no other museum in the world. These objects, stories, and intersections come alive in the exhibition, as well as in this remarkable catalog, contextualized by brilliant and perceptive authors and framed by the fine editing and broad contextualizing of curators John W. Troutman and Kenneth Cohen.

The National Museum of American History began taking popular culture seriously in the 1970s and has wrestled ever since with the inherent rigidity and stresses of scholarly institutions collecting popular artifacts. The collection now spans centuries

and genres, and it is a humbling honor to steward Paul Simon's guitar, Billie Jean King's dress from that gendered match, the Handmaid's costume worn by actress Elizabeth Moss, Ella Fitzgerald's archive, and items from BLM protests that shook the world in summer 2020, including Bubba Wallace's shirt.

This exhibition and book show that the strength of American entertainment lies in the diversity of its voices, rich complexities of its creations, struggles it embodies, and injustices it exposes. It articulates and demonstrates our deepest challenges, and illuminates and sets forth our highest ideals—and also reveals that which we fear discussing or remembering.

For more than 150 years, US entertainment in its broadest definition has been the stage where barriers have been broken, stereotypes reinforced or challenged, and our uneven and paradoxical journey as a democratic republic both reflected and shaped—and most certainly shared. Such places and spaces have allowed for personal, private, and communal expression and inclusion while also serving as arenas for fights and activism for representation. At a time in the nation's trajectory marked by disruption, crises, change, and uncertainty, this work inspires us to uphold and defend the American experiment and to move a nation forward—ideally not backward. And with its mission to use history to empower people to create a more just and compassionate future, the museum is poised to help us all better understand the power of entertainment as a force for change—and how we choose to use it as such.

ENTERTAINMENT: A CONVERSATION STARTER

KENNETH COHEN AND
JOHN W. TROUTMAN

On May 15, 1862, in the midst of the Civil War, a brass band celebrated the opening of the new Union Base-Ball Grounds in Brooklyn, New York, by making an overt political statement: they played "The Star-Spangled Banner." The song would not become the official national anthem for another seventy years, but its celebration of the US flag made it a popular tune during the fight against the Confederacy and a pointed selection for christening a baseball park named for the Union.

Despite today's calls to "keep politics out" of sports and entertainment, the history of playing "The Star-Spangled Banner" at sporting events reveals how entertainment, sports, and politics are inextricably linked in US history. Following its charged introduction in 1862, the song was played only periodically at baseball games until a moving performance during game 1 of the 1918 World Series in Chicago. It was a turbulent moment: as a flu pandemic raged alongside World War I, Chicago's Federal Court House building was bombed the day before the game, allegedly by antiwar activists who had seen nearly one hundred of their fellow protesters sentenced to prison the previous week. As a result, according to the *New York Times*, "the mind of the baseball fan was on the war," which explained both the remarkably small and quiet crowd and why a US Navy band's playing of "The Star-Spangled Banner" during the seventh-inning stretch grew into a spontaneous all-stadium chorus that "marked the highest point of the day's enthusiasm." Fans who might have come to the ballpark to escape their worries were roused and rallied by music that inspired a political expression of patriotism in reaction to recent events.

"The Star-Spangled Banner" has been played at every World Series game since then. In 1931, it became the national anthem. During World War II, it became customary to play it before all regular-season games. While the anthem's history at sporting events has turned on efforts to rally the home front during wartime, its almost-daily performance in the 1950s and 1960s turned it into a rite so mundane that the nationalism it generated became widely viewed as apolitical. Then, before game 5 of the 1968 World Series, as the country was embroiled in conflict over the Vietnam War and shocked by the assassinations of Martin Luther King Jr. and Robert F. Kennedy, José Feliciano played an innovative, soulful, and searching rendition of the anthem. Steeped in blues and folk music traditions, and played on a guitar built by an immigrant family from Mexico, Feliciano's performance provoked an emotional response. The *Los Angeles Times* reported that NBC "received a rash of calls from irate viewers." One spectator in the stadium called it "a disgrace, an insult" and said he'd "write my senator about it." Feliciano was surprised. "I just do my thing, what I feel," he said. "I love this country very much." Despite the outrage of some listeners, his version struck a chord with many others: it was the first performance of the national anthem to break into the pop charts.

Feliciano's performance was eclipsed by another appearance of the anthem in the national discourse eleven days later, when the US sprinters Tommie Smith and John Carlos raised their black-gloved fists in protest against civil and human rights violations during their medal ceremony at the Olympic Games in Mexico City. Since then, other athletes have provoked debate by breaking convention during the playing of "The Star-Spangled Banner"—though Feliciano paved the way for broader acceptance of personal interpretations from musicians like Jimi Hendrix, Whitney Houston, and Lady Gaga. Yet, in all these cases, too, the song has mobilized people, either for or against the meaning of its public performance. The debate is not about whether the national anthem should be political. It's about which side of the political conversation you are on.

Through the incomparable collections of the Smithsonian Institution, *Entertainment Nation* considers the ways popular entertainment and sport have animated this conversation. While we savor our personal and often highly emotional experiences with music, sports, stage, and screen, the examples in this book illustrate how popular entertainment also reflects and contributes to collective discussion of the events and issues of the day. Even

those who see commercial entertainment as offering a break from grim reality acknowledge that it is inescapably tied to the real world. "The world is a challenging and serious place," one would-be entertainment escapist told the *Washington Post* in 2017, "but you have things you like that can help you navigate it." In other words, the entertainments we love offer less of a break from reality than a road map of it, helping each generation explore the pressing questions of their time.

Just as important, entertainment provides venues—physical and virtual—where people meet and engage each other, so nobody has to make this journey alone. The centrality of this convening power of entertainment is indicated every time musicians, actors, and athletes express the hope that their performance will "start a conversation." In 1985, the country singer Willie Nelson saw that the efforts of his small circle of friends to advocate for policies to assist family farms would go nowhere if all they did was "sit around and talk to farmers and each other." He planned the first Farm Aid concert as part of a strategy to "talk to everyone else," and that conversation continues today through the panels and advocacy planning that are part of the event. Similarly, quarterback Colin Kaepernick protested

↘ Concerto Candelas Guitar, custom built for José Feliciano and used to play the national anthem at game 5 of the 1968 World Series.

↓ Program for the first Farm Aid concert in September 1985, with a design reminiscent of earlier farmer's almanacs.

↑ Actors Laura Dern, Nicole Kidman, Zoë Kravitz, Reese Witherspoon, and Shailene Woodley of *Big Little Lies* in the press room at the 75th Annual Golden Globe Awards, Beverly Hills, California, January 7, 2018.

↖ Gown worn by Zoë Kravitz at the 2018 Golden Globe Awards, later auctioned to support the Time's Up Legal Defense Fund, which helps survivors of sexual violence seek justice.

racial injustice by taking a knee during the national anthem before NFL games in 2016 in the hope that this gesture would spark "the real conversations that are uncomfortable for a lot of people" but are necessary "to really effect change." When actor Debra Messing explained why she and many other stars wore black gowns to declare "Time's Up" on discrimination and sexual harassment at the Golden Globe Awards in 2018, she said, "We want people to start having this conversation that women are just as valuable as men." Of course, entertainment can spark conversations on important issues regardless of the performers' intent, and sometimes over their vociferous objections. But debate only underscores entertainment's enduring function in drawing together Americans from all walks of life to navigate their world in conversation with one another.

Entertainment Nation reveals how, for at least the past 150 years, commercial entertainment has shaped the United States by fostering conversations about significant national issues. Based on the long-term exhibition of the same name at the Smithsonian's National Museum of American History, this catalog couples stunning photography of beloved artifacts in the national collection with surprising insights that expose the interrelated relevance of music, sports, television, theater, and film in American life—showing that our personal pop culture preferences connect us to ongoing discussions about the past, present, and future of the country.

LEARNING TO LISTEN

The urge to reject or downplay the cultural and political relevance of entertainment is as old as entertainment itself. In fact, the Smithsonian has long been a public forum for such arguments. A brief history of that contention helps to explain the scope of the collections in this catalog, and what is at stake in admitting or denying the power of entertainment to convene important discussions about the state of the nation.

For most of its first century, the Smithsonian ignored popular entertainment. From its founding in 1846, and the opening of its original National Museum in 1881, the Smithsonian focused on amassing collections that traced the evolution of technology and people, as defined by its early staff. The collection of entertainment artifacts concentrated on examples from western Europe. Horns, violins, harpsichords, and pianos dominated the musical instrument holdings. The early sports collections documented the expansion of middle-class leisure and recreation in the industrializing United States, as exemplified by mass-produced figure skates, roller skates, and tennis rackets. The Smithsonian's earliest theater costumes were contributions to a "Period Costume Exhibit" in 1914, in which the gown worn by Charlotte Cushman in the role of Queen Katherine in Shakespeare's *Henry VIII* in the mid-nineteenth century was displayed as if it were a historically accurate representation of sixteenth-century regal garb. Meanwhile, objects such as musical instruments used by nonwhite peoples were typically exhibited in ways that affirmed the racial hierarchies underlying the "science" the curators then subscribed to.

These collections were presented as evidence of "progress" over time, with the latest Western technologies unquestioningly

situated as the most "advanced" examples. This effort, as described in 1881 by the assistant director of the Smithsonian's National Museum, "to present all peoples, civilized and savage" in a way that "should illustrate human culture and industry in all their phases," was political. It was white supremacist. But people who marginalize or reject voices and accomplishments different from their own often fail to recognize that subjugation as a political act.

Just as early Smithsonian curators shaped and interpreted their entertainment collections to uphold racial and cultural hierarchies, they ignored the political implications of popular entertainment as a form of "low" culture not worthy of the institution's attention beyond its place in the evolution of technology. This catalog offers dozens of examples of important social and political statements made through entertainment by a diverse array of Americans in the nineteenth and twentieth centuries. Yet it was only in the 1970s, in the wake of the civil rights movement and Vietnam War protests, that a new generation of Smithsonian curators began to appreciate, collect, and interpret artifacts attesting to the power of entertainment in people's everyday lives. By then, most of the entertainment collections had moved from the original National Museum to the Museum of History and Technology (later renamed the National Museum of American History), which opened in 1964. The new approach met with objections from senior historians like Merle Curti at Columbia University, who thought "the emphasis on sports and the popular arts may downgrade the contributions of hard work, and especially 'high culture.'"

It was bad enough, in these critics' eyes, that the Smithsonian was condescending to collect Judy Garland's ruby slippers from the filming of *The Wizard of Oz*, or sheet music written by Irving Berlin, or the figure skates worn by early Olympic champion Sonja Henie. When curators started to collect objects representing contemporary pop culture, the gloves really came off. A gift from the boxing champion Muhammad Ali in 1976 drew ire from veterans' groups and conservative Texas Senator John P. Tower because of Ali's activism and his refusal to fight in Vietnam. Two years later, curators explained the acquisition of two upholstered chairs from the set of the controversial sitcom *All in the Family* as an effort to share how "producer Norman Lear made conflicts and wounds in American life the targets of the show's biting comedy," in contrast to past shows "portraying happy families living in a world without social strife." But letters poured in from people furious at the Smithsonian for celebrating a show they saw as "a monument to bigotry, slobbishness, and a sneer at all decent American values." Significantly, these indignant reactions were not dismissive of entertainment's power to start a conversation. They were arguments over whether the museum was on the right or the wrong side of it.

For others, the expansion of the entertainment collections signaled an ignoble drift away from the presidents, generals, and inventors they wanted the museum to lionize. As one Louisiana resident wrote in 1986, "Now that you have the musical horn of that distinguished American Dizzy Gillespie to go with Archie Bunker's chair, surely you must desire the jock strap worn by John C. Hicks. As a museum, you have succeeded in giving s—— a bad name." A Washington newspaper columnist responded similarly after Fred Rogers, the host of *Mister Rogers' Neighborhood*, donated one of the iconic red sweaters he wore on the set. The writer mockingly requested a ceremony at the museum where he could donate something equivalent, "a pair of dirty white shoes that I picked up some years ago in search of comfort."

These complaints, as well as the handful of letters praising the museum's "commendable" incorporation of entertainment and suggesting other items to add to the collection, demonstrate the ongoing debate in the United States about the value of popular culture and entertainment. As *Entertainment Nation* shows, some people have wrung their hands over the influence of performers playing to the masses since at least the mid-1800s, when P. T. Barnum organized tours for Jenny Lind and Charles Stratton (known as Tom Thumb). These critiques have generally argued that such performers and genres are unimportant because they don't represent the allegedly more refined and uplifting tastes of powerful elites—or that they might encourage cultural and even political revolt by eroding reverence for "high culture." In either case, those who dismiss or condemn the relevance of entertainment often overlook the politics embedded in their own undemocratic position. One *Smithsonian* magazine subscriber jokingly bemoaned that the acquisition of a jacket worn by Henry Winkler in the role of Arthur Fonzarelli on *Happy Days* ruined his strategy of "putting the magazines on my coffee table with a studied casualness so that visitors to my home will see them and be quietly impressed with my taste, my culture, my appreciation for the finer things." The Smithsonian could no longer help maintain his efforts to claim status with the Fonz in the building.

Despite such objections, two key developments fostered further collecting and consideration of commercial entertainment by the Smithsonian. The first was the rise of the academic study of popular culture in the late 1960s. Well-researched scholarship on popular entertainment provided intellectual support for the new curators' approach, ironically combating elitism with the gravitas of peer-reviewed professorial arguments. At the same time, popular demand for entertainment artifacts began to grow. In 1970, MGM auctioned over 350,000 props, costumes, and other items from old movies (after years of just throwing things away), and the sale triggered a collecting boom. This trend was also fueled by a rise in nostalgia amid the disillusionment that spread as a result of an economic recession, Watergate, and foreign policy failures during the 1970s. While nostalgic collectors drove up prices and competition for the museum's acquisitions, they also explain why the debate over this collecting that raged in print and letters did not play out in the museum's galleries. Instead, when the first major display of the pop culture entertainment collections went up as part of the museum's bicentennial exhibit in 1976, reports documented "the popularity of the entertainment and sports artifacts."

Then came *M*A*S*H*. In 1983, the museum staged *Binding Up the Wounds*, an exhibit exploring one of the longest-running television shows in US history. It drew so many visitors that the museum had to deploy timed tickets for the first time. The *New York Times* led a parade of positive reviews, approving how the exhibit combined artifacts from the show with points about "not just the American experience in the 1950's in Korea, the setting of *M*A*S*H*, but also the social issues facing the United States in the 1970's, when the series was made, issues that include feminism, racism, alcoholism and antiwar activism."

Driven by both popular interest and a critical approach, the museum continued to stage exhibits featuring specific iterations of commercial entertainment, including Negro League baseball, Hollywood, *Sesame Street*, and the electric guitar. Today, its collections and research embrace the manifold cultural traditions and social perspectives that make American entertainment such a globally compelling conversation starter. *Entertainment Nation* builds on this past, as the Smithsonian's first long-term exhibit and catalog to consider how commercial entertainment genres have worked together across time, to provide a medium for the dialogues that have shaped American history.

HAVING A SAY

This catalog explores not only the ways in which American popular entertainment has generated conversation about politics and society but also what has and has not changed about those conversations and how we participate in them. Juxtaposing artifacts used by performers and audiences in different eras and genres of entertainment points to connections and continuities that have been overlooked in the past, as well as notable distinctions and changes in the content and process by which people join in the discussion. This catalog represents an effort to address popular entertainment as a whole. Museums and scholars have typically focused on a specific genre or period, or a single show or event. Recognizing commercial popular entertainment as an integrated ecosystem makes the scale and scope of its relevance harder to ignore. There is a reason photographer Annie Leibovitz thought the "perfect backdrop" to the album cover for Cyndi Lauper's *She's So Unusual* was a sign for a wax statue of Puerto Rican baseball Hall of Famer Roberto Clemente.

An activist who fought segregation and insisted on the media using his Spanish name (rather than "Bobby"), Clemente was also a humanitarian who died in a plane crash delivering food and supplies to Nicaraguans hit by an earthquake in 1972. He would likely have sympathized with Lauper's view of the album's hit song, "Girls Just Want to Have Fun," as a feminist anthem that would do political work under the cover of a catchy dance tune: "It'll be something that will bring us all together and wake us up," Lauper said. "It would be a movement right under all the oppressors'

↑ Album cover for *She's So Unusual*, photographed by Annie Leibovitz in front of a Coney Island Wax Museum advertising a lifelike model of Roberto Clemente.

→ Dress worn by Cyndi Lauper on the cover of her 1983 debut album, *She's So Unusual*.

← Woody Guthrie playing guitar during World War II. He pasted slogans on his instruments to underscore the messages of his songs.

↙ President Barack Obama looks at a jersey worn by Jackie Robinson as he tours the National Baseball Hall of Fame and Museum in Cooperstown, New York, May 22, 2014.

noses, and no one would know about it until there was nothing they could do to stop it."

During World War II, folk musician Woody Guthrie famously adorned his guitar with the slogan "This Machine Kills Fascists." American media discussed Joe Louis's fists in the same way during the run-up to his fights with Nazi Germany's champion, Max Schmeling. But entertainment's pervasive role in mobilizing political conversations is accurately rendered only when we take into account all the other ways entertainment has been used to fight for freedom, equality, and dignity. *Entertainment Nation* is filled with artifacts that reflect these struggles, which were sometimes overt and sometimes more subtle, from props and costumes used in *M*A*S*H*, *Roots*, and *The Smothers Brothers Comedy Hour* to the tennis rackets wielded by Althea Gibson and Billie Jean King. This catalog also reaches further back in time to demonstrate that entertainment has long fueled discussions about inclusion and justice—from Jackie Robinson's ending the segregation of major league baseball in 1947 to the pathbreaking Afro-Cuban singer Graciela, whose performances led to greater integration of New York nightclubs in the early 1940s, to the African American musicians who played the first industrially produced banjos a century before that. Even in the 1820s and 1830s, the power of sport to epitomize the promise of American democracy explains why Americans started to call elections "races."

Of course, entertainment has been used to foment repression and bigotry as well as to inspire democratic change. Early film could promote empathy by helping viewers imagine themselves in someone else's shoes, but it also perpetuated racist stereotypes

↓ Political cartoon depicting the 1836 presidential election as a horse race, with candidates' faces pasted onto the horses' heads and symbols of their strongest supporters riding them.

POLITICAL RACE COURSE - UNION TRACK - FALL RACES 1836

Nº 1. Old Tippecanoe . Nº 2. The Kinderhook Poney . Nº 3. Tennessee White .
Nº 4 Black Dan of Massachusetts

NOT. COOL.

GO TRIBE!

← Graphic comparing Native American sports mascots to other forms of minstrelsy. It was designed by Aaron Sechrist for a symposium on sports mascots held at the Smithsonian's National Museum of the American Indian, 2013.

that arose from minstrelsy, whether blackface or the lesser-known but equally dehumanizing yellow-face (East Asian) and brown-face (Latin American), and the red-face that spawned numerous Native American sports team mascots. P. T. Barnum's circus acts encouraged debate about whether the nation was a virtuous republic or an evil empire, but both positions were rooted in a belief in white supremacy. Well into the twenty-first century, the movie hero on the white horse was almost always a white man. Persistent efforts by diverse communities have only just started to change this approach to casting.

Many other entertainments are hotly debated because they offer mixed messages or because their meanings have shifted over time. Lance Armstrong's bicycle from the 2000 Tour de France signaled his accomplishments as a cancer survivor until 2013, when he admitted to doping. The legacies of *Sex and the City*, with its narrative framed by newspaper columns crafted on an Apple PowerBook now in the Smithsonian collection, include its destigmatizing of women's sexual desires, although its focus on white heterosexual women limited its impact. These examples, like others in the catalog, shows us the unsettled and ongoing nature of the conversations that popular entertainment provokes.

The cunning power of entertainment lies in its invitation to makers and audiences to have a say, under the cover of "leisure" and the pursuit of enjoyment. Although artists and athletes may craft works or perform with a specific intent, their work can generate diverse, unpredictable, and moving responses, and this interaction can influence people's thinking about important issues precisely because it merges politics with pleasure. If popular entertainment is a forum in which performers and audiences use their skills and their voices to explicitly or implicitly advocate on the issues of the day, this catalog considers who has held the microphone and who has had to shout to participate. Its focus on entertainment's connection to struggles for freedom and equality

means it does not shy away from calling out performances and audiences that have supported oppression—or unabashedly siding with those who have fought against it.

Recognizing the power of entertainment requires examining not only the messages it conveys but also how people have used it to communicate. Each chapter of this catalog illustrates a specific tension that structures our meaningful engagement with entertainment. The first chapter, "Harmony and Discord," addresses the tension between unity and division that is inherent in almost every conversation, simply by virtue of the fact that there are two or more sides in the discussion. Chapter 2, "Signal and Noise," introduces the strategies and technologies that entertainers use to reach audiences and invite conversation. "Comedy and Tragedy" explores how entertainments sway audiences by appealing to emotions rather than explicitly stating a position. Chapter 4, "Gaining and Losing Ground," highlights artifacts that detail the twisted trajectories of conversations over time, as audiences and performers oscillate between success and failure in their effort to make a point and realize their goals. The final chapter, "Heroes and Villains," looks at how some individual performers come to transcend a single issue and generate broader conversations about values, including what is right and good, and what is wrong and evil.

Precisely because these artifacts tell us so much about the conversations between the people who made and enjoyed (or reviled) them, almost every object in this catalog could have been placed into any of the chapters. Our choices reflect an effort to illuminate surprising facets of famous items, to amplify unexpected resonances between objects, and to highlight angles that deserve more public attention. But considering how an artifact might fit into other chapters, or comparing items across the chapters, only underscores entertainment's power to engage us in something bigger than ourselves.

← Sarah Jessica Parker as Carrie Bradshaw in season 5 of *Sex and the City*.

↓ Apple PowerBook used by the character Carrie Bradshaw to record her commentaries in the Emmy Award–winning cable television comedy *Sex and the City*, which ran from 1998 to 2004.

HARMONY AND DISCORD

HARMONY AND DISCORD

The concepts of harmony and discord refer to the relationships between simultaneously sounded musical notes. However, they can also refer to the relationships between beautifully wrought affirmations of community and humanity on one hand, and sharp reflections of social and political turmoil on the other. Along these lines, entertainments can express resilience, genius, and optimism, as well as traumatic upheaval, oppression, and loss—sometimes in the same moment or refrain. The uneasy coexistence of harmony and discord is an important way entertainment speaks to us, signaling its potential to shape and complicate our perceptions of the world through exposure to others' perspectives.

Using entertainment to reach people in this way dates back to the founding of the nation. During and immediately after the American Revolution, entertainers rallied supporters across boundaries of wealth, age, gender, and race in theaters and at horse races—places where entire communities gathered. Everyone in the audience could sing "Hail Columbia," an early version of the national anthem, before seeing a play that challenged Thomas Jefferson's foreign policy (*The Embargo*, opened in 1808) or mocked Alexander Hamilton's extramarital affair (*The Apology*, 1798). At racecourses, shared interest in the graceful power of thoroughbreds was channeled by the partisan and ideological messages of horses named "Democrat" and "Anti-Democrat," or, in 1832, "Andrew Jackson" and "Nullifier," amid South Carolina's efforts to nullify, or ignore, federal import tax legislation supported by President Andrew Jackson. Indeed, the importance of racetracks in shaping political debate was one reason why Americans started calling elections "races" in this period. Early political cartoons reflecting this metaphor suggest that despite racial and gendered restrictions on citizenship and voting rights in the period, hardly anyone was excluded from these trackside conversations. In the racetrack's accessible environment of democratic debate, black jockeys and fans saw an opportunity to resist subjugation and surveillance by meeting, speaking their minds, and otherwise "taking freedoms," as white commentators frequently phrased it.

Generations of Americans have followed suit, using entertainment as a platform for bringing people together to discuss contentious topics, to press for civil rights, and to draw attention to other critical issues facing the country. Such initiatives have not always succeeded in realizing change, of course, and entertainment has also been used to foment bigotry. The artifacts presented in this chapter document efforts in both directions, illustrating the range of messages that entertainers have tailored to resonate with people through harmony and discord.

IBTIHAJ MUHAMMAD HIJAB, FENCING MASK, AND LAMÉ JACKET

At the Summer Olympic Games in Rio de Janeiro in 2016, New Jersey–born Ibtihaj Muhammad became the first American to compete while wearing hijab. Winning a bronze medal in the team sabre competition while proudly wearing the stars and stripes on her fencing mask, Muhammad advocated for a more inclusive nation at a time when presidential candidate Donald Trump was calling for stricter travel bans from predominantly Muslim countries, recalling the targeting of Muslim Americans after the 9/11 attacks in 2001. "Anyone who has paid attention to the news at all would realize the importance of having a Muslim woman on Team USA," Muhammad said at the time, recognizing how competing as an Olympian situated her in the conversation about what it means to be American—an issue that often lies at the heart of entertainment's persistent interplay of harmony and discord.

↑ Ibtihaj Muhammad celebrates a point over Ekaterina Dyachenko in the women's sabre team semifinals at the Rio Olympics, August 13, 2016.

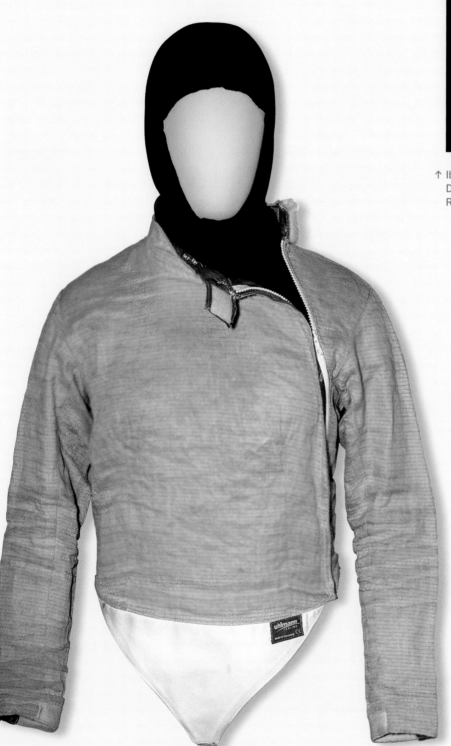

ALOHA BLUES

Sometimes the harmony and discord expressed in music represent not simply a relationship between simultaneously sounded notes, but also a tension between social or political turmoil on the one hand and striking affirmations of resilience on the other. Such was the case in the formation of two distinctive guitar-based traditions: the modern Hawaiian mele, or songs, that originated just before and after the 1893 overthrow of the Hawaiian Kingdom, and the blues-steeped songster tradition developed by Southern Black musicians in the Jim Crow era. Both were full of spellbinding compositions and innovative techniques, and both became global sensations by the mid-twentieth century. Though originating in different regions and from different peoples, these musical traditions share the remarkable capacity to represent, often in

→ Sheet music for "Aloha ʻOe," composed by Queen Liliʻuokalani, 1912.

the same breath, extraordinary expressions of community belonging, innovation, love, and genius, as well as traumatic upheaval, migration, and loss.

When Liliʻuokalani, the future queen of the Hawaiian Kingdom, composed "Aloha ʻOe" in 1878, she wrote it as an account of a farewell romantic embrace. Liliʻuokalani was well versed in composition, having written several mele that quickly became popular throughout the islands. Her songs combined traditional Hawaiian poetics with compositional and melodic strategies adopted from the Western hymns that Christian missionaries from the United States and elsewhere introduced to the islands upon their arrival in the early 1800s. The composition of "Aloha ʻOe" thus reflected the royal family's openness to foreign influences—but only to the degree that such influences reinforced Hawaiian values of solidarity and resolve.

"Aloha ʻOe," having emerged from harmonious and multitudinous origins, gained powerful new resonances from the discord that was soon to come. In 1893, Queen Liliʻuokalani was overthrown by a group of US-backed oligarchs, many of whom were descended from those earlier missionaries. When Liliʻuokalani resisted the takeover, she was imprisoned in her palace, where she continued to compose mele—this time to rally her people. Meanwhile, "Aloha ʻOe" was culturally appropriated by those who overthrew her kingdom. The sheet music in our Smithsonian collections was marketed by Tin Pan Alley publishing companies as a romantic advertisement for the spoils of the overthrow. Intended for sale thousands of miles away from the Islands for performance in family parlors, it signaled the availability of an exotic and newly annexed US territory and its cultural traditions. For generations of Native Hawaiians, however, performances of "Aloha ʻOe" grew to signify not simply a love song but a tribute to the last recognized monarch of the Hawaiian Kingdom and a celebration of independence and cultural integrity.

Other objects in the Smithsonian collection also represent this tension in modern Hawaiian music. The composer Sam K. Nainoa was best known for his close association with the Hawaiian "steel" guitar. Born in the 1870s and growing up on Oʻahu, Nainoa and his cousin Joseph Kekuku spent hours playing music together. Nainoa originally focused on the violin, Kekuku on the guitar. Both instruments had been introduced to the Hawaiian Islands decades earlier by missionaries and sailors. But Kekuku crafted picks to pluck the guitar strings, and with his other hand he began running a steel bar over them, creating a glissando effect that could mimic the falsetto singing that had become popular in Hawaiian music. After refining this new technique, he introduced his friends to the kīkā kila, or Hawaiian steel guitar, and the technique quickly spread across the archipelago. After the overthrow brought disenfranchisement and limited economic choices for Native Hawaiians, many began traveling the world, performing mele with lyrics in Hawaiian—a language banned in Hawaiian schools. These performances on Hawaiian guitars influenced the sounds of vernacular music throughout the world.

In the United States, they transformed guitar playing in blues, country, and other genres.

Sam Nainoa became an adept steel player, and his Rickenbacker Hawaiian guitar—one of the earliest mass-produced electric guitars, manufactured circa 1934–1936—was donated to the Smithsonian by his descendants. Its simple, sleek, and refined design belies its cultural load. In Nainoa's day, the sound of the Hawaiian steel guitar could function at once to kindle non-Hawaiians' fantasies about an exotic island paradise and to fortify the resolve of modern Hawaiians to celebrate their home and cultural traditions.

In the US South, a guitar culture developed by Black songsters was equally transformative and complex. At the vanguard of this culture were, once again, two guitarists who honed their musical skills as children. John Smith Hurt, later known professionally as Mississippi John Hurt, was raised in Avalon, Mississippi. At around age nine he began teaching himself to play guitar, inspired by the music of the community frolics, picnics, and congregations of his youth—from ragtime, blues, ballads, and fiddle numbers to pop tunes and gospel music. Meanwhile, near Chapel Hill, North Carolina, another nine-year-old, Elizabeth Nevills Cotten, was developing a technique on the banjo that involved playing a right-handed instrument upside down. When she transferred the technique to the guitar soon after, the result was mesmerizing: her index finger plucked the bass notes as her thumb plucked a melody line. Her finger wore deep grooves into the wooden body of her 1950 Martin 000-18 guitar, shown on page 27, which she played for the last four decades of her life. These two musicians grew up eight hundred miles apart and were unknown to each other until they met and performed at festivals in the 1960s. However, when we hear the recordings of Hurt and Cotten today, side by side, their unique repertoires and techniques produce astonishing harmony.

Like Kekuku and Nainoa in Hawaiʻi, Hurt and Cotten grew up in contexts where overt resistance to authority could have dangerous consequences. Among the inequities and horrors of the Jim Crow South, both were forced to quit school by the fifth grade to support their families. Cotten worked as a domestic for white households. Hurt sometimes lined track for the local railroad, but mostly, like other members of his family, he worked full time as a farmer. He spent nearly his entire life in Avalon, just seven miles from where Emmett Till was murdered: in fact, one of the local white fiddlers who often demanded Hurt play with him testified as a character witness on behalf of one of Till's killers. In one sense, Hurt and Cotten challenged these insufferable and dehumanizing conditions by crafting an expressive musical body of work founded upon a rich tradition of regional Black songcraft, harmonized through their innovative guitar techniques, that celebrated Black Southerners' dignity and verve.

The power of their craft slowly became venerated within the white-controlled music industry, but tensions remained. In the 1940s, Cotten was working as a domestic for the family of the

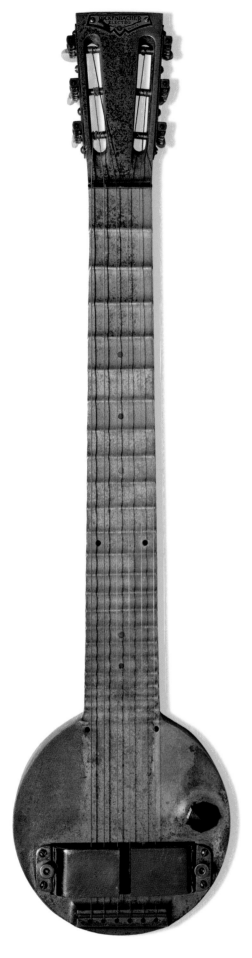

← Sam Nainoa's Rickenbacker A-22 "frying pan" Electro Steel guitar, ca. 1934–36.

→ Sam Nainoa with an acoustic guitar, finger picks, and a steel bar, demonstrating the Hawaiian steel guitar technique, date unknown.

ethnomusicologist Charles Seeger. They "discovered" her talents one day when she picked up their guitar. After Peggy Seeger shared one of Cotten's compositions, "Freight Train," in her folk music circles, two British songwriters copyrighted it as their own and landed a hit. (The copyright was eventually restored to Cotten.) Hurt made a few records in 1928, just before the Great Depression gutted the music industry. He continued to work on farms and play for local gatherings over the decades. He was "discovered" in 1963 when white folklorists, having heard some of his earlier records, tracked him down in Avalon. He vaulted to fame that year at the Newport Folk Festival, where he performed songs such as "See See Rider," "Frankie," and "Candy Man"—now considered Hurt classics—while playing this borrowed 1890s Emory guitar. Even the musicians' later acclaim, however, was tempered: the mostly white, urban progressive audience of the folk revival movement celebrated both Hurt and Cotten as "authentic" and "traditional" rather than recognizing their modern innovations. Nevertheless, Cotten recorded immensely influential albums and toured until she passed away in 1987. Hurt quickly recorded a slate of brilliant live and studio albums but was exploited by white managers. He died in 1966.

The musical lives of Lili'uokalani, Kekuku, and Nainoa, like those of Hurt and Cotten, were awash in waves of harmony and discord. While liberatory in some contexts and confining in others, their music—like the other examples in this chapter that explore festering inequities alongside calls for national unity and justice—reveal the day-to-day tactics and tensions as well as the far-reaching implications of entertainment as a site of deeply important personal, cultural, and political work.

John Troutman

↖ Photograph of Mississippi John Hurt by Charmian Reading, showing Hurt performing in 1966 for the March against Fear, a 220-mile march from Memphis, Tennessee, to Jackson, Mississippi.

↑ Elizabeth Cotten, photographed by John Cohen in Washington, DC, ca. 1960.

↑ Emory guitar played by Mississippi John Hurt at the 1963 Newport Folk Festival.

→ Elizabeth Cotten's 1950 Martin 000-18 guitar.

This bass drum, measuring nearly two and a half feet tall, was used in the Fillmore Citrus Association Mexican Band, which performed during the 1920s and 1930s throughout Ventura County in Southern California. Its sponsor, the Fillmore Citrus Association, was a consortium of growers that lobbied for the citrus fruit industry. The association also managed the processing and distribution of citrus produce, helped set prices and wages, managed housing for laborers, and organized public activities like fairs.

During the 1930s, citrus was Southern California's principal agricultural product, and growers established company housing in order to recruit and retain workers with families. As a result, large barrios, or *colonias*, of Mexican and Mexican American families developed around the citrus farms. In towns like Fillmore, employers controlled just about everything, from labor to housing, shopping, and even leisure pursuits like the band and local baseball teams.

These leisure activities were part of the growers' efforts to retain their labor force, and they helped build community between older and newer workers. It is telling, however, that the Fillmore Association also sponsored an American Band, separate from its Mexican Band, as part of an unsuccessful effort to discourage workers from organizing unions across racial and ethnic lines. The Fillmore Citrus Association Mexican Band performed in Anglo, Mexican, and cross-cultural settings, including parades, concerts, birthday parties, and other community celebrations like the Fourth of July and Dieciseis de Septiembre (September 16, Mexican Independence Day). In 1931, the band's renown earned it a two-hour concert broadcast on a major Los Angeles radio station.

The musical style of this type of *orquesta* was similar to that of the brass bands of the eastern United States. But in addition to waltzes, polkas, tangos, and foxtrots, it played familiar Mexican numbers. The band director, Manuel Lucero, had studied music formally in Mexico. Scholars have noted that the interest in *orquesta* reflected a desire among Mexican migrants and their US-born children for social mobility. In the context of an agricultural labor market that was tightly controlled and often ignored workers' rights and limited their opportunities, the band's genre and style became a vehicle for gaining status by blending American and Mexican culture. Members hoped their performances across the region would identify them as modern culture brokers—a role that could open up networks leading to greater economic prosperity. So, while the association believed the band was good for morale and promoted "Americanization," to band members, instruments like this drum represented the pursuit of upward mobility through a selective adoption of elements of US culture that kept them in control of their Mexican identity.

L. Stephen Velasquez

← Fillmore Citrus Association Mexican Band bass drum, made by the Ludwig Drum Company, ca. 1920–40.

→ Fillmore Citrus Association Mexican Band, 1931.

↑ John Philip Sousa, photographed by Brown Brothers Studio, ca. 1925.

→ JOHN PHILIP SOUSA BATON

From 1892 until 1932, John Philip Sousa's wildly popular military-style Sousa Band toured the United States and inspired the rise of marching bands across the country. By composing and conducting performances of patriotic music—such as his famous anthem "The Stars and Stripes Forever"—Sousa promoted a unifying sense of nationalism. The son of immigrants, Sousa received this conductor's baton as a gift. It features an American eagle atop a crest referencing his family's Iberian roots.

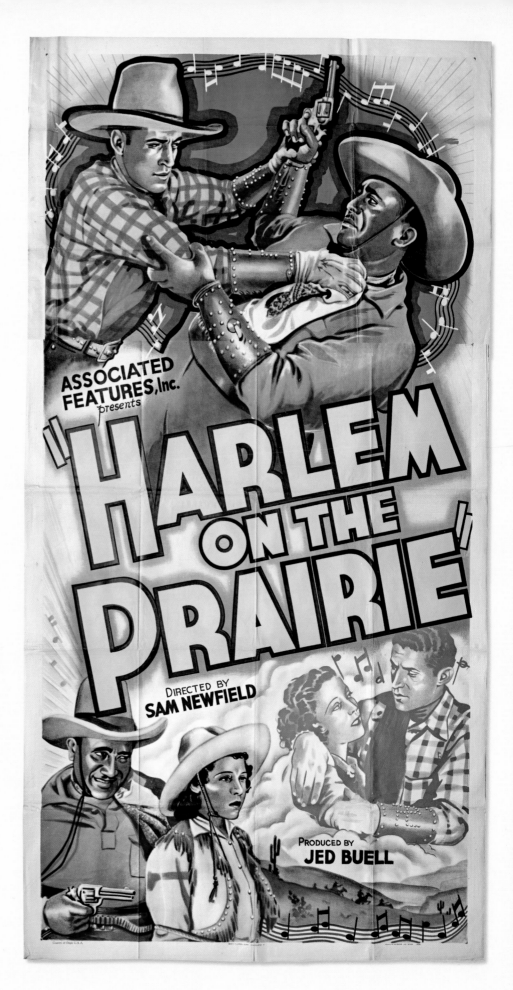

→ **HARLEM ON THE PRAIRIE MOVIE POSTER**

Harlem on the Prairie was the first all-Black western of the talkies era. Starring jazz musician Herb Jeffries as a singing cowboy, the 1937 film made an African American character the hero on the white horse. Unlike other movies aimed at Black audiences, Jeffries's film played in mixed-race, segregated theaters too. In these venues, Black moviegoers were restricted to the balconies, but, along with white audiences, they glimpsed the powerful possibilities of centering African American characters.

GENDER BENDING ON THE AMERICAN STAGE

Following a long theatrical tradition, gender impersonation was a popular feature of the American stage in the nineteenth and early twentieth centuries. During this era of vast social change, women entered the workplace in greater numbers, sought educational opportunities, and agitated for political rights. Emerging ideas about sexuality spurred debates and anxieties about gendered behavior and sexual transgression. These issues inevitably entered the theatrical world, too.

Among the actors acclaimed for their gender-bending roles were Charlotte Cushman, Bessie Bonehill, and Julian Eltinge. Although subversive in some ways, they did not perform drag routines as we know them today, celebrating a queer and transgender sensibility: they more often reinforced conventional gender ideals and sexual norms. Born several generations apart, all three of these performers achieved international stardom by managing to inhabit cross-dressing roles without unsettling their audiences.

Charlotte Cushman was among the leading dramatic performers of the mid-nineteenth century, celebrated in the United States and internationally. From her debut as Lady Macbeth in 1836, she played a variety of strong women characters. However, she was best known for her "breeches roles," including such traditionally

↑ Lithograph showing Charlotte Cushman as Romeo and her sister Susan Cushman as Juliet, London, 1846.

← Ceramic statuette based on the Cushman lithograph, produced in Staffordshire, England, ca. 1852.

male parts as Romeo and Hamlet. In 1857, Cushman defied convention by playing Cardinal Wolsey in Shakespeare's *Henry VIII*, sometimes alternating this role with that of Queen Katherine, the first of Henry's wives. Her costume for the ambitious, scheming churchman—richly embroidered scarlet vestments, cape and train, and biretta—highlighted Wolsey's power and disguised Cushman's female body. Cushman's physicality, intensity, and deep voice enabled her to project a commanding masculine presence on the stage. Although some critics thought her too forceful, most praised her blend of male and female attributes, the "rare union and perfect balance of her passion and intellect."

Offstage, Cushman rejected a womanly appearance and heterosexual relationships. She loved women throughout her life and helped establish an expatriate community of artistic "bachelor women" in Rome in the 1850s. Her private life was no secret, but Cushman managed her public reputation skillfully. At this time, passion between women was widely considered an element of platonic friendship, not yet pathologized as lesbian sexuality, and commentators described Cushman's "strong and generous affections" as evidence of sisterly loyalty.

Such acceptance had waned by the late nineteenth century, when references to "manly" women described them

→ Costume worn by Charlotte Cushman in the role of Cardinal Wolsey in Shakespeare's *Henry VIII*, ca. 1857.

as embodying the movement for women's rights and posing a threat to male power. The new field of sexology redefined same-sex desire as deviant homosexuality, presenting it as an abnormal medical condition and a psychological inversion of biological gender. A woman wearing pants onstage now could be a cause for alarm. Women performers deflected audiences' discomfort through more stylized and fanciful portrayals of men, often in settings of leisure and luxury.

British-born Bessie Bonehill epitomized this shift in her performances as a male impersonator in the 1890s. Singing and dancing in English musical halls and variety shows, Bonehill played comic roles such as newsboys, sailors, and jaunty young men-about-town. When American vaudeville pioneer Tony Pastor brought "Bonnie Bessie" to New York in 1889, she was a sensation. In her hit show, the musical comedy *Playmates*, she starred as a dashing cashier who falls in love with his employer's daughter, and she played six other male roles with flurries of costume changes. One outfit, with frilly lace collar, green velvet jacket, and these matching knickers and raffish hat, worn for her role as a foppish youth, combined the looks of Robin Hood and Little Lord Fauntleroy.

Bonehill confidently navigated the growing public anxieties over gender and sexual nonconformity. Her press notices portrayed her as a devoted wife and mother who lived on a farm and led a blameless life. Like Cushman, whose performances in Civil War sanitary fairs aided Union soldiers, Bonehill enhanced

→ Breeches and cap worn by Bessie Bonehill in *Playmates*, 1894.

← Collectible cabinet card advertising Bessie Bonehill in *Playmates*, 1894–95.

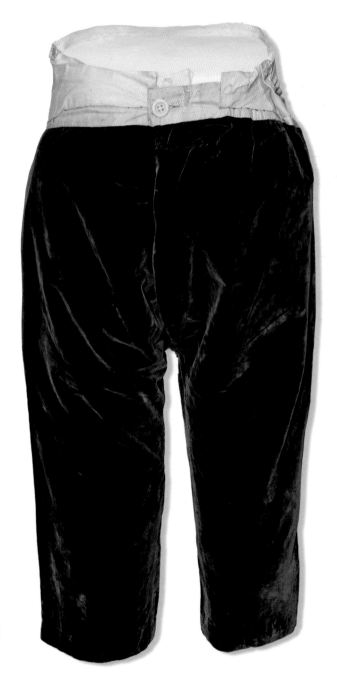

her motherly reputation by supporting worthy causes. Combined with her innocence and boyishness onstage, her characters' racy hints and misbehavior came across as lovable, not immoral. As one critic said, "She looks like a handsome boy and dances like a sprightly girl."

For men impersonating women, the situation was more fraught. Women's cultural and legal advances in the late nineteenth century placed greater pressure on men to display their manliness. Body building, athletics, and scouting were pastimes seen to shore up men's strength as they faced the perceived threats of the women's movement and the growing strains of white-collar work and urban life. Although a "gay world" existed in many cities, and men had played women's roles in theaters for centuries, most men sought to distance themselves from visible displays of effeminacy, on and off the stage.

Still, Julian Eltinge achieved early renown as a female impersonator in vaudeville revues and minstrel shows and eventually graduated to Broadway and film. In *The Fascinating Widow,* a 1910 musical comedy created as a vehicle for his talents, Eltinge made eleven costume changes as a woman. "Ambisextrous," one critic called him, and audiences may have viewed him as transgressive. Yet Eltinge appeared in the guise of affluent white womanhood, the contrived plots turned on heterosexual romance, and women spectators noted that he wore the latest Paris fashions. At the end of each show, Eltinge always took a bow dressed in a man's suit, affirming his masculine identity.

Even more than Cushman and Bonehill, Eltinge cultivated his personal reputation and participated in a burgeoning culture of celebrity and consumption. Playbills and advertising postcards depicted him as both an elegant woman and a well-dressed man. He published *The Julian Eltinge Magazine* as a souvenir program with beauty tips, started his own cosmetics brand, and appeared in corset ads. He "outshines the women at their own game," one magazine declared. Yet his offstage persona was that of a "he-man" who enjoyed boxing, fishing, and smoking cigars. Revealing no sexual intimacy with men or women, he claimed to be devoted solely to his mother.

Over time, Eltinge's body aged and his Gibson Girl style went out of fashion. Although a queer sensibility guided a brief urban "pansy craze" of cross-dressing in the 1920s, social anxieties about homosexuality continued to mount, as police arrested cross-dressers and shuttered same-sex night spots. Gender impersonation persisted, but performers could no longer gain wide popularity from it. Only in the later decades of the twentieth century, when feminist and LGBTQ movements brought sweeping changes to American culture, did such gender-bending move beyond gay parties and drag balls back into the mainstream of entertainment and everyday life.

Kathy Peiss

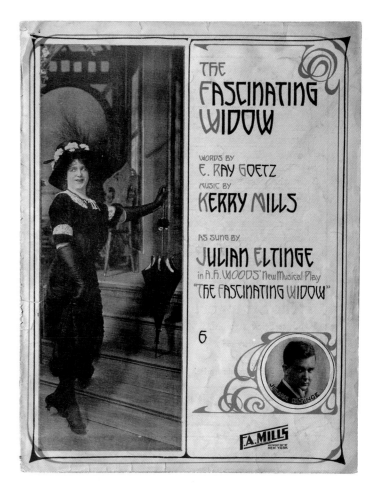

↗ Sheet music and postcard for Julian Eltinge's performance in *The Fascinating Widow*, 1910–11.

JULIAN ELTINGE
In the Fascinating Widow,

← PROMOTIONAL PHOTOGRAPH OF TSIANINA REDFEATHER

After surviving culturally oppressive federal boarding schools for indigenous children as a child in Oklahoma, Muscogee singer Tsianina Redfeather established a successful career performing American Indian–themed semiclassical music on concert stages across the country. Both Native and non-Native audiences thronged to see her. In 1926 she packed the Hollywood Bowl for her performances in *Shanewis*, an opera based on her life. She used her appeal to advocate for voting rights, educational reform, and other issues affecting reservation communities.

→ MISTER ROGERS SWEATER

In every episode of the public television series *Mister Rogers' Neighborhood*, Fred Rogers sang "Won't You Be My Neighbor?" while changing into one of these cardigan sweaters. The gentle and unhurried host revolutionized children's television, speaking directly about self-esteem, feelings, and getting along with others. Rogers believed that thoughtful television programming could aid children's social and emotional development, helping to create a more humane society.

↓ Fred Rogers on the set of his popular children's television show, ca. 1992.

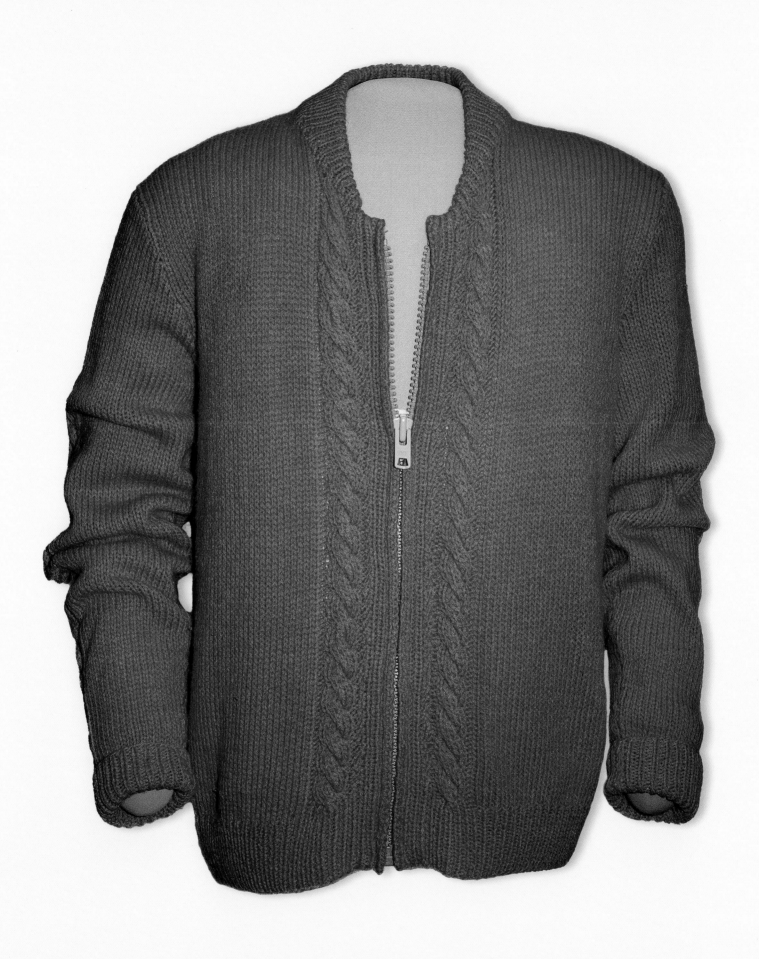

THE UNASSUMING ORIGINS OF POLITICAL SATIRE ON TV

↑ Tom (left) and Dick Smothers pose with a drum featuring the name of their variety show.

Clean-cut folk singers in matching red blazers, Tom and Dick Smothers broke new ground for television comedy with their popular variety show, which aired on CBS from 1967 to 1969. Drawing ideas and talent from the 1960s counterculture, *The Smothers Brothers Comedy Hour* took subversive aim at American politics and got canceled for it, but American television would never be the same. The Smothers Brothers proved that TV comedy could function as a forum just as well as sober reporting and analysis on the nightly news. Its irreverence laid the foundation for later shows such as *Laugh-In, Saturday Night Live, Chappelle's Show*, and *The Daily Show with Jon Stewart*.

In the early 1960s, most working comedians were relatively apolitical and inoffensive, even in the trendy nightclubs of San Francisco and Greenwich Village. Touring these clubs and college campuses, the Smothers Brothers created a humorous folk-music act that was more charming and silly than polemical. Between their performances of traditional songs on Tom's acoustic guitar and Dick's upright bass, the brothers engaged in banter about sibling rivalry with puns and malapropisms that had little more edge than family teasing around the dinner table. When their 1961 debut album *The Smothers Brothers at the Purple Onion* became a surprise success, it spawned a recording career and brought the duo national popularity. They soon appeared on bigger stages and late-night television.

↗ Blazers worn by the Smothers Brothers in the 1988 revival of *The Smothers Brothers Comedy Hour*.

When CBS offered the brothers the chance to host their own variety show, it was half in recognition of their potential and half out of desperation: the "kamikaze hour" time slot they were offered was opposite the NBC ratings juggernaut *Bonanza* on Sunday evenings. With expectations set low but a major network backing them, the brothers assembled a dream team of seasoned television comedy writers and young talent eager to experiment and make their mark. Crafting a new kind of variety show, one that wove together musical performances and skits with absurdist antiestablishment set pieces and mock editorials, made the careers of writers Mason Williams, Pat Paulsen, Rob Reiner, Bob Einstein, and Steve Martin.

The *Comedy Hour* proved a remarkable success, besting *Bonanza* in the ratings to become the most influential television series of the late 1960s. The most surprising aspect of the show's success was its ability to bridge the generation gap. Tom and Dick were far from hippies; their familiar, homespun sensibility and variety-show format were as attractive to older viewers as the cutting-edge skits and exciting guest stars were to youngsters. Nevertheless, the show was packed with winks and nods to contemporary cultural shifts: innuendo-drenched interviews with flower child Goldie O'Keefe (Leigh French); provocative performances by popular musicians like The Who and Jefferson Airplane; jokes referencing the sexual revolution, the Civil Rights Movement, policing, the draft, and the war in Vietnam; and even a tongue-in-cheek presidential campaign waged by the deadpan Paulsen.

But when the *Comedy Hour*'s politics became more explicit in its second season, the show created problems for CBS. The network began cutting left-leaning jokes about abortion, Christianity, and drugs, sketches pillorying prudish network censors, and Pete Seeger's performance of his song "Waist Deep in the Big Muddy"—a thinly veiled critique of President Lyndon B. Johnson's Vietnam policy. LBJ himself called the chair of CBS, William Paley, to complain about the show's treatment of his administration, although he later wrote the Smothers Brothers a remarkable letter praising their satire. Seeger's very appearance on the *Comedy Hour* generated controversy, as it constituted his return to network prime time after seventeen years of being blacklisted for stonewalling the hearings of the anticommunist House Committee on Un-American Activities.

CBS fielded thousands of letters and calls from the show's viewers every week, either decrying or praising its deliberately provocative sketches, gags, and guest appearances. More worrisome for the network, however, was the pushback from affiliate stations across the country. Banding together, they forced the network to begin providing closed-circuit previews of episodes and reserved the right to censor content they deemed offensive to local tastes. This pressure enraged the Smothers Brothers, who reacted by continuing to push the boundaries. By 1969, CBS was looking for reasons to fire them. Mired in conflict over controversial segments, like Harry Belafonte's performance of "Don't Stop the Carnival" accompanying footage of police brutality at the 1968 Democratic Convention in Chicago and David Steinberg's sermonettes mocking organized religion, the Smothers failed to deliver tapes on schedule, giving CBS a justification for canceling their contract.

Though the Smothers Brothers lost their show, their satire won in the end. Within years of their program's demise, equally sharp lampoonery was generating conversation and controversy in shows like *All in the Family*, *M*A*S*H*, and *Saturday Night Live*. Tom Smothers's incredulous observations about the inhumanity and injustice of American society were echoed in Jon Stewart's exasperated monologues on *The Daily Show*. Like Paulsen, Stephen Colbert's alter ego excoriated contemporary politics by delivering absurd, if only slightly exaggerated, editorials straight-faced on *The Colbert Report*. Colbert, too, launched a mock campaign for president in 2008. Despite, or perhaps because of, their matching blazers and haircuts, the Smothers Brothers' greatest contribution to American culture was making room for television comedy to be a little transgressive.

Ryan Lintelman

THE WHITE HOUSE
WASHINGTON

November 9, 1968

Dear Messrs. Smothers:

I am very grateful for your kind and thoughtful letter.

To be genuinely funny at a time when the world is in crisis is a task that would tax the talents of a genius; to be consistently fair when standards of fair play are constantly questioned demands the wisdom of a saint.

It is part of the price of leadership of this great and free nation to be the target of clever satirists. You have given the gift of laughter to our people. May we never grow so somber or self-important that we fail to appreciate the humor in our lives.

If ever an Emmy is awarded for graciousness, I will cast my vote for you.

Sincerely,

[signature: Lyndon B. Johnson]

Messrs. Tom and
Dick Smothers
7800 Beverly Boulevard
Los Angeles, California 90036

← Letter from President Lyndon B. Johnson to Tom and Dick Smothers, 1968.

→ STEPHEN COLBERT JUMPSUIT

Stephen Colbert took the stage at the 2010 Rally to Restore Sanity and/or Fear on the National Mall in Washington, DC, wearing this patriotic jumpsuit inspired by daredevil stuntman Evel Knievel. Colbert and his *Daily Show* foil, Jon Stewart, planned the event to satirize intensifying political polarization and the far-right rallies led by media personalities like Glenn Beck. Colbert rose to fame as the mock-conservative host of *The Colbert Report*, which parodied the paranoia of Beck and other hosts on Fox News.

↑ A digital image on canvas of writer-comedian Stephen Colbert in his guise as the host of the Comedy Central network series *The Colbert Report*.

This neon sign was featured in the opening sequence of NBC's *Late Night with David Letterman*, which aired from 1982 to 1993. Letterman's offbeat, absurd, and irreverent humor made him a Generation X successor to Johnny Carson, even though he famously lost the role of *Tonight Show* host to Jay Leno after Carson's retirement. The style of the neon lettering hinted at Letterman's classic Midwestern charm while signaling a sarcastic commentary on the promotional business of late-night TV—a combination that imbued Letterman's interviews, sketches, and stupid pet tricks with a countercultural edge.

COMMENTARIES BY A DUST BOWL REFUGEE

Woody Guthrie was known for his songwriting, especially "This Land is Your Land," written in 1940. But starting in the 1930s, he wrote other poignant songs, like "Pastures of Plenty" and "Dust Bowl Refugee," that dealt with the plight of migrant workers driven to California from Oklahoma by the Dust Bowl. He also wrote children's songs, like "Riding in My Car," with the help of his daughter Cathy. In all, he is thought to have composed almost a thousand songs, mostly drawn from his own life experiences and from newspaper articles. Of these, he recorded a few hundred, leaving behind many lyrics for which others have composed music.

But Guthrie was much more than a songwriter. He was an artist who worked in many formats and could lace his political commentary into any of them. He wrote three novels, the most famous of which was the autobiographical *Bound for Glory*. In the 1930s, he presented a radio show in California and wrote articles for the communist newspaper *The Daily Worker*. Some of these articles included his own political cartoons. He also made oil paintings, including one portrait of Abraham Lincoln, along with watercolors and pen-and-ink drawings.

Guthrie suffered from Huntington's chorea, a degenerative brain disease that started affecting him during the 1940s. This condition led to great bursts of creativity followed by barren periods. For instance, when Guthrie stopped by the New York office of Moses Asch, who founded Folkways Records, he would sometimes record a few compositions, but he once recorded seventy-five tracks in a single day. In April 1946, he sat in Asch's office turning out dozens of pen-and-ink drawings. This drawing comes from that period.

↑ Woody Guthrie performing at the Shaffer Farm Security Camp in Shaffer, California, 1939.

→ Woody Guthrie, photographed by Sid Grossman, ca. 1946–48.

While the vast majority of his drawings depicted his family life, others, like this one, harkened back to his family's departure from the Dust Bowl town of Pampa, Texas, and his experiences in California. Migrants were told that things were good in California and that they could find work. But in reality, if they were not turned back at the state border (as described in his song "Do-Re-Mi"), most had to settle in squalid labor camps where food was scarce. They faced harassment and persecution from the authorities and vigilante groups. The drawing here speaks to all these dangers.

As Guthrie's disease progressed in the late 1940s and 1950s, his work grew more abstract and simplified. His lyrics became childlike, with run-on, made-up words, and simple, repeating rhymes. Yet his less detailed and more faceless drawings from this period create a sense of anonymity in the figures, inviting us to fill them with portraits of diverse people who continue to experience oppression.

Jeff Place

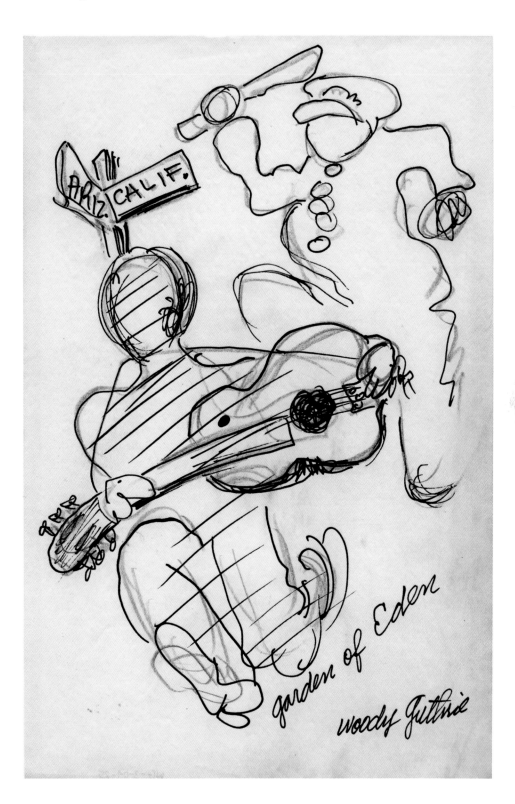

→ Drawing by Woody Guthrie, mocking California's reputation as a "Garden of Eden," depicts a police officer chasing a person with a guitar toward Arizona, 1946.

When the operatic soprano Jenny Lind toured the United States in the 1850s, she sparked a craze dubbed "Lindomania." Crowds unable to get tickets to her concerts sometimes rioted outside the halls where she performed. Some thought that her mass appeal—and the use of her likeness on a flood of consumer merchandise, from sheet music to trivets—diminished the value of her art. Others thought it demonstrated that in a republic, art was for everyone.

→ COSTUME FOR TEVYE FROM *FIDDLER ON THE ROOF*

This costume was worn by actors Harry Goz and Zero Mostel in the role of Tevye, the narrator of *Fiddler on the Roof*. Tevye struggles to respect tradition and accept change as his community faces revolution and anti-Semitism in turn-of-the-century Russia. His mariner's cap embodies this conflict, simultaneously referencing the working-class styles of the period and the adoption of this type of hat by Jewish men whose traditional yarmulkes were banned.

↓ Zero Mostel as Tevye in *Fiddler on the Roof*, ca. 1970.

In her 1939 recording of "Strange Fruit," Billie Holiday hauntingly evoked the image of Black lynching victims as "strange fruit hanging from the poplar trees." The devastating protest anthem raised awareness among white Americans and led more of them to ally with African American activists in support of antilynching and other antiracist causes.

↑ Billie Holiday, photographed by Herman Leonard, ca. 1949.

← *BIRTH OF A NATION* MOVIE PROGRAM

D. W. Griffith's 1915 film *The Birth of a Nation* depicted the aftermath of the Civil War as an epic battle to maintain white supremacy. White actors in blackface portrayed newly free African Americans as treacherous villains, and Ku Klux Klansmen were presented as the film's heroes. Screened by Woodrow Wilson at the White House despite protests and boycotts organized by civil rights activists, the movie fueled the rebirth of the Klan and triggered attacks on Black communities.

↑ INCARCERATION CAMP BASEBALL AND MITT

Players broke in this mitt and baseball at the Gila River incarceration camp in Arizona. There, people imprisoned during World War II simply for having Japanese heritage built a six-thousand-seat stadium, organized teams, and arranged games among themselves as well as with local clubs. As a leading historian of Japanese American baseball, Kerry Yo Nakagawa, put it, baseball was no mere diversion at Gila River but "an important symbol of American brotherhood"—a statement of unity from Americans disowned and incarcerated by their country.

← Fans watching a game at the Manzanar incarceration camp in California, 1943.

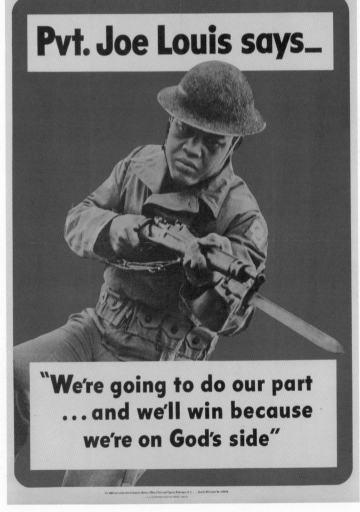

← Poster advertising the Joe Louis–Max Schmeling rematch, 1938.

↓ 1942 US government poster featuring Joe Louis as part of an effort to maintain morale during World War II.

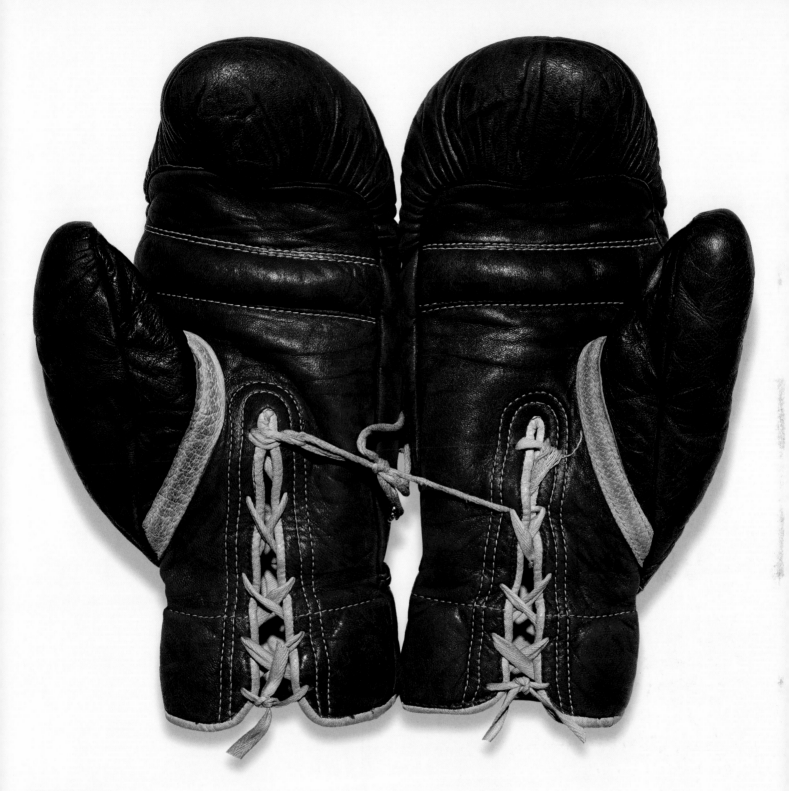

↗ JOE LOUIS GLOVES

Joe Louis wore these gloves during his first fight against
Germany's Max Schmeling in 1936. Although he lost that
bout, he rebounded two years later to knock out Schmeling—
hailed by Hitler as an icon of white supremacy—in the
first round of their rematch. While most of the United States
celebrated that win as a victory for democracy over fascism,
it electrified Black communities with hope for progress
against racism at home. Leaders from Martin Luther King Jr.
to Maya Angelou later described how Joe Louis inspired a
generation of African American activists.

"PROUD TO BE A BLACK AMERICAN"

After the men's two-hundred-meter dash at the 1968 Olympic Games in Mexico City, the three medalists—Tommie Smith and John Carlos of the United States and Peter Norman of Australia—created an iconic moment in sports history. Wearing this warm-up suit, his gold medal around his neck, a black glove on his right hand, a black scarf around his neck, and carrying a box with an olive branch inside, Smith joined Carlos and Norman on the Olympic medal ceremony podium. As "The Star-Spangled Banner" began playing, Smith and Carlos raised their black-gloved fists and bowed their heads in silent defiance of Olympic protocol. Norman stood solemnly beside them, supporting their protest by wearing a badge created by the Olympic Project for Human Rights (OPHR), the organization created in 1967 through which Olympic athletes discussed how to use the platform of the 1968 games to draw attention to racial inequality.

The following day, in a studio interview with the sports announcer Howard Cosell, Smith explained the significance of the protest gestures. Every detail carried a message. The arc formed by the athletes' gloved, upstretched fists symbolized "the power within Black America" and "Black unity." Smith's scarf signified "Blackness," while their black socks, worn without shoes, represented the poverty plaguing Black America. Later, John Carlos mentioned that their bowed heads were a gesture of prayer for Black America. Carlos had also worn beads that symbolized the chains used during slavery, while his unzipped warm-up suit symbolized the casualness with which the US government was moving to end racial discrimination. When Cosell asked Smith if he represented all Black athletes, Smith responded, "I can say I represented Black America." Cosell followed up by asking him if he was "proud to be an American." Smith replied, "I'm proud to be a Black American."

For decades, scholars, pundits, and activists have rightly situated this protest in the context of the civil rights and Black Power movements of the late 1960s. However, it also occurred during the Cold War battle for international influence between the United States and the Soviet Union, which infiltrated most aspects of society, including sports. With their protest, Smith and Carlos violated two long-standing principles of US foreign policy during the Cold War: first, that representatives of the United States should not criticize their country on foreign soil; and second, that if African Americans addressed racial inequality in the United States, their pronouncements had to express faith in the US democratic, capitalist system to solve these problems.

Beginning in the late 1940s, US State Department officials estimated that almost half of the Soviet Union's anti-American

← Tommie Smith (center) and John Carlos (right) raise their fists on the medal podium at the 1968 Summer Olympic Games in Mexico City.

With their protest, Smith and Carlos violated two long-standing principles of US Cold War–era foreign policy: first, that representatives of the United States should not criticize their country on foreign soil; and second, that if African Americans addressed racial inequality in the United States, their pronouncements had to express faith in the US democratic, capitalist system to solve these problems.

propaganda focused on racial discrimination. As independence movements proliferated throughout Africa, Asia, the Middle East, and Latin American during the 1950s and 1960s, the Soviets made effective use of US segregation to gain the allegiance of people of color in nations around the world. In response, the United States seized the passports of Black activists, including W.E.B. Du Bois and Paul Robeson, which effectively prevented them from addressing international audiences, and began a campaign of sending middle-class African Americans abroad to try to position African Americans as the preeminent citizens of the African diaspora rather than as victims of racial discrimination. African American athletes such as Althea Gibson, Jesse Owens, Bill Russell, and Rafer Johnson were prominently featured in these campaigns. This strategy was effective because it suggested that despite racial inequality, some African Americans had achieved the American dream.

Initially, most African Americans were supportive of these campaigns because they seemed to portend a more integrated and fair society. However, by the late 1960s the struggles of the civil rights movement and violent responses to it increasingly called into question these Cold War narratives. The success of middle-class African American athletes patently did not lead to widespread access to better housing, education, or prestigious and well-paying employment. As a result, one unintended consequence of the failed US attempt to use African American athletes as symbols of racial progress was to politicize athletes such as Smith and Carlos, who became committed to pushing for change and staged a powerful counternarrative that night in Mexico City.

Damion Thomas

→ Team USA warm-up suit worn by Tommie Smith at the 1968 Summer Olympic Games in Mexico City, manufactured by Wilson Sporting Goods Co.

↑ Kenneth Guscott (left), Bill Russell (center), and Marvin Gilmore (right) speak at NAACP headquarters on July 8, 1964.

↓ **BASKETBALL AWARDED TO BILL RUSSELL**

Celtics center Bill Russell received this basketball when he became the first NBA player to reach 10,000 rebounds. A statue now stands in Boston honoring the philanthropic contributions of the eleven-time NBA champion and five-time MVP. But in 1972, Russell refused to attend the ceremony retiring his number, citing racist treatment from media and fans. The former player and first African American coach in the NBA has been a lifelong civil rights activist, supporting the nationwide protests staged in 2020 in reaction to the murders of George Floyd and other victims of police brutality by likening them to "the strange and bitter crop of injustices" that Billie Holiday sang about eighty years earlier.

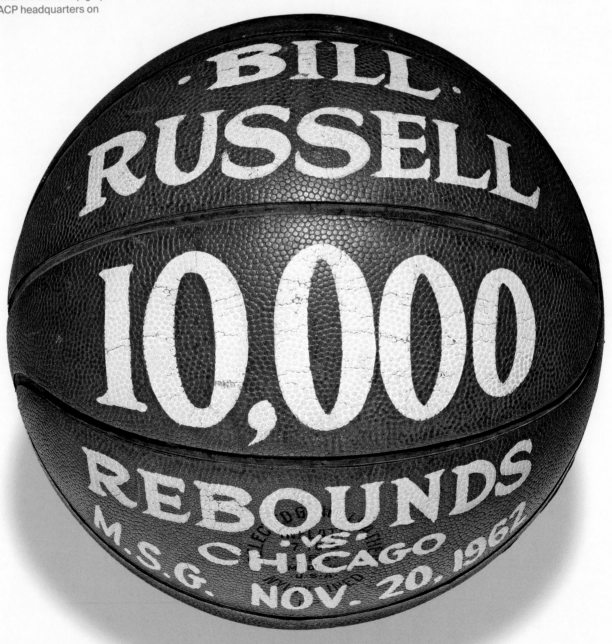

← TATA CEPEDA BOMBA DRESS

Brought to Puerto Rico by enslaved West Africans, bomba is a dance of resistance as much as of joy and liberation. Because the music's rhythmic drumming follows the movements of the dancer, bomba has long been used to communicate defiance that would have been policed if spoken. Margarita "Tata" Cepeda comes from a family steeped in bomba. Her grandmother Caridad Brenes Caballero drew from traditional Afro-Puerto Rican fashions to create this bomba dress, including the use of a pañuelo (headscarf).

THE *BUT* THAT FOLLOWS THE STAR-SPANGLED BANNER

After his debut album Get Lifted *thrust him onto the national scene in 2004, John Legend quickly became one of the most in-demand songwriters and collaborators for ground-shifting music, film, and television. At the same time, his poignant political and cultural commentary on social media and his extensive work on behalf of social justice and philanthropic campaigns has made Legend a significant voice in national conversations. In November 2017, during a wide-ranging interview after he received the Smithsonian's American Ingenuity Award, Legend discussed the American flag as a symbol and a flashpoint for controversy, most recently over NFL quarterback Colin Kaepernick's decision to protest systemic racism by taking a knee during the anthem's performance before games.*

I think these conversations are important, but the song is more of a symbol. . . . I mean, we can get into the literal lyrics of the song— that's one thing—and we can say, "Do these particular lyrics and does this particular song represent the country in the way that we think a song that is supposed to unite us should?" And I think my argument would be that it doesn't. But it is our national anthem. I mean, it is. I've sung it, we've all sung it. And it is a stand-in for another idea, of what it means to be American, or what it means to be patriotic, [or] what it means to support the troops.

← The Star-Spangled Banner, flown over Fort McHenry in Baltimore when it was attacked by British soldiers in 1814 and the inspiration for the national anthem.

And I think when we talk about patriotism and what it means to be American, that's a conversation that we have to explore as well. Because, you know, a lot of times, particularly with Black folks, we've had tension with the idea of loving America. Because we love it in the sense that we were born and raised here, we helped build the country, but America has not been good to Black folks for a long, long time. And so we've always wanted America to actually live up to the ideals that Thomas Jefferson talked about, even as he was sexually assaulting his mistress—who was actually a sex slave. All the ideals discussed by our founders, even in that moment they weren't living up to these ideals.

Black folks have borne a lot of that pain and that struggle from America not living up to its ideals. And so, whenever we think about what these symbols mean—it's like it's hard to even think about American history without thinking about the *but* behind every symbol that we revere. Because you talk about Thomas Jefferson—there's a *but* after him. You talk about the White House—it was built by slaves. You know, there's *buts* after everything for us, and we can't enjoy it in the same way that everybody else can without thinking about the *however,* the *but.*

It's just part of everything, every experience that we have in this country and every conversation about the history of this country. Even looking at [Black] World War II soldiers coming back home, they were fighting for freedom around the world, [they] would come back home and get treated like second-class citizens, and can't drink from the same water fountain, and [their kids] can't go to the same schools as their white counterparts in their hometowns, and they don't get treated with respect when they get back home. So, when folks are talking about respecting the troops, I wonder if they're including the Black veterans when they're talking about that. When they're talking about this country being the greatest country in the world, what does that mean? And are we living up to that? And these are conversations that are not about the national anthem, you know. They're about America, and do we believe in the myth of America, or do we address the fact that all the things that we value and the ideals that we have laid out in our founding documents, all of them came with a *however* for too many people in this country.

John Legend

↑ John Legend performing at the Macy's Fourth of July Fireworks Spectacular, broadcast on July 4, 2020.

→ ROYALTY AGREEMENT FOR GERTRUDE "MA" RAINEY'S "WALKING BLUES"

Blues singer Gertrude "Ma" Rainey toured for two decades before Black talent scout and burgeoning industry mogul J. Mayo "Ink" Williams brought her to the white-owned Paramount Records, where she quickly became a top artist. Williams formed the Chicago Music Publishing Company to purchase the rights to his artists' work in return for royalty payments, as this 1923 contract demonstrates. This arrangement thwarted Paramount's control over Black artists, but Williams's inconsistency in delivering royalties could keep them singing the blues.

ROYALTY AGREEMENT

CHICAGO MUSIC PUBLISHING COMPANY
CHICAGO MUSIC CO.
Music Publishers

Main Offices:
PORT WASHINGTON, WIS.

Chicago Office:
OVERTON BUILDING
South State St.
CHICAGO, ILLINOIS

AGREEMENT made this ....12th.... day of ...December... 192 3 ....between the XHICAGOXXMUSICXXCO.... Chicago Music Publishing

Co. AGENT of the City of Port Washington, Wisconsin hereinafter designated as the "PUBLISHER" and.............
Chicago, Illinois

............GERTRUDE RAINEY & LOVIE AUSTIN...hereinafter designated as the "COMPOSER".

WITNESSETH

1. The COMPOSER hereby sells, assigns, transfers and delivers to the PUBLISHER, its successors and assigns, the original musical composition written and composed by........GERTRUDE RAINEY....................

and bearing the title of........WALKING BLUES..

including the title, words and music thereof, TO HAVE AND TO HOLD, the same absolutely unto the PUBLISHER, its successors and assigns forever, together with all rights therein, or any copyrights now subsisting, for all countries, that the COMPOSER now has or may be entitled to or that he hereafter could or might secure if these presents had not been made, including the publishing rights, the performing rights, the rights to use the same for mechanical reproduction, the right to make, publish and perform any arrangement or adaptation of the same, and all copyrights and the rights to secure copyrights and extensions and renewals of copyrights in the same, or in any arrangements or adaptation thereof.

2. And the COMPOSER hereby convenants, represents and warrants that the composition hereby sold is an original work and that neither said work nor any part thereof, infringes upon the title of or the literary or musical property or the copyright in any other work, and that he is the sole writer and composer and the sole owner thereof, and of all the rights therein, and has not sold, assigned, set over, transferred, hypothecated or mortgaged any right, title or interest in or to the said composition or any part thereof, or any of the rights herein conveyed, and that he has not made or entered into any contract or contracts with any other person, firm or corporation whomsoever, effecting said composition or any right, title or interest therein, or in the copyright thereof, and that no person, firm or corporation other than the COMPOSER has or has had, claims or has claimed any right, title or interest in or to said work or any part thereof or any use thereof or any copyright therein, and that said work has never been published, and that the COMPOSER has full right, power and authority to make this present instrument, sale and transfer.

3. IN CONSIDERATION hereof and in reliance upon the truth of each and every representation by the COMPOSER herein made, the PUBLISHER agrees to pay to the COMPOSER the following royalties, towit:

(a) Two cents (2c) upon each and every complete printed pianoforte copy of the said work sold by the PUBLISHER in the United States and Canada only. It is, however, distinctly agreed and understood that in the event the PUBLISHER sells, assigns, transfers and delivers the musical composition covered by this contract to any other individual, partnership or corporation whomsoever, the COMPOSER agrees to accept as royalties due him one quarter (¼) of the royalties actually received by the publisher.

(b) And the COMPOSER agrees that the PUBLISHER shall be under no obligations to pay any other sum whatsoever except as in this agreement provided that no royalties shall be paid upon the following: complimentary copies; copies sold but not paid for; copies sold and returned to THE PUBLISHER; copies sold or given away as new issues or for advertising purposes; professional copies; copies included in folios or books or published in newspapers, magazines or other periodicals; copies sold in foreign countries or mechanical royalties collected therein; band, orchestra, medley or other arrangements of or containing said work or any part thereof.

THE PUBLISHER will pay to the composer a sum equal to one-fourth of any and all royalties that the PUBLISHER shall actually receive from the use of said musical composition for mechanical reproduction less ten per cent (10%) for cost of collection in the form of all player rolls, records, discs, or other devices for the mechanical reproduction of the musical composition.

← Gertrude "Ma" Rainey with the Wild Cats Jazz Band, ca. 1928.

GLORIA ESTEFAN DRESS AND EMILIO ESTEFAN CONGA

The Estefans—Gloria singing and Emilio on keyboards and congas—had years of success with the Miami Sound Machine, performing and recording in Spanish for Latin American audiences. But when they started producing rhythmic Cuban-inspired pop tunes in English, like the 1987 hit "Rhythm Is Gonna Get You" (the video for which featured Gloria in this costume), their multimillion-selling singles made them the nation's most successful crossover artists. Yet they remained true to what Gloria described as "our responsibility to our people, our culture."

BARACK OBAMA BASKETBALL TOURNAMENT BRACKET

President Barack Obama filled out this NCAA men's basketball tournament bracket for a 2016 ESPN television special, also completing an example for the women's competition. In doing so, he joined tens of millions of Americans from all walks of life who enjoy "March Madness" by attempting to predict the victors of the single-elimination tournaments featuring the nation's best college basketball teams.

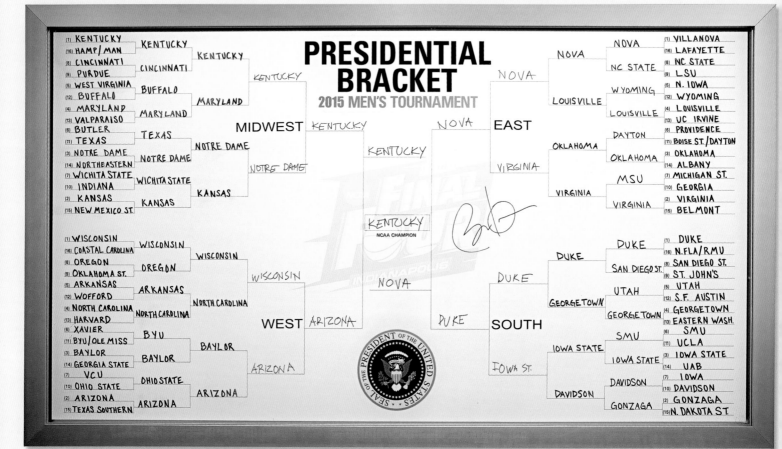

Jersey worn by Bill Baker, skate worn by Buzz Schneider, and stick used by Phil Verchota during the 1980 Winter Olympics in Lake Placid, New York.

JERSEY AND EQUIPMENT FROM THE "MIRACLE ON ICE"

The USA hockey team's stunning 4–3 medal-round upset of the Soviet Union at the 1980 Winter Olympics in Lake Placid, New York, was made even more compelling by ongoing Cold War tensions between the two nations. The young American team's victory over their more experienced rivals, followed by a gold-medal win over Finland two days later, was quickly politicized to boost American confidence amid a flagging economy, the expansion of Soviet influence in Asia and Central America, and the taking of fifty-two Americans as hostages in Iran after the fall of its American-backed regime.

MINNIE FISKE WHEAT DRESS

When actor Minnie Maddern Fiske wore this satin dress in the title role of the 1901 play *Miranda of the Balcony*, she revealed a long-standing tension between Americans' admiration of European culture and their assertion of cultural independence. Embroidered with sequined sheaves of wheat, the iconic dress gave a distinctively American flavor to a play based on a British novel, even though the dress had won a prize at the 1900 Paris World's Fair for its French designer.

↑ Minnie Maddern Fiske, photographed by Otto Sarony, 1907.

↑ JOHN L. SULLIVAN BANNER

Fans in 1882 commissioned this silk banner as a copy of the one that Irish American boxer John L. Sullivan hung in his corner for a title-winning bout in Mississippi earlier that year. Sullivan coupled his Irish patriotism, as represented by the Green Harp flag, with white supremacy, reflected in the placement of the Confederate battle flag in the top left corner of the United States flag. Sullivan's explicit refusal to fight Black challengers established a color line upheld by every white American champion for the next fifty-five years.

"WE JUST HAVE TO COME TOGETHER"

Randy Moss was one of the greatest deep-ball receiving threats in NFL history. He retired in 2013 after a fourteen-year career in which he was a six-time Pro Bowl selection and ultimately ranked second in career touchdowns by a wide receiver. At his 2018 Hall of Fame induction ceremony, he wore this tie, embroidered with the names of thirteen murdered policing victims. The sartorial selection immediately sparked conversation, with Moss explaining that "I've been dealing with racism my whole life. We all know what's going on. By having these names on my tie, in my Hall of Fame ceremony, I wasn't there voicing, but I protested silently." Moss had the tie made by a tailor in Georgia shortly after he learned he had been elected to the Hall of Fame, and he wanted to "say to those families that regardless of right or wrong, their loved ones would not be forgotten, and they would know they're not alone."

Moss has also expressed his respect for police officers by wearing this West Virginia state police cap to events and appearances, including the 2017 Super Bowl and interviews with ESPN and NBC between 2014 and 2018. Moss started wearing the hat in the early 2010s, after he got to know state troopers in the security detail of former West Virginia governor Joe Manchin, with whom Moss frequently attended public events promoting youth programs and charitable causes throughout the state. When a trooper was killed in 2012, Moss told the officers he wanted a hat to "honor your guys."

Moss has observed that "some guys criticize" his connections to police and his support for the Black Lives Matter movement. "I get it from both sides," he said when he donated these materials to the museum. But he also sees himself as uniquely positioned to promote dialogue despite receiving hundreds of hate mail messages after the induction ceremony. He told ESPN that "Sunday night [after the ceremony], I'm driving home, and I get a direct message on my Instagram from an officer telling me, 'Hey, buddy, I disagree with the criminals that you have on your tie.'" Moss responded to the officer, "Yeah, some broke the law, but not all of them." He explained, "'People make mistakes. But you shouldn't lose your life for a lot of the reasons that people have been.' Now, the police officer agreed with me that those people should still be here. He agreed that they shouldn't have lost their lives. That kind of made me feel good. We communicated about it and agreed on something."

Moss himself experienced racially motivated attacks and policing while growing up in Rand, West Virginia, and was charged with misdemeanors for assault and bumping a police car early in his career. He says this history informs his ability to broker productive communication. "I know police have tough jobs. I've honored them for that," he has said. "But I can't ignore the other part of it. There are things that shouldn't be happening. We just have to come together to admit what's going on and try to fix it."

Kenneth Cohen

↑ Randy Moss posing with the bust created to represent him in the Pro Football Hall of Fame, at his 2018 induction ceremony.

GREG GUNN

TAMIR RICE

AKAI GURLEY

PAUL O'NEAL

ERIC GARNER

FREDDIE GRAY

WALTER SCOTT

SANDRA BLAND

AKIEL DENKINS

ALTON STERLING

MICHAEL BROWN

TRAYVON MARTIN

BRENDON GLENN

PHILANDO CASTILE

TERENCE CRUTCHER

↙ Tie worn by Randy Moss at his Pro Football Hall of Fame induction ceremony in 2018, and West Virginia State Police cap worn by Randy Moss, 2014–2018.

THE MEANING OF MAKING
EVERYONE DANCE

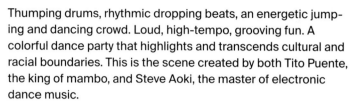

↑ Tito Puente holding his drumsticks in front of a backdrop of singing birds, in a composition crafted in 1984 by the Puerto Rican photographer ADAL.

← Timbales played by Tito Puente at the 1996 Summer Olympics closing ceremonies in Atlanta, Georgia.

Thumping drums, rhythmic dropping beats, an energetic jumping and dancing crowd. Loud, high-tempo, grooving fun. A colorful dance party that highlights and transcends cultural and racial boundaries. This is the scene created by both Tito Puente, the king of mambo, and Steve Aoki, the master of electronic dance music.

Though both are musicians, there are few immediately obvious commonalities between the timbalero and the DJ. But their multicultural backgrounds laid the foundation for soundtracks that created similar experiences for their fans.

Puente was born in 1923 in New York City and raised by Puerto Rican working-class parents in Spanish Harlem. He learned to play multiple instruments at an early age and dropped out of high school to join one of the most influential Latin bands in New York, the Machito Orchestra. During World War II he served in the Pacific theater with the US Navy and played in a jazz band with other sailors. On returning to the United States, he enrolled in the Juilliard School, the famed musical conservatory in New York. His music drew from Cuban and African traditions but often layered them with jazz and other sounds.

Steve Aoki grew up in California during the 1970s and '80s, raised by parents who migrated from Japan in the 1960s. His father started the chain of Benihana Japanese restaurants, and Steve went to college, where he majored in gender studies and sociology. He played in a punk band as a teenager and then created the music label Dim Mak and started working as a DJ while in college.

The tools of their trade in the Smithsonian collection—the timbale drum set Puente played at the closing ceremonies of the 1996 Olympic Games and Aoki's 2010s mixer set—helped these musicians challenge assumptions, culturally and musically. Puente's timbale set is signed in Spanish and English, and decorated with the logo of the Atlanta Games and the 100th anniversary of Olympic Games bringing the world together, just as his beats and rhythms brought spectators and athletes of all nations to their feet and encouraged them to dance together. Similarly, Steve Aoki's mixer and turntables represent a style of music and performance that blends familiar and diverse genres in creative ways, with rising beats and synthetic tones that encourage lively movement. The worlds of sound created by both Puente and Aoki meld multiple musical traditions, temporarily blurring political and social boundaries as they urge a wide range of listeners to move to a complex, shared beat.

This music also shares a common history. At the time of the Atlanta Olympic Games, when Aoki had just graduated high school, the United States was becoming an increasingly diverse and global nation. Drawing on the radical social politics of the

← Steve Aoki performing at the 2021 Electric Zoo festival on Randall's Island in New York City.

↓ Pioneer CDJ-2000 multiformat players and DJM-800 mixer emblazoned with "Dim Mak," the name of Aoki's music label, used by Steve Aoki in the early 2010s.

1960s and '70s, many progressives called for a more inclusive society, and although conservatives argued that a multicultural society would be morally and politically weaker, an explosion of new entertainment media and forms embraced and demonstrated the power of cultural plurality. "Crossover" acts of the 1990s, especially Latin performers, challenged cultural stereotypes. Often termed the "Latin wave," Caribbean and Latin music with English lyrics joined punk and new wave on mainstream pop radio stations, MTV, VH1, and even network television.

At that time, Asian American communities were even less visible in popular culture than they are today, but Aoki found power in the margins. His music infused punk and hardcore styles with an awareness of social justice. Songs like "Equal in the Darkness" exemplify Aoki's belief that "music is a platform to talk about more sophisticated issues in society."

The two performers' backgrounds and interests straddled different worlds, as reflected in their creation of sounds, rhythms, and harmonies that connect people. "When we perform for the audience, we give them good vibrations and happiness. They forget their problems because they see that we're giving it from our hearts," Puente once said about how his music pulled his audiences together. Aoki, too, frames his music as a mode of drawing diverse audiences and individuals into engagement. "I create music to create a conversation," he says. As performers who shaped and were shaped by the opportunity of the 1990s, they created music that testifies to the optimism of that moment as well as to the persistent power of diverse musicians to unite global audiences through innovative cross-cultural rhythms.

L. Stephen Velasquez

SIGNAL AND NOISE

SIGNAL AND NOISE

Entertainment has long offered the opportunity to share and blend ideas from different communities and cultures, reaching across boundaries with fresh performances and new messages through an increasing range of media and platforms. Entertainers such as Awkwafina and Lil Nas X first emerged on YouTube, SoundCloud, Twitter, and TikTok—social media and streaming platforms that enable emerging artists to overcome a lack of industry connections or resources and reach mass audiences. Entertainers on these platforms are known for innovative performances that express their roots, bridge artistic genres, and address pressing issues—from sexism, racism, and homophobia to eating disorders and bullying.

Yet developing stirring and imaginative content isn't always an inclusive or democratic process. The history of entertainment technologies shows that such signals have not always penetrated the dense background noise of conformity. Photography, for instance, emerged about the time of the Civil War and inspired a craze for affordable, collectible lifelike images of celebrities. Around the world, diverse audiences collected photos of performers, often those who shared their political affinities. By the 1950s, however, the rise of television had amplified the noise and reduced the signal. The centralized power of a few national networks, and the outsized influence of the small and homogeneous circle of executives who ran them, contracted the field of well-known entertainers.

This chapter highlights the strategies deployed by entertainers who seek to share new ideas and pressing truths, and the challenges of sharing those ideas. Through artifacts illustrating technologies that facilitate connection with audiences, as well as the cultural and institutional barriers that impede it, we see the effort required to break through the noise with a signal that generates new conversation.

PROP MANACLES WORN BY LEVAR BURTON IN *ROOTS*

LeVar Burton wore these foam-lined manacles while playing Kunta Kinte, an enslaved African, in the televised adaptation of Alex Haley's book *Roots*. Over eight consecutive nights in January 1977, the miniseries presented the story of Kinte and his descendants. With its searing depiction of slavery and its empathetic and dignified portrayals of Black characters, exceptional for television at the time, the show transfixed millions of viewers and engaged the nation in an unprecedented conversation about the impact and legacy of slavery. And because Haley's work was informed by painstaking genealogical research, *Roots* spurred Black pride and interest in the links between family, national, and global histories.

↑ LeVar Burton as Kunta Kinte in the 1977 television miniseries *Roots*.

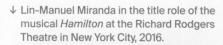

LIN-MANUEL MIRANDA COSTUME FROM *HAMILTON*

Lin-Manuel Miranda wore this green silk suit to emphasize Alexander Hamilton's growing financial interests during the second act of the 2015 original Broadway production of *Hamilton: An American Musical*. Featuring performers of color interpreting the nation's founding era through rap and hip-hop, the show broke Broadway conventions and box office records, won eleven Tony Awards, and was cited in debates on immigration, Puerto Rican statehood, and the January 6, 2021, attack on the US Capitol.

↓ Lin-Manuel Miranda in the title role of the musical *Hamilton* at the Richard Rodgers Theatre in New York City, 2016.

→ Cover of *Minnie Pearl's Scrapbook*, ca. 1955.

↑ MINNIE PEARL $1.98 HAT

In 1940, Nashville's *Grand Ole Opry* radio program debuted Sarah Ophelia Colley's homespun comic character Minnie Pearl. Hailing from the mythical hamlet of Grinder's Switch, Tennessee, and greeting her national and live audiences with a down-home "How-deeeee!" while wearing a straw hat adorned with fake flowers and a $1.98 price tag, Pearl used quaint yet hilarious anecdotes to make rural audiences feel at home at a time when many were moving to cities and felt unsettled by the changes wrought by modern life.

BROADCASTING REMAPS BOUNDARIES

On a cool day late in 1954, the media entrepreneur and civil rights advocate Raoul A. Cortez posed for a photo with city leaders in San Antonio, Texas. The occasion was the groundbreaking for a new television studio that would be home to KCOR, the first Latino-owned, all-Spanish-language television station in the continental United States. The call letters COR honored Cortez.

Cortez understood the power of broadcasting to challenge borders and boundaries. With KCOR, he created a media home for Spanish-speaking ethnic Mexican communities in south Texas, both despite and in answer to the long history of anti-Mexican violence, disenfranchisement, and discrimination there. He used not just broadcasting but also its architecture to underscore the message that KCOR would be "La Voz Mexicana." The station's antenna was the tallest structure in the city, redefining the San Antonio skyline and allowing the voices of Spanish-language broadcasters to travel hundreds of miles. The midcentury modern Aztec-style sculpture at the station building entrance underscored the ethnic Mexican identities of the owner and employees and became the station's icon. According to employees, the mask served as a constant reminder that, as Mexican Americans, they had an important place in the city and in broadcast television.

Although KCOR's reach was confined to South Texas, it provided the seed for a national network that brought together diverse Latina/o viewers from Miami to Los Angeles. In 1960 Cortez sold the station to Mexican media entrepreneur Don Emilio Azcárraga Vidaurreta and a group of US investors that included Cortez's son-in-law. Under the new owners, KCOR became the kernel of the Spanish International Network (SIN), which knitted together stations across the country to become the first Spanish-language network in the United States. In 1976 it was the first US television network to launch a satellite, in order to beam programming from Mexico. This broadcasting link rebuilt a linguistic and cultural connection disrupted by the borders and treaties imposed in the nineteenth and early twentieth centuries. In a provocative ad in *Variety*, SIN linked its primacy in satellite technology to an earlier first, reminding readers that "Spanish language and culture" had existed in America before the English arrived at Plymouth Rock. SIN's later transformation into Univision continued KCOR's legacy of making Spanish-speaking communities visible in the United States.

Kathleen Franz

↓ Raoul A. Cortez with San Antonio, Texas, city officials at the groundbreaking for the KCOR studio in 1954.

↙ Concrete sculpture of an Aztec mask attributed to artist Pedro Teran, more than three and a half feet tall, placed at the entrance to the KCOR building, ca. 1955–57.

↑ DR. STRANGELOVE PRESSBOOK

This 1964 Columbia Pictures pressbook provided local theater managers with promotional materials for Stanley Kubrick's *Dr. Strangelove*. Promising a blend of "hot-line suspense" and satire, the pressbook courted controversy by advertising the movie's "wild" content and potentially "pinko" (communist) intonations. The film garnered acclaim for its satirical look at the absurdity of a world preserved by the threat of mutually assured nuclear destruction.

IRVING BERLIN HAT

In 1942 the US military recruited Irving Berlin, a Russian Jewish immigrant known for composing all-American pop music, to mount a morale-boosting song and dance extravaganza. Berlin borrowed from a similar production he had staged during World War I, which explains why his costume included this hat in the style of the First rather than the Second World War. The 1942 show, *This Is the Army*, featured Berlin's patriotic hymn "God Bless America" and became a Broadway and Hollywood hit.

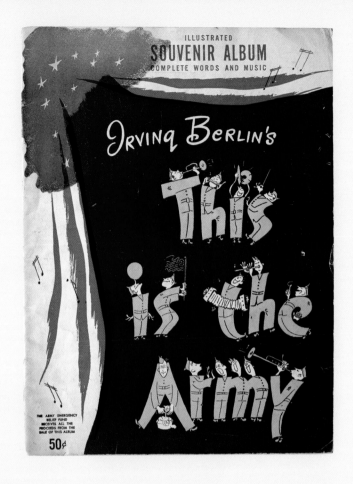

← Team photo of the Rockford Peaches, 1945.

ROCKFORD PEACHES

↑ ROCKFORD PEACHES PENNANT

During World War II, entertainment rallied a home front enduring wartime sacrifices. In 1943, major league baseball executives organized the All-American Girls Professional Baseball League (AAGPBL) to provide competitive versions of the national pastime in towns where men's minor league and company-sponsored teams had lost players to military service. The Rockford Peaches and other AAGPBL franchises thrived until minor league baseball began to expand after the war. Then professional baseball, like many other wartime opportunities for women, largely disappeared in the postwar "return to normalcy."

→ STUDIO MICROPHONE FROM WANN

The first radio broadcasts began in the 1920s, but it was not until the late 1940s and 1950s that hundreds of new local stations gave a radio voice to communities of color ignored by national radio networks. In Annapolis, Maryland, the radio station WANN became an institution and an important platform for the local Black community.

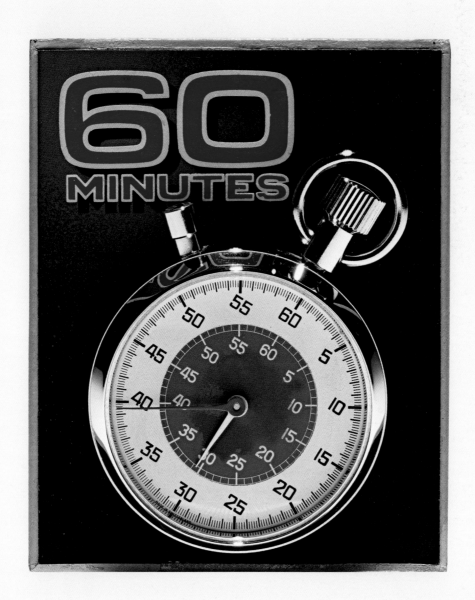

↗ *60 MINUTES* STOPWATCH

This stopwatch opened and timed the weekly
CBS newsmagazine *60 Minutes* from 1970 until
1998. Premiering in 1968, the show pioneered
investigative television journalism. Its one-hour
broadcasts soon became a Sunday night staple
and ranked among television's top-rated
programs for decades. Through interviews with
newsmakers both notable and notorious,
research that generated on-camera gotchas,
and Andy Rooney's humorously cranky
concluding commentaries, *60 Minutes* blurred
the line between news and entertainment but
offered greater depth than nightly news sound
bites and one-line newspaper quotes.

BOB ROSS EASEL

Artist Bob Ross hosted *The Joy of Painting* on PBS from 1982 to 1994. Asserting that everyone had artistic talent, he taught viewers how to create beautiful landscapes through simple steps, using easy oil-painting techniques. Ross's relaxed demeanor and positive catchphrases—such as "We don't make mistakes; we just make happy accidents"—continue to attract viewers in syndication and online. Yet even Ross did not completely avoid political commentary, as when he painted "a crooked tree" and remarked, "We'll send him to Washington."

↑ Bob Ross holding up his paint palette and brushes in his studio, ca. 1991.

BUILDING A GREAT SOCIETY ON SESAME STREET

→ Cast shot of season 7 of *Sesame Street*, ca. 1970.

→ Muppets Oscar the Grouch, Bert, Ernie, and Cookie Monster, along with a *Sesame Street* sign, ca. 1969–79.

On November 10, 1969, a new kind of children's television program premiered on public television stations across the United States. In the opening scene, an African American man named Gordon walked down an urban street with a multiracial girl named Sally, welcoming her to the neighborhood. "Sally, you've never seen a street like Sesame Street. Everything happens here. You're gonna love it," Gordon said as they passed by time-worn brownstones, fire hydrants, and trash cans. Before long, Sally met an eight-foot-tall yellow bird, a mischievous orange puppet who loved to sing to his rubber ducky in the bath, and a grouchy orange (later green) monster who lived in one of those trash cans on the street. In between the segments of humans and puppets interacting on the street, colorful animation, catchy music, and a guest appearance by Carol Burnett, the show taught numbers, letters, and life skills. Rather than being sponsored by companies marketing sugary cereal or action toys to children, this program was brought to viewers by the letters W, S, and E, and the numbers 2 and 3.

The most remarkable thing about *Sesame Street* wasn't its music or cast of monsters: it was the mission. For the first time, educators and child development experts worked together with creative talent to produce a national television series with a curriculum, a research team, and above all, the goal of functioning as an educational resource for minority and lower-income children. Amid the Civil Rights Movement and the tide of President Lyndon B. Johnson's Great Society social welfare legislation, the Children's Television Workshop set out to prove that television could be a powerful force for social change.

In a landmark speech at the National Association of Broadcasters' 1961 annual meeting, Federal Communications Commission chair Newton Minow had famously called the television landscape a "vast wasteland." His denunciation of the cultural bankruptcy of television became a clarion call for critics, but he also offered a solution: broadcasters should serve the public, especially children. "Is there no room on television to teach, to inform, to uplift, to stretch, to enlarge the capacities of our children?" he asked.

A young television producer named Joan Ganz Cooney believed there was. Cooney established the Children's Television Workshop, with funding from the Carnegie Corporation, the Ford Foundation, and the US Department of Education, to develop a model educational children's television program. Her research showed that despite the advances made by federal programs like Head Start, only half the nation's school districts offered kindergarten classes. The lack of preschool in disadvantaged communities, Cooney wrote, resulted in an academic achievement gap

that had lasting socioeconomic effects. Meanwhile, by 1960, 87 percent of American households owned a television, and children were watching an average of twenty hours of television every week. Cooney saw an opportunity to use that television time to educational ends.

In the summer of 1968, Cooney organized a series of seminars with experts in child development and education, animators, advertisers, children's book authors, and the puppeteer Jim Henson to draft a curriculum and shape the concept for what was then blandly titled *Early Childhood Television Program*. At this point, Henson and his Muppets were best known for their work in television advertising, which was fitting given Cooney's emerging concept for the show. Advertisers knew the medium better than anyone else. If the workshop team could harness the production values and addictive qualities of television commercials to promote reading comprehension instead of toys and cereal, this new show could help a generation of youngsters, especially in disadvantaged communities.

Some of the creative talent Cooney hired was inspired to join the team after the assassination of Martin Luther King Jr. For them, this seemed like a critical moment to harness the power of television to serve African American communities. The show would be set in an inner-city neighborhood, with authentic trash cans, stained sidewalks, and brownstone stoops that would feel familiar to its target audience. In an attempt to counter harmful stereotypes, the show's human cast would feature a stable middle-class Black family, Gordon and Susan, living harmoniously with their white neighbors and diverse Muppet residents. Early guest stars included James Earl Jones, Mahalia Jackson, and Nina Simone singing "To Be Young, Gifted, and Black." A Department of Utilization at CTW was dedicated to community outreach, setting up "*Sesame Street* centers" at churches, libraries, and community centers where those without televisions could watch the show, and to distribute related educational materials for use in schools and at home.

Besides teaching literacy and numeracy, the show also taught life and social skills: how to deal with feelings, big changes, people different from you, and conflict. In this regard, the Muppets were the show's secret weapon. Big Bird was a naive and sometimes clumsy six-year-old, Bert and Ernie were mismatched roommates who learned to navigate their differences, and Oscar the Grouch was a grumpy, trashcan-dwelling monster who was nevertheless a valued member of the neighborhood.

Sesame Street was an immediate success, lauded for its combination of education and entertainment. Research commissioned by CTW showed that regular viewers scored higher on standardized tests of reading, writing, and comprehension than nonviewers, with gains particularly noticeable among children from disadvantaged communities. Ten years after its debut, the show was drawing an audience of nine million children for every broadcast, and one study found that 90 percent of all children in low-income households were regular viewers.

> Besides teaching literacy and numeracy, *Sesame Street* also taught life and social skills: how to deal with feelings, big changes, people different from you, and conflict.

Like many other Great Society projects of the 1960s, however, *Sesame Street* has weathered criticism from across the ideological spectrum—criticism that has kept its funding and survival tenuous despite its huge following. As early as the Nixon administration, with its federal support in peril from conservative opposition to public television, CTW turned to generating revenue from books, toys, and its chart-topping soundtrack records. Some critics then accused *Sesame Street* of becoming just another children's television cash cow. More recently, although its controversial move from the PBS network to HBO has benefited the show financially, some have decried the change as a betrayal of the series' original mission. (New episodes premiere on HBO, but public television airs reruns.)

Sesame Street has also struggled over the years to fully achieve its mission to represent a diverse and multicultural nation. Debate raged behind the scenes and among critics when the Muppet character Roosevelt Franklin, a speaker of African American Vernacular English, was added to the show in 1971. Performer Matt Robinson championed the character, who was popular among viewers, as an intelligent, hip, and unmistakably Black member of the Muppet cast, but some reviewers and researchers feared that Franklin's dialect and mannerisms reinforced stereotypes and taught bad habits. When Latina/o activists demanded greater representation, three characters were added for the 1971 season: Rafael, Maria, and Luis. In 1991, the bilingual Muppet Rosita joined the cast. Julia, a Muppet with autism spectrum disorder, is a more recent addition. As the other characters learn about her condition, they also learn that she's just as valued a friend as any other; they may just have to play with her a little differently.

Sesame Street's casting, merchandising, and sometimes even its messages remain subjects of debate today. In 2021, after Texas senator Ted Cruz tweeted that Big Bird's advocacy for COVID-19 vaccination constituted "government propaganda," a *Saturday Night Live* skit portrayed Cruz saying, "For fifty years, I stood by as *Sesame Street* taught our children dangerous ideas, like numbers and kindness." The joke hinged on recognizing that the show has always blended occasionally controversial efforts to be relevant with completely uncontroversial educational content—a mix that explains the broad following of the longest-running and most influential children's television program in US history.

Ryan Lintelman

← Learning kit for *Sesame Street* episodes, including an LP record and parent/teacher guides, created by the Children's Television Workshop, 1970.

↓ Blouse and skirt worn by Loretta Long in the role of Susan on *Sesame Street*, ca. 1970s.

← ROSITA PUPPET

Despite its inclusive mission, the children's television series *Sesame Street* premiered in 1969 without a single Latina/o character and consequently faced immediate criticism from activists. Human characters Luis Rodriguez and Maria Figueroa first appeared in 1971, and twenty years later Rosita, performed by Carmen Osbahr, joined the cast as the show's first Latina Muppet character. Designed to resemble a fruit bat, Rosita, La Monstrua de las Cuevas, teaches viewers Spanish-language skills and speaks about her Mexican heritage.

→ *HOWDY DOODY* MARIONETTE

This was one of three marionettes used on *The Howdy Doody Show*, which entertained an in-studio peanut gallery and millions of kids at home from 1947 to 1960. As television ownership among American households soared from 9 to 87 percent during those years, Howdy sold his rapt audience on sponsors' cereal, candy, and toys, along with dozens of his own licensed products. Soon, concerned parents and activists called for banning advertising and expanding educational content in children's television programming.

PELÉ JERSEY

Soccer star Edson Arantes do Nascimento became known as Pelé while growing up in his native Brazil. Widely considered the greatest player of the world's most popular sport, Pelé retired in the mid-1970s after playing for the North American Soccer League's New York Cosmos. On a team named for and aspiring to universal appeal, he led an international cast of all-stars who won a championship and jolted attendance from 3,500 to 35,000 per game. Pelé's Cosmos brought soccer into the mainstream of US sports while highlighting the global and immigrant communities that were the game's hotbed.

↓ Pele playing for the New York Cosmos against the Dallas Tornado at Downing Stadium, New York City, June 15, 1975.

In 2010 Arizona empowered police in the state to question any member of the public about their immigration status, in effect targeting any Spanish-speaking person with brown skin as a candidate for incarceration and deportation. The Phoenix Suns decried the law as a violation of "our basic principles of equal rights and protection under the law." In protest, the team wore jerseys normally reserved for Noche Latina, game nights begun by the National Basketball Association in 2006 to celebrate Latina/o players and fans. This one was donned by All-Star center Amar'e Stoudemire.

↑ A Phoenix Suns fan holds up a sign supporting the team's protest against an anti-immigration law in Arizona during the Suns' May 2010 playoff game against the San Antonio Spurs.

MISS REPRESENTATION

For Asian Americans and Pacific Islanders, trying to find a version of yourself in media programming and advertising is not difficult. But the images often look like those in a funhouse mirror—oddly familiar, but distorted, exaggerated, and sometimes even grotesque. And the characters have sometimes been difficult to stomach. It doesn't help to see non-Asian actors playing the roles. Many people in the United States have heard of blackface, but not "yellowface" or "brownface": they probably failed to notice the prosthetics used on Jonathan Pryce's eyes in *Miss Saigon*, intended to make him look the part of a "Eurasian" pimp, or the skin darkener Ashton Kutcher applied to play a Bollywood producer in a snack commercial. Scripting Asian characters to speak with a heavy accent or in "broken" English has been a common tactic to emphasize their foreignness. Of course, to play the Chinese Hawaiian fighter pilot Allison Ng in Cameron Crowe's 2015 film *Aloha*, Emma Stone skipped the accent, tape, and tanner, and just whitewashed the role. In sum, the mirror held up to Asian Americans and Pacific Islanders in Hollywood has not reflected real individuals.

The stereotypical nature of these roles has been manifested not only by artificial changes to the actors' physical appearance but also by costumes. By comparing Diosa Costello's costume from the Broadway run of Rodgers and Hammerstein's *South Pacific* in 1950 and Constance Wu's Cinderella-like gown from the 2018 film *Crazy Rich Asians*, we can explore how American culture has persistently missed representations and misrepresented Asian American and Pacific Islander women—and ask whether things are finally changing.

Diosa Costello was born Juana de Dios Castrello in Guayama, Puerto Rico, on April 23, 1913. Widely known as the Latin Bombshell, she thrilled American audiences in Broadway romances such as *Too Many Girls* (1939) and *Crazy with the Heat* (1941). "I was the original J.Lo," Costello quipped when donating materials to the National Museum of American History in 2011.

But in 1950, Costello took on a different kind of role as Bloody Mary in *South Pacific*. While Costello's comic performance was described as "beautiful" by the *New York Times*, Bloody Mary was not supposed to be Latina—or African American, like Juanita Hall, the powerhouse performer from whom Costello inherited the role.

In fact, the character, like the whole musical, was based on James A. Michener's first book, *Tales of the South Pacific*, which won a Pulitzer Prize. Michener in turn appears to have drawn

Bloody Mary—a local souvenir vendor and matchmaking mother—from at least two women he knew while stationed in Vanuatu during World War II: a Samoan Scottish hotel owner and a woman of Tonkinese (Vietnamese) descent. French colonists had imported Tonkinese laborers to harvest coconuts and cacao on several of those islands. Working nine-hour days on multiyear contracts in segregated conditions made the South Pacific anything but paradise to the Tonkinese. According to Michener's biographer, Stephen J. May, the real Bloody Mary was a worker who had attempted to organize her fellow indentured laborers. Imagine if that storyline had taken center stage in a Broadway musical!

Instead, the Bloody Mary of Michener's book and *South Pacific* is a stereotyped character who reflects European romanticism and stereotypes (come on, look at the costume!) more than the immigrant and native histories that have shaped Pacific Island cultures. Leave it to the white male author, a visitor to the islands, to make it clear who gets to tell the story: "No one knows the Pacific better than I do," Michener later wrote in his memoir *The World Is My Home*. "No one can tell the story more accurately."

← Theater still photograph of Diosa
Costello in the role of Bloody Mary, in
the Broadway musical *South Pacific*,
ca. 1950.

→ Costume worn by Diosa Costello in
the role of Bloody Mary, 1951.

↓ Lobby card advertising Universal Pictures' film adaptation of the 1961 musical *Flower Drum Song*, 1962.

↓ Constance Wu in the wedding scene from the film *Crazy Rich Asians*, 2018.

It would be years before Asians, Pacific Islanders, and Asian Americans were accurately represented in any Hollywood production. The first movie to feature an all-Asian cast was *Flower Drum Song*, adapted in 1961 from the 1958 Rodgers and Hammerstein musical (itself adapted from a 1957 novel of the same name by Chan Ying Lee). The next—the movie adaptation of Amy Tan's *The Joy Luck Club* in 1993, directed by Wayne Wang—did not appear until 1993. *Crazy Rich Asians* hit the big screen twenty-five years after that, in 2018 (directed by Jon Chu and adapted from Kevin Kwan's 2013 novel). At this rate, American audiences will be able to get their next fix of an all-Asian cast in 2036. Progress!

Crazy Rich Asians is rooted in tensions over class and status. The central character, Rachel Chu, is a Chinese American university economist with working-class roots who finds herself a fish out of water as she seeks acceptance from her boyfriend's extremely wealthy Singaporean family. The clothing in the film highlights each character's class position. Those who recently elevated their rank by attending American schools demonstrate their new-found status with a gaudy and conspicuous personal style. In contrast, Rachel's boyfriend and his family, with a long-established social position and wealth, wear understated, elegant clothing defined by cut and formality rather than color and audacity.

With help from friends who understand the codes of local high society, Rachel cycles through dozens of outfits until she finds the right gown to wear to a wedding. The one she selects becomes a kind of uniform, signaling her claim to inclusion. The film's director, Jon Chu, saw Rachel's gown resonating with audiences. In an interview for the *Los Angeles Times*, he commented: "I remember seeing moms make it for their little girls, I remember seeing women wear it with a sense of pride. It became literally a fairy-tale dress for people. We talked about how this would make her feel and how powerful it would be for her—and that it's also her *choice* to wear."

One mother who was inspired by the film, Ha Truong, herself the daughter of Vietnamese refugees, shared her thoughts on making a version for her five-year-old daughter, Olivia: "Being an Asian American, oftentimes, you don't see that Asian part of yourself in America, and neither do your peers. . . . It's refreshing to see someone on the big screen my daughter and my son can relate to. So many stories haven't been told—and hopefully this means more are to come."

Theodore S. Gonzalves

→ Gown worn by Constance Wu
in the role of Rachel Chu in
Crazy Rich Asians, 2018.

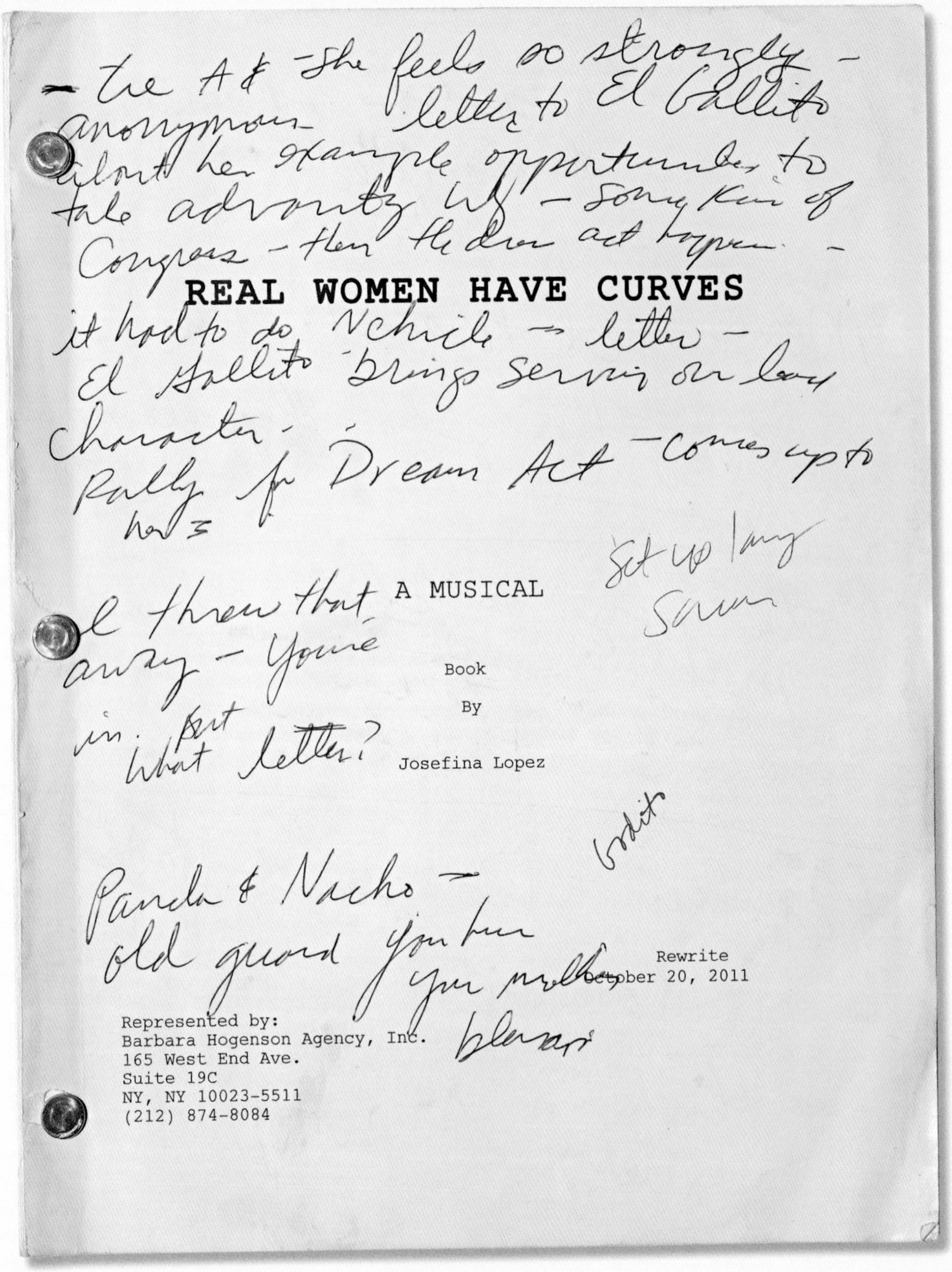

REAL WOMEN HAVE CURVES

[Handwritten annotations across top of page:]

~ the A & she feels so strongly ~ anonymous letter to El Gallito about her example opportunities to take advantage of ~ Sony Kim of Congress ~ then the dream act topyou ~

it had to do w/chile → letter ~ El Gallito brings Serving on lay Character ~ Rally for Dream Act ~ comes up to her 3

el threw that away ~ You're in. But what letter?

Set up lang Sarra

Panda & Nacho → old guard you bun yu moth...

edit

blenari

A MUSICAL

Book

By

Josefina Lopez

Rewrite
October 20, 2011

Represented by:
Barbara Hogenson Agency, Inc.
165 West End Ave.
Suite 19C
NY, NY 10023-5511
(212) 874-8084

↑ **DRAFT SCREENPLAY FOR** *REAL WOMEN HAVE CURVES*

Writer Josefina López inspired breakout conversations about Latina/o immigrant experiences in her coming-of-age play—and subsequent 2002 film, and forthcoming musical—*Real Women Have Curves*. The main character, Ana Garcia, channels Lopez's own memories of growing up as an undocumented immigrant in East Los Angeles, resisting her mother's traditional expectations that she conform to a thinner body type and work in her sister's struggling garment shop. Instead, Ana follows her dream of going to college, saying, "How dare anybody tell me what I should look like—or what I should be." The plot of this early draft of the musical's script references the Dream Act, which would provide pathways to US citizenship for young undocumented immigrants.

→ Movie poster for *Real Women Have Curves*, 2002.

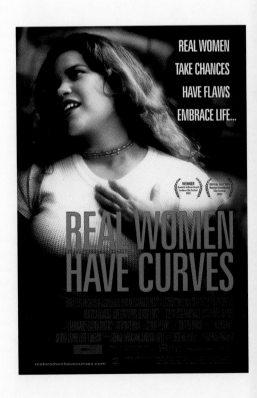

REAL WOMEN
TAKE CHANCES
HAVE FLAWS
EMBRACE LIFE...

**REAL WOMEN
HAVE CURVES**

realwomenhavecurves.com

↑ Sandy Koufax pitching, photographed by Leigh Wiener, 1963.

↙ **SANDY KOUFAX GLOVE**

Hitters saw this right-handed glove at the beginning of Sandy Koufax's pitching wind-up, just before they saw a ball thrown by "the Left Arm of God." The pride of the Dodgers, and of Jewish fans across the nation, Koufax was the first major league player to pitch four no-hitters and win three Cy Young Awards. In 1965 he turned religious practice into a national story when he declined to pitch the first game of the World Series because it coincided with the Jewish high holy day of Yom Kippur. Some fans complained, and others burst with pride.

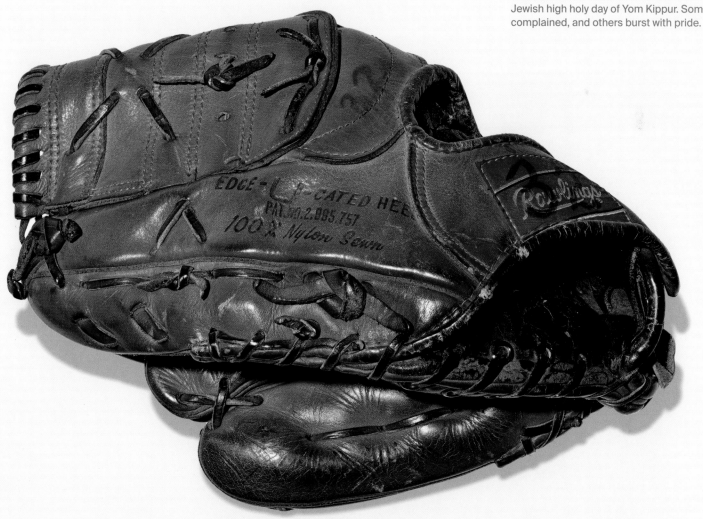

↑ Skateboarder Cindy Whitehead,
photographed by Ian Logan, 2020.

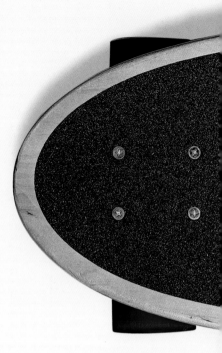

↖ CINDY WHITEHEAD SKATEBOARD

Cindy Whitehead's rebellious nature and free spirit fit with America's view of the stereotypical skateboarder, but her fight for gender equity in the sport sets her apart. Whitehead, who turned pro at age seventeen in the mid-1970s, constantly fought for acceptance and recognition in the male-dominated sport. Her "Girl Is Not a 4 Letter Word" brand emerged in the 2010s with gear designed to empower girls and women in skate.

THE AUTHENTICITY OF ELLEN

Show business is brutal to a celebrity's personal freedom. No matter how talented a person may be, management of their image determines whether they sink or swim. Historically, one of the most lethal blows to a career has been being outed as LGBTQ+. On screen, men such as Victor Buono, Paul Lynd, and James Coco could be campy as long as they kept their private lives secret. Greta Garbo and Marlene Dietrich made it cool to be bisexual in the 1930s, but by the 1980s, only women with heterosexual credentials (like Julie Andrews, Lucy Lawless, and Eva Longoria) risked playing lesbian or masculine characters. Likewise, only straight men, such as Billy Crystal in the popular sitcom *Soap*, might safely impersonate a gay character. Real-life gay people like Rock Hudson and Meredith Baxter took roles that foregrounded masculinity or domesticity to throw off suspicion.

Enter Ellen DeGeneres with her popular sitcom, *Ellen,* which ran from 1994 to 1998. Through just a few seconds of one episode in season 4, she became a major contributor to dismantling Hollywood's hypocrisy around queerness.

When *Ellen* aired, gay activism, gay liberation, and Gay Pride celebrations were chipping away at discrimination. But in everyday life during the 1990s, it was still dangerous to be out. LGBTQ+ people risked verbal harassment, termination of employment, and physical assault. Sex between men or between women was still a criminal offense in many jurisdictions. Making jokes about gay people was as common and acceptable as making jokes about your mother-in-law. The popularity of *Ellen*, which focused on the relationships between DeGeneres's charming and funny onscreen character and her circle of friends and family, inevitably led to interest in the actor's private life. As questions circulated, DeGeneres replied to the whispers with creative confrontation: she scripted an episode in which she publicly outed herself via a hot mic.

That brave and controversial act nearly ended her career. The show's ratings declined, and sponsors withdrew their advertising. She received hate mail and threats. When ABC canceled *Ellen* the following year, her career initially suffered. Soon, however, her creative talent prevailed, along with the rapid acceptance of LGBTQ+ rights. In the following years, sodomy laws were overturned, more and more public figures came out, and Gay Pride parades spread to cities across the country. DeGeneres returned to work in several high-profile TV, film, and stage projects as a

performer, writer, and producer. Her long-running, award-winning afternoon talk show debuted in 2003. Precisely because her trailblazing has led to more out-and-proud celebrities, the media now largely covers her like any other star—with headlines about where she goes with her wife, how much her home is worth, and whether she really is as nice as she seems.

DeGeneres has used her celebrity and wealth to support social and environmental issues, including LGBTQ+ rights, gay youth, transcendental meditation, animal rights, and HIV and AIDS advocacy. In recognition of her entertainment contributions and humanitarianism, President Barack Obama awarded her the Presidential Medal of Freedom in November 2016. This is the custom-made suit that DeGeneres wore for the ceremony. The suit captures not only DeGeneres's unique lesbian style but also her determination to be honest about her identity. Her tailored jacket of preppy maroon plaid and dapper buttoned-up shirt demonstrate her belief that when you are your authentic self, it makes it safer for others to be theirs.

Katherine Ott

← Barack Obama awarding Ellen DeGeneres with the Presidential Medal of Freedom, November 22, 2016.

→ Suit worn by Ellen DeGeneres at her Presidential Medal of Freedom ceremony, 2016.

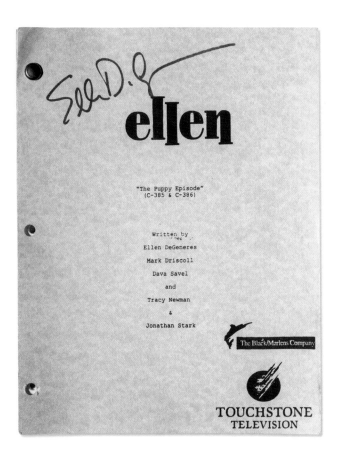

↑ Autographed script for "The Puppy Episode" of the television show *Ellen*, in which DeGeneres comes out as gay, 1997.

↗ AVENUE Q PUPPETS

With its cast members, style, and structure
drawn from *Sesame Street*, the musical *Avenue Q*
parodied the television show's encouragement
of self-improvement, multicultural harmony, and
kindness. Running on Broadway from 2003 to
2009 and then for another decade off Broadway,
the grown-up puppet and human citizens of
Avenue Q explore real-life issues head-on
through songs like "Everyone's a Little Bit Racist"
and "If You Were Gay, It Would Be OK."

→ **JASON COLLINS JERSEY**

"I didn't set out to be the first openly gay athlete in a major American team sport," Washington Wizards Center Jason Collins said when he came out in an essay he wrote for *Sports Illustrated* in 2013. "But since I am, I'm happy to start the conversation." Collins wore number 98 in memory of Matthew Shepard, whose brutal 1998 murder prompted anti-LGBTQ+ hate crime legislation.

PRINCE'S GUITAR

It's their first date. Apollonia and The Kid are window-shopping on a downtown sidewalk. We see her from the back. The name on the store window is "Lorraine's." Was Apollonia checking out wedding gowns? She follows The Kid down the block. Something else has grabbed his attention. In a window display, the most gorgeous guitar you have ever seen seems to be suspended in air on a mannequin. "Do you see something you like?" Apollonia asks. He doesn't answer. For all she knows, he could have been spying on the item for weeks. She knows exactly what to get him.

That instrument, known as Prince's Cloud guitar for its ethereal look, appears three times in *Purple Rain*. The first is in that sidewalk scene. The second is when Apollonia surprises The Kid by giving him the instrument—before telling him she'll be joining his rival's band. And the third is when The Kid takes the stage to belt out the title song, dedicated to his father. Prince could have easily ordered a prop for those scenes, a facsimile that matched the distinctive shape, color, and gold-plated hardware of his own guitar. But the Cloud guitar needed to be more than a prop. As Prince's first custom-built guitar, it—like his first film—had to be both visually and musically stunning.

The breathtakingly unique shape of an existing custom-built bass guitar served as Prince's inspiration. Jeff Levin, a luthier at New York City's Matt Umanov Guitars who had started his own line of instruments, designed and built a bass for himself as a one-off in 1972. Prince found the bass for sale in 1976, fell in love with it, and bought it. It was subsequently played in Prince's music

videos by André Cymone ("Why You Wanna Treat Me So Bad?") and Sonny Thompson ("My Name is Prince" and "The Most Beautiful Girl in the World").

The photographer and former Prince guitar tech Joel Bernstein recalls that Prince described Levin's bass design as "erotic" and noted "he wanted to have it right away." Levin says his design was influenced by the early-twentieth-century design of the Gibson F-style mandolin, itself inspired by carvings on older violins. The similarities are evident. The scroll on the original Gibson—elongated into a horn on Levin's bass—has a regal flourish. That element is reflected in the bass's headstock design and the swirl around the output jack.

Prince approached a Minneapolis guitar shop, Knut Koupee Enterprises, to incorporate that bass guitar's looks into the design of a new six-string electric guitar that would realize his ambition for *Purple Rain*'s overall visual style. In concert with Prince's outfit of commanding high heels, a high-collared purple trench coat with padded shoulders, and a shirt with Edwardian ruffles, the Cloud guitar completes a modern take on Gilded Age luxury blended with pathbreaking onstage gender-bending. The instrument's white surface stands out against the deep purple coat, and its soft and curving shape is contrasted by its piercing scream.

Prince had several Cloud guitars built over the years. When he donated one to the National Museum of American History in 1993, he did not provide many details about it. After his death in 2016,

John Woodland, the luthier charged with the care of the guitar collection at Prince's Paisley Park Studios, studied it further. Colleagues at the Smithsonian's National Museum of Natural History ran the instrument through a CAT scanner, a device typically used at the museum to examine archaeological specimens. The scan seemed to confirm Woodland's theory that the body and neck of the guitar were built from parts manufactured by a Minneapolis guitar company called O'Hagan, and that Knut Koupee's luthiers repurposed and reshaped them to create the new design for Prince.

Meanwhile, Smithsonian conservators analyzed the instrument's paint. They discovered six layers of paint colors and preparatory grounds underneath the final coat of yellow. This discovery seemed to confirm Prince's penchant for changing his guitars' colors to match his aesthetic of the moment. Together, these clues date the instrument to 1983 and suggest that this was the first Cloud guitar ever built for Prince—the once-white instrument featured in *Purple Rain* (1984).

The guitar's origins reveal how luthiers helped craft Prince's iconic and constantly shifting aesthetic, steeped in androgenous sexuality. Perhaps that aesthetic explains why, twenty-three years after Apollonia asked The Kid if he saw anything he liked in the store window, Prince sang in "Guitar": "I love U, baby. But not like I love my guitar."

Theodore S. Gonzalves

← Prince's yellow Cloud guitar, custom built by Knut Koupee Enterprises, Inc., ca. 1983.

→ Prince performing live at the Fabulous Forum in Inglewood, California, February 19, 1985.

WIDENING ONE'S SCOPE

↗ American Mutoscope Company
coin-operated mutoscope from
the late 1890s.

The first commercial motion pictures were not projected on a screen in a theater. Instead, people watched on devices designed for individual viewing in storefront parlors. The first of these devices, Thomas Edison's kinetoscope, created an appetite for this novel form of entertainment. To cash in on what seemed like an insatiable demand for these early films, several small companies in the 1890s competed to develop new viewing technologies. One of these, the mutoscope, was invented in 1894 by William Kennedy Laurie Dickson and Herman Casler. It catapulted their fledgling company—later known as the American Mutoscope & Biograph Company—to the forefront of the moving-picture industry in the United States. Like the kinetoscope, the mutoscope was a peephole motion-picture viewing device. But rather than illuminating a strip of film as the kinetoscope did, mutoscopes used a flip-card mechanism, in which black and white photographs affixed to sturdy cards created the illusion of moving images.

The American Mutoscope Company began producing its own content in earnest in 1896, when the company moved its operations to a building in New York City and Dickson began photographing from the rooftop. Those early moving pictures, including two views of Union Square, along with *Skirt Dance by Annabelle*, *Sandow*, and *A Hard Wash*, represent the impulses of early cinema in the US to both captivate and titillate. Urban scenes offered viewers the thrill of visiting places they'd never been. Moving pictures of the dancing Annabelle and the almost-naked body of the weightlifter Eugen Sandow flexing his muscles enabled a new form of voyeurism.

The mutoscope's technological limits, which kept pieces to less than a minute long, meant that filmmakers often resorted to quick sight gags, many of which drew on degrading racial, ethnic, and gender stereotypes. In *Biddy the Irish Wash Woman,* a man dressed as a woman doing laundry falls into a washtub, inviting viewers to laugh at a gender-bending performance that reinforced stereotypes of Irish women as unfeminine. In *A Hard Wash,* an African American mother scrubs her child futilely, as if to suggest he will never come clean.

As the technology evolved to shoot longer films and to project them on a screen, not only did moving images become a lucrative industry that revolutionized commercial entertainment, but they also became a powerful transformative force in American life and culture. The Biograph Company, as it was subsequently called, abandoned the mutoscope and devoted its energies to film production and exhibition, and in the span of two decades it produced more than three thousand short films. Americans flocked to nickelodeons, small storefront theaters that charged a nickel for admission. By 1910, one in four Americans visited these makeshift theaters each week.

Movies had a profound impact on the way ordinary people understood space and time. Even in their earliest days, motion pictures quite literally opened up the world. In viewing distant places (like Union Square or Niagara Falls), well-known personages (like bodybuilder Eugen Sandow or President William McKinley in a picture titled *McKinley at Home*), people experienced the world as smaller and more accessible. Moving images also enabled viewers to feel as if they were actually present at historical events, like Edison's maudlin 1895 *Execution of Mary,*

Queen of Scots. Other examples included both reenactments and actual footage of the Spanish-American War.

Although moving images continued to rehearse degrading stereotypes, the arrival of longer films led to more complex narratives, creating more progressive possibilities as well. Movies enabled viewers to take on what we might call "prosthetic memories"—feelings of personal connection to historical events through which viewers didn't actually live. Such experiences expanded viewers' own horizons, informing their politics, worldviews, and understanding of themselves. Because films enabled viewers to see the world through someone else's eyes, they had the potential to create empathy in viewers—to foster a sense of unexpected connection to people who might seem very different.

Alison Landsberg

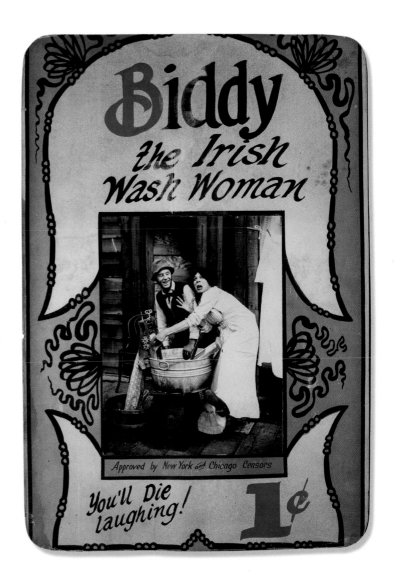

↑ Advertisement for a mutoscope film featuring a cross-dressing actor in a stereotyped performance of an Irish laundress, ca. 1920s.

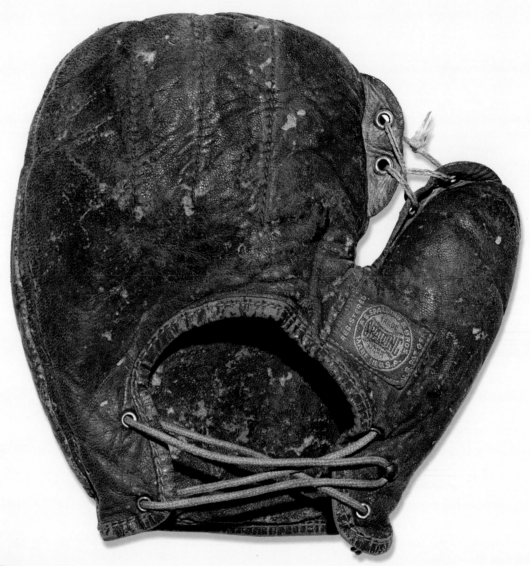

↖ EARLY MITT AND 1883 BASEBALL

Baseball gained popularity after the Civil War, as gloves made the game safer, and the mass production of balls and other equipment made it more affordable. At the same time, early sportswriters linked the game to lasting values of teamwork and discipline. Traditional yet modern, baseball became the "national pastime" by appealing to fans across generational, regional, class, gender, and racial lines. However, white men responded to its popularity by racially segregating the game and pushing women out of playing, both professionally and recreationally.

↙ **LINDSEY STIRLING VIOLIN**

After judges on television's *America's Got Talent* voted the dancing violinist off the show in 2010, Lindsey Stirling started posting music videos online. She paired mash-ups of electro-pop styles with lively steps and twirls in settings often drawn from video games or movies. Her posts inspired millions, then billions, of fans worldwide and revealed how audiences and entertainers could forgo traditional tastemakers and gatekeepers to build powerful connections directly through digital platforms.

↑ Lindsey Stirling performing at the Uptown Theatre in Napa, California, January 29, 2015.

↗ DOLBY CINEMA PROCESSOR

In the mid-1970s, computer-generated special effects and innovative audio technologies expanded the possibilities of movie storytelling. Dolby Laboratories' audio processors, installed in cinemas, produced multichannel, immersive sound experiences that came to provide their own draw. Such technological developments led to the rise of blockbuster movies—big-budget films offering visually and aurally striking experiences that drew record-breaking crowds. This Dolby Laboratories CP100 unit processed the audio for the 1975 London premiere of The Who's *Tommy*.

↘ FAIRLIGHT COMPUTER MUSICAL INSTRUMENT

Launched in 1979, the Fairlight CMI (computer musical instrument) enabled musicians to convert human voices, environmental sounds, and even previously recorded songs into digital audio files that they could manipulate, integrate into new compositions, and polyphonically play through the Fairlight's integrated audio workstation and synthesizer keyboard. Captivated by this new technology, jazz piano great Herbie Hancock used this Fairlight CMI to create his 1983 futuristic-sounding hit "Rockit."

→ CABLE TV BOX

In the 1970s and 1980s, cable television expanded because its advocates successfully fought regulations that had protected the major networks from competition. As millions of households replaced their roof-top antennas with set-top cable boxes like this Jerrold Starcom II model, they gained access to a mind-boggling thirty-seven channels. The new stations included specialized entertainment channels like MTV and ESPN as well as channels like BET and Galavision that aimed to serve Black and Latina/o audiences underrepresented on network television.

↑ Duke Ellington playing with a band, photographed by Robert Houston, ca. 1970.

↓ **DUKE ELLINGTON ORCHESTRA MUSIC STAND**

By 1961, Duke Ellington's renown as a bandleader, composer, and musician allowed him to negotiate contracts that excluded performances before segregated audiences. But gains made by the Civil Rights Movement also led Ellington to participate in the US State Department's "jazz diplomacy," a global campaign showcasing the country's most premier Black and brown jazz musicians in an effort to counter Soviet arguments that racism undermined US claims about the moral superiority of capitalism and democracy. Duke Ellington Orchestra members used this music stand during their 1963 State Department–sponsored tour of the Middle East and South Asia.

ELLA FITZGERALD RED SUIT

Born in Virginia in 1917, Ella Fitzgerald launched her musical career in the nightclubs of Harlem. Her highly technical and virtuosic improvisation and scat singing won her broad acclaim and made her one of the best-known jazz performers. As a result of this success, she was one of the first Black women to appear in global advertising campaigns. She wore this suit in an iconic photograph by Annie Leibovitz, taken around 1988, that featured in an American Express campaign.

↓ Ella Fitzgerald, photographed by Annie Leibovitz, ca. 1988.

WHAT CELEBRITY PHOTOGRAPHY SAYS

Today, celebrity status is dependent on photography. Studios, agents, producers, marketing executives, advertisers, paparazzi, and even the famous themselves use photography to create and promote public personas and feed insatiable audiences. The use of photography to create, maintain, and sometimes ruin celebrity status has its roots in the mid-nineteenth century, when new photographic processes enabled the large-scale reproduction of paper prints from glass negatives. The resulting images were sold, given away, and collected in the form of cartes de visite and cabinet cards, which allowed the famous to reach audiences in new ways, and also empowered ordinary people to judge the famous.

Made possible by new processes in the 1850s that enabled multiple prints to be made from a single glass plate negative, cartes de visite are photographs printed on paper about the size of a business card and mounted on card stock. These inexpensive reproductions allowed individuals to purchase and collect portraits made from life. Originally designed to facilitate and reflect social connections (hence their reference to the practice of leaving visiting cards), cartes de visite quickly evolved into a means of bringing celebrities into the homes and social circles of ordinary people. Cabinet cards emerged at the end of the 1860s as a slightly larger version of the cartes de visite.

Mathew Brady's New York City photography studio, known as Brady's National Portrait Gallery, used the new technology to create a visual who's who of the era. It was a place to see, be seen, and even have one's own portrait made by the celebrated photographer. His Broadway gallery was just down the street from the American Museum of P. T. Barnum, who is often credited with pioneering the commercialization of pop culture and influenced Brady's approach to business.

Entertainment entrepreneurs like Barnum used the power of photography to publicize performers' faces and bodies to

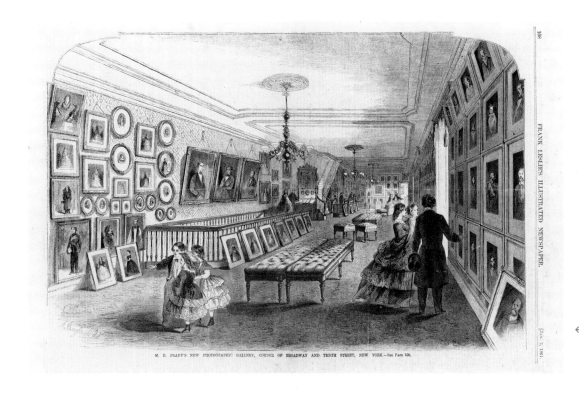

M. B. BRADY'S NEW PHOTOGRAPHIC GALLERY, CORNER OF BROADWAY AND TENTH STREET, NEW YORK.—See Page 106.

← Mathew Brady's New York City photography gallery and studio, printed in *Frank Leslie's Illustrated Newspaper*, January 5, 1861.

audiences nationwide. But Barnum also had a favorite cabinet-card portrait of himself, made by the Boston-area photographer George K. Warren. Warren kept the negative for this image on file and made prints for Barnum to give away. Warren, like Brady and other photographers, fueled the collecting frenzy by offering celebrities free photographic portraits. With the name of the photographer's studio printed on the cards, this strategy capitalized on the subjects' fame to advertise the photographer.

Abraham Lincoln recognized the political potential in this commercial blend of photography, entertainment, and celebrity. In October 1859, after delivering his famous Cooper Union address, in which he argued that twenty-one of the thirty-nine signers of the Constitution—"a clear majority of the whole"—would want slavery to be contained, Lincoln headed to Brady's studio for a portrait. The self-conscious and gangly Lincoln was put at ease when Brady asked if he might adjust the president's shirt to make his neck seem shorter. The resulting carte de visite was widely collected. The image was also used by newspaper illustrators and turned into campaign pins. Lincoln later introduced Brady as the man who helped make him president. After his assassination, the image was used to make mourning badges.

In contrast to sitters like Lincoln, Brady and his staff of photographers stayed silent on the issue of slavery by not directly depicting enslaved people in their widely published images of

↑ Carte de visite of P. T. Barnum, photographed by George K. Warren, ca. 1870.

→ Badge of mourning for President Abraham Lincoln, made after his assassination in 1865, repurposed from a photograph by Mathew Brady.

the Civil War. Warren, however, arranged an album in his Boston gallery that included members of his family who were deeply involved in the Union Army, as well as celebrities who shared that allegiance. Within this assemblage is a carte de visite portrait by Brady of the Italian opera singer Agostino Susini and his younger American-born wife, the opera singer Isabella Hinckley, as well as one of another American opera singer, Clara Kellogg. Hinckley was famous for a rendition of the "The Star-Spangled Banner" sung for Lincoln at the American premiere of Verdi's *Masked Ball* in February 1861, when seven Southern states had already declared secession and Lincoln was due to be inaugurated just weeks later. Kellogg, born in South Carolina, was a soprano who had won acclaim in Europe, sided with the Union, performed for Lincoln, and befriended Union generals.

Assembling albums of cartes de visite was often a conscious expression of the collector's politics, values, and ideas. Karl Schenk, who became the president of Switzerland in 1865,

assembled an album of prominent figures in the American Civil War, including generals and elected officials. On one page, below a photograph of the abolitionist Henry Ward Beecher, who had organized Lincoln's Cooper Union address, he placed the portraits of John Wilkes Booth and Sergeant Boston Corbett, with the word *Mürder* inscribed between them. The elegant portrait of Lincoln's assassin was a reproduction of a photograph circulated to promote his successful acting career. Corbett was famous for shooting a cornered Booth, who was meant to be captured alive. Taken for questioning, Corbett became a national hero when Secretary of State Henry Stanton declared him a patriot and freed him from facing a court-martial. Like many other celebrities, Corbett went immediately from his questioning to Mathew Brady's Washington, DC, studio to have his portrait made.

Shannon Perich

↗ Cartes de visite featuring singers Isabella Hinckley and Clara Louise Kellogg, from photographer George K. Warren's album, ca. 1860.

→ Page from Karl Schenk's album featuring California secessionist and Tennessee-born Senator William Gwin, Henry Ward Beecher, John Wilkes Booth, and Sergeant Boston Corbett, ca. 1865.

Senator *Gwin*.

Beecher.

Wilkes Booth.

Sergt. BOSTON CORBETT, 16th N. Y. C
Who shot J. WILKES BOOTH, April 26, 186

THE MARATHON

← Nipsey Hussle performing at the Warfield Theatre in San Francisco, California, June 27, 2018.

↓ Chain set including including Cuban links and pendants of Malcolm X and All Money In (the name of Nipsey Hussle's record label).

So life is what you make it
I hope you make a movement
Hope your opportunity survives the opportunist
Hoping as you walk across the sand you see my shoeprint
And you follow, til it change your life, cuz it's all evolution
And I hope you find your passion, cause I found mine in
    this music
But I hope it's not material cause that's all an illusion.

Nipsey Hussle, "Bigger than Life"
Quote selected by family of Nipsey Hussle

Nipsey Hussle, born Ermias Asghedom, was a force in the West Coast hip-hop scene. Raised in the Crenshaw district, he brought South LA to life with his unique sound and brand of storytelling through rap. Nipsey's music championed themes of Black empowerment, self-determination, and the lessons he learned growing up in one of America's toughest cities. His impact, however, reached far beyond his music.

As an independent artist, Nipsey charted his own rise from local fame to national stardom. After developing a loyal following with his celebrated mixtape catalog, he used unconventional strategies to monetize his success. He made headlines with his 2013 Proud 2 Pay campaign, charging $100 for limited-release copies of his Crenshaw mixtape. While that success highlighted his individual business savvy, Nipsey went against the grain by promoting his

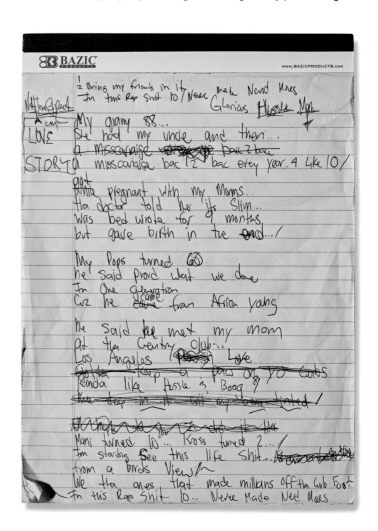

own brand of entrepreneurship grounded in collectivist principles, a strong sense of place, and obligation to community.

Nipsey carried a powerful sense of purpose that was ambitious, calculated, and contagious. His strategy was about the long game, or the "marathon," as he called it. He applied that metaphor to his personal and public life, mentoring and inspiring a generation to become politically engaged and displaying an integrity and authenticity not often found in his industry. An avid reader, Nipsey rebranded a pro-Black political ethos founded on community, self-sufficiency, and mutual aid by updating it for youth detached from traditional symbols of communal life and mired in extreme inequality. His lyrics offered moments of reflection along with stories of resilience, personal motivation, and collective pride—never preaching to his audience but instead sharing a life lived. Whether over a soul sample or a synth-driven track, Nipsey's gritty sound and authenticity made his message felt.

Nipsey attributed his broader vision to his experience visiting his father's home country of Eritrea, where he witnessed long-standing cultural traditions and communal survival strategies that shifted his perspective on the violence and excesses of Los Angeles. Putting his values into practice, Nipsey created his own label and initiated business projects that revitalized his neighborhood. His community-based business ventures included transforming a local strip mall into the flagship store for his multimillion-dollar brand, The Marathon Clothing. He supported neighborhood kids through STEM initiatives and hired formerly incarcerated people to staff his local businesses. As an activist, Nipsey brokered public-safety initiatives with local politicians.

Nipsey's untimely passing in 2019, at thirty-three years old, shook the spheres of entertainment and social justice alike. Beyond his rising rap stardom, Nipsey was recognized as a hip-hop intellectual and mentor of his own generation. Memorials sprang up across the country and personal stories flooded the news media. From entertainers and athletes to local shop owners and community members, many shared remarkably personal stories of being changed by Nipsey's sharing his love of books, his sound advice, or his generous support. For Nipsey, these were not good deeds but part of the work—effort he put into creating community with people when the cameras were turned off. On his passing, the organic, homegrown movement he was building was introduced to a broader audience, and they were moved. His "marathon" spirit of dedication, self-reliance, and community empowerment lives on. He is remembered as a hip-hop icon who represents a mission bigger than rap.

Tsione Wolde-Michael

← Lyric notebook on which
 Nipsey Hussle drafted lyrics
 for *Higher*, 2019.

→ Suit and shoes worn by
 Nipsey Hussle in the
 Grammy award–winning
 music video *Higher*, 2019.

COMEDY
AND
TRAGEDY

COMEDY AND TRAGEDY

Entertainment moves us. It keeps our attention because it sparks our emotions. This power is symbolized by the theatrical masks of comedy and tragedy, a legacy of ancient Greek theater. This chapter uses comedy and tragedy as a reference while exploring how entertainers can not only make us laugh out loud and weep in sorrow, but also scare us to death, enchant us with a soulful riff, and elate us by winning. More importantly, the artifacts showcased in this chapter reveal how performers have historically played to our passions to make a point, not just a profit.

Although entertainment brings audiences together and seeks to inspire a moment of shared sentiment, rarely does everyone end up feeling the same way. Because audience members bring with them their own desires and proclivities, a performance can incite a wide range of emotional responses and outcomes. Such competing and contested swirls of affect amplify both the connections and divisions among audiences. In 1849, English actor William Macready's subtle exposition of emotion, in contrast to more popular, melodramatic styles of expression, was so closely tied to elitism that his performances at New York's Astor Place Opera House led to debates between elite and working-class spectators inside the theater. The argument boiled over into a riot that destroyed the Opera House and ended with the state militia shooting into the crowd. Nearly 150 years later, in 1984, Bruce Springsteen's song "Born in the U.S.A." generated a similarly polarized emotional reaction among its audiences. In Springsteen's lyrics about a Vietnam war veteran returning home to encounter unemployment and indifference, some found a caustic indictment of economic policy and politicians' disregard of veterans' needs. Several Republican political campaigns, meanwhile, embraced it as a nationalistic anthem that cele-brated the country's can-do spirit without irony.

The following pages illustrate entertainment's enduring power to move us to action through the emotions that it conjures in an audience. Whether the tensions and contradictions of that experience lead us to conversation or to cruelty is up to us.

SAVION GLOVER TAP SHOES

One constant of American comedy has been a laugh line intended to reinforce social hierarchy. Tap dancer Savion Glover has said that "the history of tap dancing is that it was always the butt end of a joke," because it is partly rooted in blackface minstrelsy's mocking distortion of African American performative traditions. Wearing these shoes, Glover challenged the stereotypes embedded in tap dancing in his award-winning show *Bring in da Noise, Bring in da Funk*. Through awe-inspiring athleticism and innovative percussive techniques, his performance illustrates how Black Americans have transformed tap from a stylized and stigmatized type of dance into a rhythmic genre that expresses creative independence.

→ Promotional poster for Savion Glover's *Bring in Da Noise, Bring in da Funk*, ca. 1995.

JERRY SEINFELD PUFFY SHIRT

Even when we think entertainment is just helping us laugh off the daily grind, the release can say a lot about our views of the world and ourselves. A 1993 episode of the NBC comedy series *Seinfeld* became a fan favorite when Jerry inadvertently agreed to wear this shirt, designed by his neighbor Kramer's girlfriend, on the *Today* morning television show—only to be mocked by *Today*'s host, Bryant Gumbel, for looking like a pirate. *Seinfeld*'s engagement with such self-absorbed and superficial problems led critics to label it a "show about nothing." But the program mined human foibles and frailty for comic gold, reflecting people's tendencies to make something out of nothing.

↑ Still from *Seinfeld* episode "The Puffy Shirt," aired September 23, 1993.

COMEDY IS TRAGEDY REVERSED

Entertainers can never be sure how audiences will react to their work. And because most performers and producers depend on ticket and advertising sales, disapproving audiences can drive them to adjust their message, face new competition, or at least accept that their original message didn't quite get through. Two examples, more than a century apart, show how audiences have asserted their opinions by transforming tragedy into comedy, and comedy into tragedy.

First, the rare painting seen inside the circle on the wagon door below captures the emotional appeal of one of the most powerful American stories ever put to paper, Harriet Beecher Stowe's *Uncle Tom's Cabin*. The worn artwork is hard to discern, but pictures the story's enslaved heroine, Eliza, clasping her young son to her chest as she flees toward the Northern free states across a dangerously semifrozen Ohio River, with a slavecatcher's hounds in close pursuit. Painted onto wagon doors that opened to reveal the stage set for a dramatic adaptation of the tale, the image was an advertisement. It promised audiences a gripping story of life and death, as well as freedom and enslavement.

Originally, tragedy laced that politically minded drama. *Uncle Tom's Cabin* was published in a newspaper in weekly installments in 1851. Its characters, including Eliza and Uncle Tom, the elderly man whose moral sense underpins the story and who is murdered near the end of the tale, illustrated the humanity of enslaved people who faced horrific family separation and physical violence.

↓ Panels from a wagon belonging to a traveling troupe that performed *Uncle Tom's Cabin* in New England during the 1890s.

Though the story did not advocate for racial equality, it was influential at a time when fewer than 10 percent of voters in the North supported candidates vowing to abolish slavery. Its popularity led to its publication as a stand-alone novel, which became the best-selling American book of the era. Whether or not Abraham Lincoln actually said, upon meeting Stowe at the White House during the Civil War, "So, you're the little woman who wrote the book that started this great war," the alleged comment captures the book's influence.

Its popularity quickly led to stage adaptations, but there were two different versions. One endorsed Stowe's abolitionist message. The other, in the words of one reviewer, seemed to "make it quite an agreeable thing to be a slave." Transforming the African American characters into blackface minstrel comedy acts, and changing the ending so that Uncle Tom survives, this rendition of the drama turned the novel's title character from a tragic martyr into a symbol of subservience. The dominance of proslavery iterations after the Civil War reveals how widespread and deep-seated racism remained, even in the North, where most performances were held. By the 1890s, as segregation was enacted into law, broadside advertisements like these were common. Hundreds of "Tom Shows" played in villages, towns, and cities across the country. The wagon panels in the museum's collection belonged to one of the rare troupes that still played the story "as originally written." But they came to the museum after the show

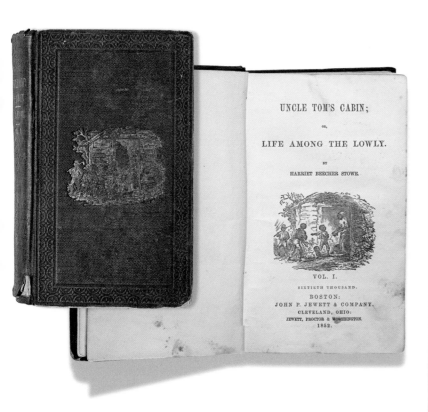

↑ First edition of *Uncle Tom's Cabin*, published as a novel in 1852.

→ Broadside advertisement for the "Original Southern Version" of *Uncle Tom's Cabin*, presented onstage by the W. I. Swain Company, ca. 1900.

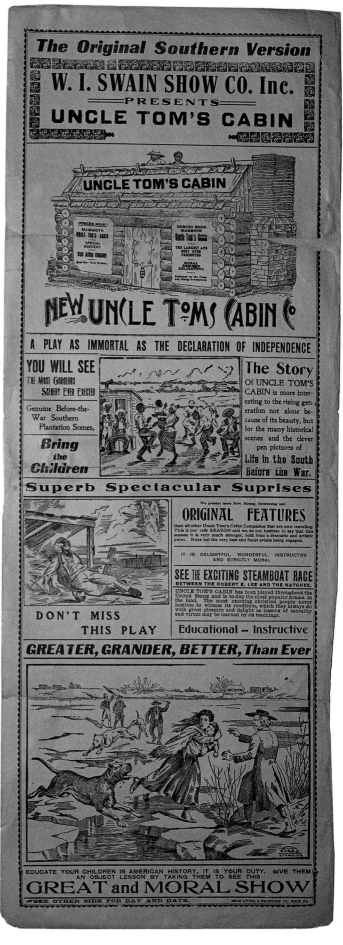

← Carroll O'Connor as Archie Bunker and Jean Stapleton as Edith Bunker in an *All in the Family* episode titled "Everybody Does It," aired January 1975.

→ Edith and Archie Bunker's chairs, end table, ashtray, and prop beer can, from the set of *All in the Family*, 1970–78.

went broke in 1900 just outside Brattleboro, Vermont. White theater audiences for the most part preferred racist comedy to abolitionist tragedy.

Decades later, many white viewers took the opposite approach in their response to Norman Lear's critically acclaimed television series *All in the Family*. The show's lead character, Archie Bunker, was a white warehouse worker and part-time taxi driver who felt passed over by the activism and liberal domestic policies of the 1960s and '70s. Worn out, like the armchair he always sat in, he reacted by spewing racist, sexist, homophobic, and other attacks on the range of people he believed threatened his place in society and at the head of his family—including his progressive daughter, her like-minded husband, and his wife, who (not coincidentally) sat in the more upright chair next to his.

Lear repeatedly defended his decision to broadcast Archie's explicit bigotry, saying the character "airs it, brings it out in the open, has people talking about it." His goal was to spark "conversation in the home" that would expose and fight hate by making it look comically backward. He liked to cite a letter he once received from a social worker who used the program to encourage people "to laugh at ourselves and view our own behavior with new insights."

But, for the most part, that's not what happened. The show's popularity ballooned because many white viewers genuinely identified with Archie's armchair commentary. And it wasn't just members of the white working class who felt this way. After Watergate, President Richard Nixon's White House tapes revealed his support for Archie's homophobic attacks and his disappointment that the show "made a fool out of a good man." "Archie for President" bumper stickers surfaced in 1973. The show generated so much debate about whether it was fighting or supporting bigotry that psychologists ran a study of viewers. They found that those who harbored greater prejudice were less likely to see the program as satire. "The present findings also seem to cast doubt on Norman Lear's . . . contention that by mixing humor with bigotry the show leads to a cathartic reduction of bigotry," the authors concluded. A show written to mock bigotry became widely viewed as a genuine airing of the grievances felt by disgruntled white Americans, who laughed with rather than at Archie.

Since then, many studies have confirmed that "entertainment is emotion." That is, people seek entertainment for the emotions it evokes. But their emotional reactions aren't always the ones producers and performers have in mind.

Kenneth Cohen

SESSUE HAYAKAWA

2017,0111.01

SESSUE HAYAKAWA PLAYING CARD

Asian immigrants to the United States often faced prejudice from those who perceived them as aliens and an economic threat. Beginning in 1882, federal laws severely curtailed immigration from China, and later from Japan, and barred these immigrants from citizenship. Despite this racism—and his typecast roles as the forbidden love of white leading ladies—Sessue Hayakawa quickly became one of Hollywood's biggest heart-throbs, and he featured in this 1916 deck of movie-themed playing cards.

MAE WEST FIGURINE

For more than six decades, Mae West urged a conversation about women's sexual liberation by playing powerfully sultry characters like the bar singer in *She Done Him Wrong*, who coined a suggestive catchphrase by asking a police officer, "Why don't you come up sometime and see me?" While her films attracted calls for censorship, she was the highest-paid woman in Hollywood by 1935. Countless mass-produced figurines of West, offered as popular carnival prizes, testify to her wide appeal not just as a sex symbol but as a pathbreaking woman in film. As she once put it, "I dominate the men in my pictures, and women—whether they admit it or not—like that."

→ Poster advertising *Every Day's a Holiday*, a 1937 comedy starring Mae West.

↓ BUSTER KEATON VELOCIPEDE

Buster Keaton rode this early form of bicycle in his 1923 film *Our Hospitality*, a satirical take on the legendary Hatfield-McCoy family feud in nineteenth-century Kentucky. Silent-film comedians helped Americans laugh through their fears of the rapid change and dislocations of modern life, often by nostalgically referencing "simpler times" (as this pedal-less bike did) and by telling stories about plucky heroes (like Keaton's character) who take on bigger bullies.

→ CHARLIE McCARTHY VENTRILOQUIST DUMMY

In Edgar Bergen's decades-long stage, film, radio, and television career, his ventriloquist dummy, Charlie McCarthy, was the unfiltered, flirtatious, and glib id to Bergen's superego. Whether trading insults with W. C. Fields or risqué repartee with Hollywood starlets, McCarthy got away with subverting social norms precisely because he wasn't a person. When a racy 1937 Adam and Eve sketch drew the ire of the Catholic Legion of Decency, it was costar Mae West who was blacklisted from NBC, not McCarthy.

← Charlie McCarthy, Edgar Bergen, and David Sarnoff, head of the Radio Corporation of America, at Sarnoff's New York office, ca. 1930.

WHAT'S SO FUNNY?

It's 1977, and you're making your debut on national television as a stand-up comic. You're a Native American. When you arrive at the sound stage, you quickly scan the script, which calls for you to appear in a sketch called "White for a Day." The show's host, none other than the legendary Richard Pryor, is supposed to come out dressed like General Custer, with arrows in his back. What could go wrong?

You could just go along with it and hope things turn out okay. You don't have a lot of time to think. If you refuse to go through with the sketch, you may not get called back for future gigs; you could even be thrown off the set. If you're Charlie Hill, an Oneida from Wisconsin, whose father serves as a respected leader of the Great Lakes Inter-Tribal Council, you say to Pryor and the show's production team, "I can't do this sketch, this is too racist."

Richard Pryor agrees. The producers strike the original sketch and the silly costuming. Instead, Pryor gives you a proper introduction for a five-minute stand-up comedy set in front of millions. Then you take the stage. "My name is Charlie Hill. *Sekoli* [hello]. I'm Oneida from Wisconsin—it's part of the Iroquois Nation. My people are from Wisconsin. We used to be from New York. We had a little real-estate problem."

There's no denying the effect of a finely crafted comedy set when performer and audience connect. Whatever pressure has been building all week long can be relieved in a few hours with a bunch of strangers in a darkened room. But comedy also calls communities—nations, even—into being. It has helped people think about belonging, identity, and power.

Crucially, however, not everyone has been in on the joke. From blackface minstrelsy and the Wild West Shows of the late 1800s, audiences have received clear direction on how to see themselves as white, as well as how to understand nonwhite Others on display for their amusement. Comic portrayals of nonwhite people as violent, lazy, lustful, stupid, or harmless hardened into common sense through repetition. These appear not just onstage but in magazines, advertisements, cartoons, logos, and lyrics. They have been projected onto "other" nonwhite people—from Asia, the Pacific, and the Americas. Stereotypes have taken the forms of team mascots, "ethnic" theme parties, and Halloween costumes. The popular sitcom *Fresh off the Boat* (2015–20) featured the young lead character Eddie Huang (played by Hudson Yang), an Asian American kid growing up in the American South. When one of his white friends cracks wise about Chinese people, Huang doesn't hold back: "I like jokes! Explain to me what's so funny so I can laugh too!"

Not being in on the joke has served as a challenge for comedians of color. Their response to garish and demeaning stereotypes has involved mining the cultural traditions of racial minorities and Indigenous peoples to transform the collective hurts of history into oblique jabs against racist thinking. Sometimes the responses have been more direct. In his book *African American Humor*, former *New York Times* critic Mel Watkins describes African American humor as a "survival tactic and buffer to social inequality" as well as an "exuberant expression of the joy and humanity of the Black folks who have created and continue to create it." In 1969 Vine Deloria Jr. claimed that Native American humor was "the cement by which the coming Indian movement is held together." Consider the brutal and inconvenient histories of child abduction, forced removal, banning of Native languages, arrest, imprisonment, killings, beatings, and torture of Native Americans. As Kliph Nesteroff noted in an oral history of Native American comedy, "The fact that many survivors could still find a way to laugh or joke was nothing short of remarkable."

One way of refuting any stereotype is to point out that what's been said about a group or a person isn't true. Yet the most brilliant comedians help us understand that stereotypes cause harm not only because they're untrue but because they deny the fullness of the subject's humanity. In *Nothing Ever Dies,* the Pulitzer Prize–winning author Viet Thanh Nguyen has noted, "While dominant Americans exist in an economy of narrative plenitude with a surfeit of stories, their ethnic and racial others live in an economy of narrative scarcity. Fewer stories exist about them, at least ones that leave their enclaves."

It's not simply that representations are scarce. Ethnic and racial Others actually see stories about themselves everywhere—in the movies, on TV and the internet, in lyrics, and yes, in comedy club routines. More often than not, those representations have been narrowed into predictable and tired stereotypes, from the hypersexualized or hyperviolent to the emasculated and feminized: the lotus blossom, the dragon lady, the Latin lover, the suffering maiden.

The Oklahoma-based filmmaker and writer Sterlin Harjo reflected on bearing witness to a person's humanity through comedy: "When Charlie Hill went on national television and simply spoke like a human being—it was a huge moment." The work of comics of color like Hill and Pryor, along with Ali Wong and others featured in this volume, invites us to find a way to confront stereotypes by insisting that there's more to all of us than what's been joked about.

Theodore S. Gonzalves

← Comedian Charlie Hill performing on *The Tonight Show Starring Johnny Carson,* aired June 18, 1991.

HARLEM GLOBETROTTERS UNIFORM

The Harlem Globetrotters basketball team was formed in Chicago in 1928. Using the name Harlem to reflect the team's African American roster, the Globetrotters traveled the country playing—and beating—white teams from small towns, but also the NBA's Minneapolis Lakers. Like Black barnstorming baseball teams, the Globetrotters deployed their supreme skill humorously in order to defuse racial tensions that could be aggravated by defeating white opponents. By the time Hubert Eugene "Geese" Ausbie wore this uniform in the 1980s, the Globetrotters had become a global family-entertainment phenomenon.

↑ Harlem Globetrotters' Geese Ausbie laughs during a basketball game, 1985.

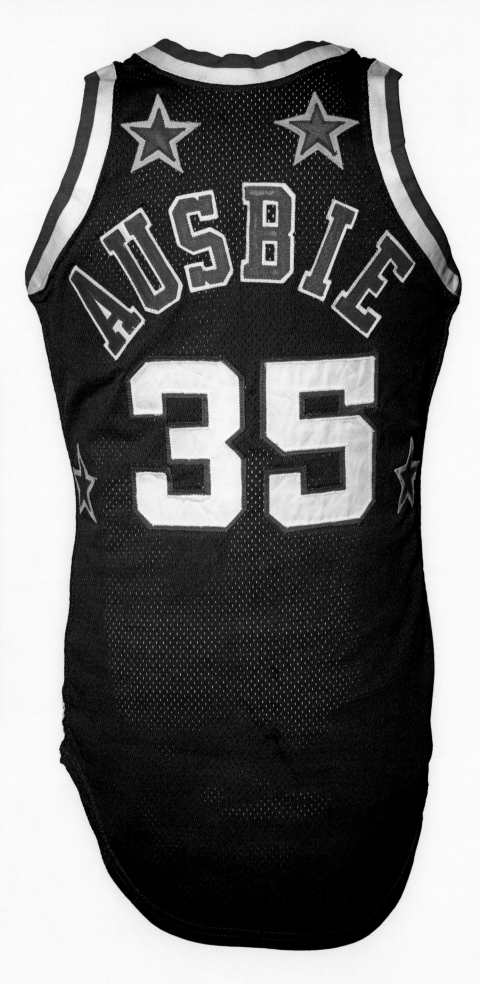

← Jack Soo as Nick Yemana in a *Barney Miller* episode titled "The Search," aired September 21, 1978.

→ **MISTY COPELAND "PANCAKED" BALLET SHOES**

When performing without tights, ballet dancers "pancake" their shoes with makeup to match their skin tone. In 2015, when Misty Copeland became the first African American principal ballerina at the prestigious American Ballet Theater (ABT), her pancaked shoes reflected her effort to expand racial diversity in ballet. Copeland has described being motivated by the hope that "little brown girls and boys [will] be able to look at me. . . and see a future for themselves in a space where they're not really celebrated."

↘ **NICK YEMANA POLICE BADGE, NAMEPLATE, AND COFFEE MUG**

In the 1970s sitcom *Barney Miller*, Jack Soo portrays Nick Yemana as a regular cop. Paperwork clutters his desk, he makes and drinks bad coffee, and he's tired of dealing with ridiculous complaints. As actor George Takei has put it, "Jack was always the quintessential All-American with an Asian American face." By being and mocking the mundane, Soo made Yemana into a groundbreaking character whose humor avoided the heavy accent, broken English, and servile or scheming roles that defined most Asian characters of the era.

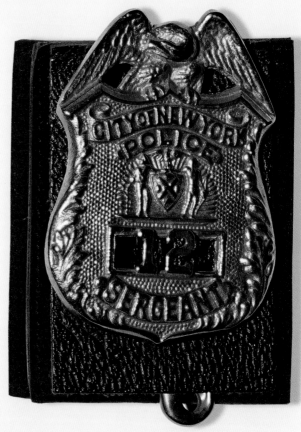

↑ American Ballet Theatre dancer Misty Copeland, photographed for *Vanity Fair* magazine in New York City, May 4, 2015.

↘ ALLIE REYNOLDS CAP

Allie Reynolds (Muscogee), like so many Native male athletes, had to live with the thoughtlessly pejorative nickname "Chief." And in 1951, after he became the first American League pitcher to throw two no-hitters in a season, a sportscaster dubbed the Yankee hurler "Super Chief." Although Reynolds could never shake off the name, in retirement he put his fame to use by founding the Red Earth cultural festival and leading other initiatives that celebrated Native peoples.

← Baseball card depicting Allie Reynolds, ca. 1951

BELIEVING IN BABY COBRA

Comedian, writer, and actor Ali Wong wore this dress for her 2016 Netflix comedy special, Baby Cobra. *Delivering a hilarious blend of autobiographical and social commentary while Wong was several months pregnant, the show went viral.*

When I filmed *Baby Cobra* I was eight months pregnant and wanted to pick clothes that accentuated my baby bump. I'm not a hider. Nobody knew who I was, so the expectations were low. When it came time to choose my outfit for the taping, I went with an $8 striped dress from H&M. Even though I was super pregnant, I still felt kind of hot in it. The truth is, people aren't used to seeing a female comic perform pregnant, especially an Asian American one. So it was fun to surprise people.

Then my look became a Halloween sensation. I couldn't believe it. It wasn't just Asian American women who dressed up as me looking extremely pregnant—so did groups of gay Black men, white men, even husbands and wives both dressed as me. It was insane!

So many Asian American women thanked me for finally giving them an easy Halloween costume. They said, "It was so nice to not wear a wig and just wear a striped dress and shove a pillow up there." I get asked about representation all the time and get tired of answering, but I think those costumes were an unexpected, delightful benefit of representation because Halloween is one of those holidays that can be really stressful!

That was the moment when I knew my life had changed. When I was a struggling comic, my father was so supportive. He grew up in a one-bedroom apartment in San Francisco's Chinatown, with no running water, and he worked hard to study and provide the best life possible for my siblings and me. He would come to my not-so-well-attended shows, and when I'd announce, "Oh, my dad is here!" after a really filthy joke, he would stand up and wave his arms in the air as if he had just won the Indy500 or conquered Mount Everest. My career was still struggling when he died. Now I think about him seeing my dress at the Smithsonian—he would probably be outside of that museum every day.

Ali Wong

← Ali Wong performing in *Baby Cobra*, 2016.

→ Dress worn by Ali Wong
on *Baby Cobra*, 2016.

AN INDEX WITH FANGS

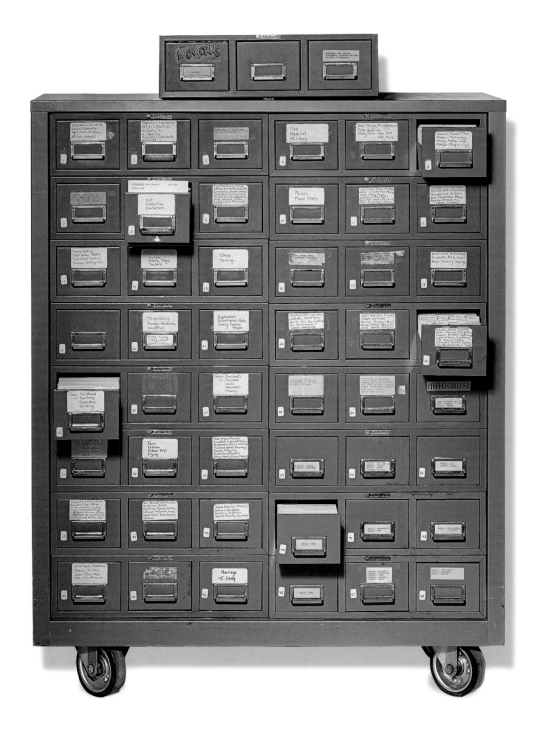

↑ Autographed photo of Phyllis Diller
on stage with Bob Hope during the
USO Christmas tour in Vietnam,
1966.

← Phyllis Diller's gag file, a card catalog
built by Art Steel Company, Inc.,
contains jokes she wrote and
collected between 1962 and 1994.

→ Costume worn by Phyllis Diller
during the 1966 USO Christmas tour.

"If cleanliness is next to godliness, my house has gone to hell."

During a career spanning six decades, Phyllis Diller broke barriers in the comedy world. She was the first female stand-up comic to become a household name, and she continued to perform her trademark self-deprecating jokes until her retirement in 2002, at the age of eighty-five.

Diller organized her jokes using this metal card catalog, which stands more than four feet tall and has fifty-one drawers. She filled it with 52,569 gag cards. Most of the jokes were typewritten, sometimes with handwritten notes added, on three-by-five-inch index cards. The jokes span the 1960s to the 1990s and are filed alphabetically under topics ranging from "accessories" to "world affairs." In addition to a joke, each card generally lists the category, date, and author of the joke. Although Diller wrote the majority of her own material, she also purchased jokes from other comedians for five or ten dollars apiece.

The gag file started as a simple book. As the collection grew, it became too difficult to find jokes in the book, so Diller created the card catalog. The indexing system made it easy for her to arrange sets of jokes about specific topics or for specific audiences.

Not only is the joke file a monument to Diller's career, it's also a time capsule. Whether it is about the student protests or inflation of the 1970s, a celebrity's many marriages, or gossip about the president, each joke gives us a glimpse into what people were worried or thinking about at a specific point in history. But the jokes often have an underlying message. Diller began her stand-up career in San Francisco as a thirty-seven-year-old mother of five. With her self-caricaturing jokes about how she couldn't cook, clean, or get along with her fictionalized husband, Fang, Diller poked fun at the myth of the idealized American wife and mother. Her stage appearance was skillfully based on that of clowns and court jesters to make her look as outlandish and harried as possible. Her roomy A-line dresses made her body look flat and shapeless, and she designed her go-go boots to hit her ankle at the skinniest point to make her legs look like toothpicks. With the addition of short, clownlike gloves, an almost transparent blonde fright wig with hairs standing on end, and a long cigarette holder, her appearance pushed the boundaries of "acceptable" womanhood as much as her jokes did.

Although she was known mostly for her comedy, Phyllis Diller's career also included starring roles in Broadway shows, piano performances with symphony orchestras across North America, the publication of five books, appearances in several USO tours, starring roles in three television series, and costarring with Bob Hope in three films. Diller even had her own line of canned chili, called Philli Dilli Chili. Her quick delivery, punctuated by her memorable cackling laugh, won her a spot in the *Guinness Book of World Records* for the most punch lines in a minute—twelve. In sum, Diller's career broke the mold for women in comedy and paved the way for other women to follow in her footsteps, but she also made mothers and housewives across the United States feel less alone in their common struggles.

Hanna BredenbeckCorp

CAROL BURNETT CHARWOMAN COSTUME

Carol Burnett wore this ragged and mismatched costume to play her signature Charwoman character on *The Carol Burnett Show,* a variety program that aired on CBS from 1967 to 1978. Exploring the thoughts of the nameless cleaning woman in pantomime, Burnett's Charwoman expressed both the constraints and the aspirations of working-class women. Whether the Charwoman was imagining herself as a torch singer or playing with toys that come to life, Burnett, who grew up in poverty, made her dreams meaningful.

↑ Comedian Carol Burnett as the Charwoman, 1972.

This signpost referenced the hometowns of the characters on the 1970s sitcom *M*A*S*H*. Based on a film of the same name, the show was set during the Korean War and followed the comedic antics of the staff at the 4077th Mobile Army Surgical Hospital, or MASH. Through its 1950s lens, the popular program used humor to address the horrors of war and leveled criticisms about the Vietnam War, helping the nation "bind up the wounds" from that conflict over the course of its eleven-year run.

↓ Members of *M*A*S*H* cast in front of the signpost, ca. 1976.

THE BUBBLING CRUDE OF THE CLAMPETTS

Come and listen to a story 'bout a man named Jed
Poor mountaineer barely kept his family fed,
Then one day he was shooting for some food,
And up through the ground come a bubbling crude.

So begins "The Ballad of Jed Clampett," the most unusual hit single of 1962. The bluegrass song by Lester Flatt and Earl Scruggs tells the story of the Clampett clan's accidental discovery of oil in their backwoods swamp, the sale of the family homestead for untold millions, and their move to Beverly (Hills, that is). The ritzy California suburb is home to swimming pools, movie stars, and—as fans of the television series *The Beverly Hillbillies* would learn—greedy and treacherous neighbors. The enormously popular CBS sitcom, which ran from 1962 to 1971, mined its unusual premise for comedy. But it also engaged viewers in conversations about wealth inequality and American values at a moment of socioeconomic reckoning, though its exclusively white perspective on these issues minimized its impact and eventually contributed to its cancellation.

Created by Paul Henning, the series drew on long-standing stereotypes and entertainment tropes to characterize the Clampetts as naive yokels whose rags-to-riches journey leaves them vulnerable to scheming and manipulation by savvy urban folk. The Clampetts are unsophisticated but also unpretentious, caring, ethical, and responsible citizens. In contrast, their Beverly Hills neighbors are often exposed as vain, superficial, and unscrupulous. Buddy Ebsen demanded that the role of Jed Clampett be written with dignity and wisdom, despite his lack of formal schooling, and he portrayed the character as an almost Lincolnesque backwoods sage.

The persistence of the yokel, rube, or hillbilly character in American entertainment—from the uncouth Jonathan in the influential early American play *The Contrast* (1787) to rural naïfs in the stories of Mark Twain and Will Rogers, the residents of Hooterville in the *Li'l Abner* comic strip, and trailer-park-dwelling Cletus in *The Simpsons*—speaks to the resilience of the trope despite enormous changes over the course of US history. Rubes were a constant presence on the vaudeville stage from the 1870s to the 1920s, an era when rapid urbanization, industrialization, and technological innovation created drastic dislocations and disorientation in lifestyle, labor, and leisure in the United States. Depictions of country folk in the big city, like the Clampetts, have persistently derived their humor from their subjects' presumed ignorance of modern urban life and its contrast with their allegedly quaint mannerisms. Indeed, period commentators noted similarities between the uncouth Hillbillies humorously crashing polite Beverly Hills society and folksy Texan Lyndon B. Johnson's coarse mode of operating within the refined

↑ The Beverly Hillbillies arriving in Hollywood in their family car in a photo from the show's first season in color, 1965.

Washington, DC, society of the Kennedy era. Like Johnson, the Clampetts were derided as nouveau riche, unschooled in the usual performances of wealth and consumption.

Yet the show's depiction of the dignity and morality of the rural poor, particularly in comparison to their wealthy neighbors, made a unique statement in popular culture at a time when Johnson's War on Poverty was drawing attention to disadvantaged communities throughout Appalachia and the rural South. Inspired by Michael Harrington's best-selling book *The Other America*, the president visited communities in eastern Kentucky in 1964 in a well-publicized tour to cast light on the economic hardships faced by Americans in regions untouched by the nation's post–World War II prosperity. Harrington's point was that the rural poor were invisible in American life, and in some ways the Clampetts did as much as Johnson to change that.

Tellingly, though, *The Beverly Hillbillies* did not explicitly engage with Johnson's policies. Having made their own fortune, the Clampetts were not concerned with economic inequality: the show's critique of wealth focused on how money is spent, held, envied, and wasted, not how (or whether) it is earned. The Clampetts' banker and friend Milburn Drysdale is obsessed with their fortune and ways to exploit it; his wife, Margaret, represents the old-money elite and cannot hide her disdain for the Clampetts' lack of sophistication or the way they spend their money. Various guest stars and bit players constantly attempt to scam and steal from the good-natured and generous Clampetts, offering weekly indictments of American society's greed.

Despite informing conversations about socioeconomic inequality among whites, this representation of the American South had nothing to say about racism or civil rights, even though the show was contemporary with the Civil Rights Movement. In this omission, as well as in the absence of any characters of color, *The Beverly Hillbillies* pandered to white viewers, like many other contemporary shows and films. But in 1970, Gil Scott-Heron's Black Power anthem "The Revolution Will Not Be Televised" foretold that "Green Acres, the Beverly Hillbillies, and Hooterville [Petticoat] Junction will no longer be so damned relevant." It was a prescient comment on the changing face of network television. CBS canceled *The Beverly Hillbillies* in 1971 alongside several other series in what was termed "the rural purge"—an attempt to redirect resources to programming that appealed to a younger, more diverse, and more urban audience. Among the replacements in coming years were *Good Times*, *The Jeffersons*, and *All in the Family*, shows that more directly addressed contemporary conversations about race, politics, and inequality.

Ryan Lintelman

→ Costume worn by Buddy Ebsen as Jed Clampett in *The Beverly Hillbillies*, 1962–1971.

↙ TOM THUMB HAT

Charles Stratton, better known by his stage name, General Tom Thumb, captured the nation's attention after his comic wit and musical talents impressed European monarchs in the 1840s. Promoted as a "distinguished man in miniature," he often performed in gentlemen's attire, including a top hat. His act raised the question: Was he mimicking a status he could never attain, or showing that all Americans could make their way to the top?

↓ Photograph of Charles Stratton with his manager, P. T. Barnum, ca. 1850.

→ KEN KESEY ACID TEST SIGN

In the early 1960s the Merry Pranksters, an itinerant group of freethinkers led by novelist Ken Kesey, used signs like this one as invitations to parties known as acid tests, where attendees experimented with the psychedelic drug LSD (legal at the time). These gatherings were part of a counterculture movement that brought antiestablishment messages into mainstream popular entertainment, especially influencing so-called acid rock bands such as the Grateful Dead.

CUBANIDAD IN EXILE

Ursula Hilaria Celia de la Caridad Cruz Alfonso was best known for her signature rallying cry of "¡Azúcar!" Her popular song "La vida es un carnaval" (Life is a Carnival) provided comfort after her death in 2003 to a global fan base who called the Afro-Cubana performer their own. A Grammy award–winning artist, Cruz recorded twenty-three gold records and 188 songs in total. Over a pulsing beat, her voice exhorts listeners not to cry but to look at the sweet side of life, which is a carnival and best lived singing. This is a fitting epitaph for a woman who tasted the bitterness of exile from her homeland, yet always showcased her cultural heritage, refusing to let it be overshadowed by the communist politics that engulfed her beloved island and kept her away from it.

Early in her career, as the lead singer for the band La Sonora Matancera, Cruz left Havana, Cuba, in 1960 for a one-year tour, never to return. As a female performer in an industry run by men, and later as a Cuban exile and naturalized American citizen, Cruz understood the importance of presentation and representation. Throughout her sixty-year career, the *bata cubana,* or Cuban rumba dress, was a symbol of her heritage and a part of her spectacular stage presence.

↑ Gold shoes custom-made for Celia Cruz by Mexican designer Miguel Nieto.

→ Cuban rumba dress worn by Celia Cruz in the 1970s and '80s.

Cruz selected this orange *bata cubana* to donate to the Smithsonian. She first wore it at Carnegie Hall and later at the Apollo Theater. With its traditional billowing sleeves and ruffled train, the gown combines the drama of the theater and the spectacle of Carnival. The nineteenth-century origins of the dress, like those of the Cuban people, reflect a blending of Spanish, African, French, and other cultures.

The dress itself is a burst of the tropics. Its deep orange color is a tribute to Cuba's national fruit, the mamey. Its ruffles are trimmed with yard after yard of white nylon eyelet ribbon, and the dress shimmers with extra glamour from more interwoven ribbons along the princess seams and collar.

"If I look into the audience and see somebody dressed better than me, I feel like I have failed," Cruz confided to Marvette Perez, then curator of Latino History and Culture at the National Museum of American History, in a 1998 interview. "People pay good money to come hear me sing, but also to see me sing, and I should always look the part." The combination of Cruz's voice and her costumes catalyzed her star power.

The Cuban flag was a powerful and visible symbol of Cruz's *cubanidad*, or Cuban identity. Her love of the island is more literally embodied in this second *bata cubana* owned by the museum, which evokes the Cuban flag with a white star at the center of the red triangle on the bodice, blue and white stripes running down the dress, and voluminous tricolored ruffles at the skirt and sleeves.

A worldwide phenomenon, yet always an exile, Cruz both transcended and embodied Cuba. Years after her death, the "Queen of Salsa" remains an icon of both Cuban culture and the sacrifices experienced by those forced to leave in the wake of the communist revolution led by Fidel Castro.

Castro denied Cruz's request to return to Cuba for her mother's funeral in 1962. The closest she came to Cuban soil was the US naval base in Guantanamo Bay, where she performed in concert in 1990. Before leaving, she slid her hand under the fence and scooped up a handful of Cuban earth. She asked to be buried with it.

Melinda Machado

← Performance costume representing the Cuban flag, worn by Celia Cruz at a Cuban Independence Day celebration in Bayfront Park, Miami, May 20, 2001.

SINGING FOR JUSTICE, DRAPED IN COURAGE

Reflecting on mass meetings during the Civil Rights Movement in an interview for the film *Eyes on the Prize*, activist-scholar-singer Bernice Johnson Reagon pointed out, "Most of the work that was done in terms of taking care of movement business had to do with nurturing the people who had come. . . . Basically songs was the bed of everything." A mass meeting served as the foundation for community care. Music, specifically congregational-style singing, nurtured the spirits of activists who had spent long days marching, protesting, and sitting in for freedom and equality. While the Civil Rights Movement was less fervent by the time Reagon, Mie Fredericks, Carol Maillard, and Louise Robinson came together to form the female vocal ensemble Sweet Honey in the Rock in 1973, an ethos of caring and nurturing infused the musical choices and performance style of the group, which, to this day, proclaims itself "a communal voice for justice and truth in the world."

Sweet Honey's a cappella songs are composed and arranged by group members. Through rhythms and harmonies drawn from the blues, jazz, soul, folk, gospel, and African musical traditions, they encourage shared emotional experiences and incorporate African American cultural traditions, history, and principles of social justice. "Moving On," a song from the group's 1985 album *The Other Side*, exemplifies these themes. An expressive solo alto voice opens the song singing, "Moving, moving on." The rest of the singers come in with "Nothing can stop me now/Nothing can hold me down/No one can keep me back 'cause we're/ Moving, moving on." The shift from *me* to *we* transforms an individual declaration into a collective chant as the singers reflect on Black freedom struggles of the past: "We've been 'buked/ We've been scorned/We've been talked about sure as you're born." The song offers a vision for collective social action: "Let's work together/Don't care how long it takes/We've come this way before 'cause we're/Moving, moving on."

Songs like this have a profound impact. Carol Maillard, one of the original members of the group, told a *Washington Post* interviewer, "We always knew that our music is very powerful. . . . The music really does reach and touch people in ways that are hard for us to comprehend because we're doing it. But what people tell us is that the vibrations, the heart, the soul, the

upliftment of the mind and the spirit, it just really reaches everybody."

Sweet Honey's lively performances and colorful attire visually reinforce the group's powerful message and illuminate cultural connections between African Americans and West Africa. Their vibrant smocks, pants, head wraps, and scarves often include adinkra symbols, which originated with the Akan people of modern-day Ghana. The costumes seen here include a black *dwennimmen* symbol, a stylistic rendering of two rams butting heads that represents strength and humility. Another symbol on the costumes is *gye nyame*, which features curves balanced around a central staff and means "fear none except for God"—a long-standing reminder of the power of faith to offer courage and comfort to those facing injustice and inequality. These symbols connect directly to Sweet Honey's ethos of care, which encourages listeners and reminds those in the fight for justice and truth that "we are the one we've been waiting for."

Crystal Moten

↘ Costumes worn by members of
Sweet Honey in the Rock,
designed by Dana Easter, 1980s.

→ JOHN COLTRANE SAXOPHONE

Jazz giant John Coltrane credited a religious epiphany with changing his life and helping him to overcome drug addiction. His deeply spiritual album *A Love Supreme* consists of a suite in four parts: "Acknowledgment," "Resolution," "Pursuance," and "Psalm." In the liner notes, Coltrane proclaimed, "All praise be to God to whom all praise is due." Coltrane began performing with this saxophone in 1965, the year of the album's release.

↑ Jazz saxophonist John Coltrane performing in West Germany, ca. 1959.

Singer Patsy Cline was one of the first women in country music to gain renown in the world of pop music. Around 1959, her mother Hilda Hensley lovingly stitched this costume for her, adorned with hot pink rhinestones. The black woolen discs sewn onto the costume celebrate her early singles records, including "Come On In," "A Poor Man's Roses," and "Stop the World." In 1963, Cline was killed in a plane crash just as her star was truly beginning to shine.

↑ Photograph of Patsy Cline, ca. 1959.

AN EMOTIONAL HISTORY OF CIRCUS ELEPHANTS

↓ Front page of the *Philadelphia Inquirer Sunday Magazine*, January 25, 1903.

↑ First American edition of *The Travels of Babar*, the second book in author Jean de Brunhoff's *Babar* series, 1934.

When the Greatest Show on Earth came to a close on May 21, 2017, the elephants weren't there. The Ringling Bros. and Barnum & Bailey Circus—a mammoth production created by the merger of two famous American circuses in 1919—had halted elephant performances a year earlier. Since the early 1800s, elephants had been the backbone of circuses, which were among the nation's preeminent forms of entertainment. The collapse of the circus signaled a shift in American culture, a shift embodied by the way elephants were presented and understood by the public.

Old Bet is widely regarded as the first circus elephant in the United States. The pachyderm was purchased by a New England ship captain in Kolkata, India (then known as Calcutta), when she was two years old, for a price of $450. On her arrival in New York City in 1796, she was sold almost immediately, allegedly for $10,000. She walked up and down the East Coast for the next twenty years, earning her owners a few cents from each astonished local who saw her.

Most Americans at the time had only encountered products made from elephants, such as ivory hair combs and billiard balls. But many spectators grew emotionally invested in Old Bet, paying to see her repeatedly over the years as she matured, each time marveling at the dexterity of her trunk, her curiosity, and her engagement with humans, especially if they offered her food.

Old Bet's popularity encouraged the development of full-fledged circuses featuring panoplies of human and animal performers, though elephants remained central attractions. After the 1860s, the expansion of railroads increased the number and traveling range of circuses. Circus managers responded to the heightened competition by acquiring more elephants and teaching them fancier tricks. A disciplined system of industrialized training and travel emerged, one that frequently traumatized the elephants and triggered what one scholar has described as "a century-long escalation in the numbers of elephants killing people and people killing elephants." When elephants lashed out, they were put on trial for murder and poor behavior in the press as well as in the courts, as if they had criminal motivations.

A number of "rogue" elephants were executed. Thomas Edison's participation in the electrocution of Topsy in 1903 was filmed. These public killings were spectacles from which circuses often profited by selling the thrill of watching enormous animals who might turn on their trainers. There were some calls to abolish such barbaric practices, but during this period even members of the early animal-welfare societies felt that killing an elephant was justified if it had harmed a human. They argued for humane and quick methods of dispatching elephants rather than changes to their treatment.

During the Great Depression and World War II, attitudes toward the exploitation of elephants and other animals began to change. In part the shift was driven by another pop culture medium—children's cartoons. Through cartoon elephants like Babar, Horton, and, most influentially, Dumbo (whose mother gets

locked away as a "mad elephant" because of her reaction when baby Dumbo is taken from her), Americans developed an interest in and affinity with the emotional capacities of elephants that gradually eclipsed the urge to control and dominate them. As this affinity grew, trainers began to see that forcing elephants and other animals to perform tricks made audiences (and, as a result, circus owners) uncomfortable. Circuses began concealing rather than publicizing the behavior of "problem" elephants. At the same time, there was increasing public concern about the dangers posed by hunters and habitat destruction to elephants in the wild. Circus attendance dropped dramatically as compassion for the animals rose.

By the late twentieth century, trainers and zookeepers recognized aggressive elephant behavior as an instinctive response that humans could mitigate by improving training and treatment. Still, at least nine circus and zoo workers were killed by elephants in the 1990s. Some cities banned circuses with elephants, and many smaller companies closed.

The Greatest Show on Earth held out longer than most, but pressure from journalists, animal rights groups, and diminished ticket sales forced Ringling to remove elephants from its shows in 2016. Even after they retired their elephants, the circus's owners were criticized for not giving them enough space and for chaining them at night. Since the 1990s, several elephant sanctuaries in the US, replete with sections of wetlands, grasslands, and forest, watering holes big enough to wade into, and heated barns, have been offering safe places for retired and rescued elephants. The evolution of attitudes toward circus elephants reflects the dynamic way in which audiences, special interest groups, and commercial entities shape American entertainment.

Shannon Perich

→ COCKFIGHTING GAFFS

Cockfighting is a blood sport that pits two roosters against each other in a potentially lethal fight, with spectators packed around the ring gambling on the outcome. In the 1800s, the razor-sharp gaffs that covered the birds' natural spurs were longer in the United States than in Europe, resulting in more bloodshed. Although illegal in many states since the colonial era, the sport remained popular long afterward, motivating protests and policies that address cruelty to animals.

↘ EARLY BOXING BELT

In the United States during the mid-1800s, the majority of prize-fighting pugilists (as boxers were known) were of Irish descent. While some of these fighters resisted the discrimination Irish Americans faced, especially in hiring and housing, by deploying racist symbols and asserting their whiteness, others focused on proclaiming their prowess as both Irish and American champions. Nobody knows who wore this trophy belt, which likely dates to the 1840s, and is one of the earliest surviving examples in the United States, but it includes harps and clovers that reference Irish heritage on either side of flags and eagles that symbolize a "United America."

↓ IVORY BILLIARD BALLS

Ivory's strength made it ideal for making billiard balls that constantly collide. But only five balls could be made from a single elephant tusk. And since heat and humidity made balls lopsided over time, they were shaved down to reshape them and then discarded when they became too small. In the decades before celluloid derivatives replaced ivory in the 1910s, manufacturers killed more than one thousand elephants per year primarily to make billiard balls.

↑ Photograph of Burroughes's and Watts's billiard balls in *The Picture Magazine*, 1893.

University of Maryland student Jim Henson transformed an old coat and ping-pong ball into this first Kermit puppet. Kermit joined the Muppets in March 1955. As Kermit's career took off in Muppet shows and movies, he gained a pointed collar and more frog-like feet but remained the cheerful and optimistic leader of his gang of eccentric strivers, inspiring fans to believe in themselves.

↑ Kermit the Frog, ca. 1977.

↖ **PROP MOSQUITO IN AMBER FROM *JURASSIC PARK***

Jurassic Park thrilled audiences with a cautionary tale of science run amok. By harvesting DNA from the blood found in prehistoric mosquitoes preserved in amber, scientists re-create predatory dinosaurs that then run rampant and destroy the safari park built to showcase them. While the presentation of the science involved was flawed (in both the movie and the novel that spawned it), the anxieties and ethical questions the story raised about the perils of progress seemed, like the velociraptors, inescapable.

← **PROP EGG FROM *ALIEN 3***

Science fiction films prey on fear while portraying the strength—and sometimes the sacrifice—that can overcome it. In the *Alien* franchise, the fortitude displayed by Ellen Ripley stood out at a time when male heroes dominated the nation's multiplexes. But the third installment of the series turns darker, as the parasitic creatures implant an alien embryo in Ripley. She commits suicide in order to prevent the new alien queen from bursting from her chest, rejecting an offer from a megacorporation that wants to breed and control aliens, not unlike the creators of *Jurassic Park*'s dinosaurs.

THE EVOLUTION OF A THRILL

For the Native Hawaiians who developed the centuries-old practice of surfing, *he'e nalu* (translated literally as "wave sliding") involved both understanding the ocean and developing a spiritual connection to it. Early European spectators, aghast at the sport's extreme nature, believed surfing had "too terrific an aspect for a foreigner to attempt." Back then, *terrific* meant something closer to *terrifying* than it does today, but this etymological relationship between thrill and danger also explains why skill, knowledge, and innovation have always been fundamental to the sport.

On dry land, the "terrific" aspect of staying upright on a fast-moving board is also central to skateboarding. Both sports attained unprecedented popularity in 1960s California. There, an abundance of baby boom teens, newly developed materials, and a growing economy—not to mention sunshine and good surf—turned surfing and "sidewalk surfing" into emblems of a youth culture.

Yet the history of surfing in California really begins with Duke Kahanamoku, a Native Hawaiian and one of the sport's earliest ambassadors. A three-time Olympic swimming gold medalist, Kahanamoku traveled the world for swim meets and shaped boards to encourage surfing in other countries as he went. The Smithsonian's Kahanamoku board is a Hawaiian plank design known as an *alaia*. It was shaped by Kahanamoku on the beach at Corona del Mar, California, in 1928 for Jerry Vultee, the aerospace engineer who designed Charles Lindbergh's Lockheed Sirius monoplane. Because Hawaiians view surfboards as personal connections to the sea, they were historically custom-made, tailored to both the body and the character of the owner.

→ Duke Kahanamoku with a surfboard bearing his name, likely on a Hawaiian beach, ca. 1915.

↙ Handmade *alaia* surfboard, measuring nine feet, four inches in length, shaped from redwood and fashioned by Duke Kahanamoku at Corona del Mar, California, 1928.

↓ Homemade skateboard fabricated by ten-year-old Jerome Gardner, ca. 1969.

Innovation has always been the beating heart of surf and skate, rooted in Native Hawaiian skill and knowledge. An abundance of baby boom teens, newly developed materials, and a growing economy—not to mention sunshine and good surf—turned surfing and "sidewalk surfing" into emblems of a youth culture.

Decades later, California kids unknowingly followed this tradition as they created handmade wooden skateboard decks. Using basic two-by-four lumber, the 1969 skateboard on page 159, shaped like a rocket, uses the wheels from a roller skate cut apart and nailed to the bottom. The donor carved the wooden plank in homage to the Apollo moon mission that year.

While the marriage of athlete and inventor was a crucial element in both early surfing and skating, the connections to aerospace engineering in particular foreshadowed massive change. The development of fiberglass, polyurethane, and Styrofoam during World War II, and especially their application to aircraft design, led to broader applications for these synthetic materials by the 1960s. They enabled the creation of lighter, shorter boards that made possible more daring tricks or just a smoother ride. These materials also facilitated the mass production of boards, transforming a DIY craft into an industry. The growth of the aviation and aerospace industries on the West Coast in the 1950s also contributed to the expansion of a middle class with money and time to devote to surfing and skating. Baby boom teenagers put some of that money into the new mass-produced boards.

The equipment used today builds on those innovations, as seen in Kelly Slater's board, manufactured by Channel Islands Surfboards, which was used to win the Rip Curl Pro Tournament at Bells Beach, Australia, in 2010. Its featherweight design allows for more control and ease of motion, emphasizing the sport's growing emphasis on agility over the strength required to surf on the one-hundred-pound boards of Kahanamoku's era. Yet it would be wrong to attribute all that change to synthetic materials alone, as it was Hawaiian surfers such as Rabbit Kekai, Kealoha Kaio, and Buttons Kaluhiokalani who pioneered the hard turns and complete rotations that increased demand for more maneuverable boards in the first place.

Innovations in surfing skills and technology carried over to skating, as seen in the skateboard used by Tony Hawk to complete his last 900-degree trick in 2016. Its lighter trucks and more durable wheels enabled Hawk to gain enough speed on a halfpipe to perform two-and-a-half revolutions in midair.

Innovation has always been the beating heart of surf and skate, rooted in Native Hawaiian skill and knowledge. In the economic prosperity of postwar California, the practice of *he'e nalu,* combined with new developments in material science, inspired a bunch of daredevil California kids to brave the terrific challenge of staying aboard.

Jane Rogers

↓ Tony Hawk skateboard featuring his Birdhouse brand deck, Independent trucks, and a combination of wheels bearing his name, 2015.

↘ Channel Islands surfboard used by Kelly Slater to win the 2010 Rip Curl Pro Tournament in Australia.

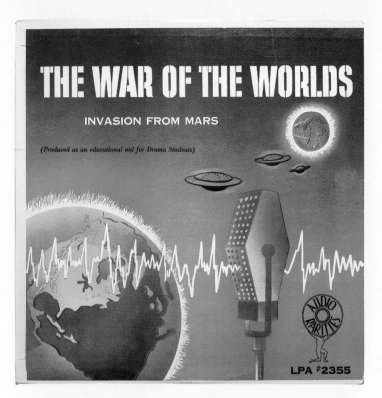

↑ *War of the Worlds* recording released as an educational aid for drama students, 1955.

↓ ORSON WELLES TYPEWRITER

On October 30, 1938, Americans tuning into CBS radio heard a horrifying report about alien invaders from Mars laying waste to New York and New Jersey. It was Orson Welles's radio adaptation of the sci-fi classic *War of the Worlds*, but some listeners—already on edge after news of Hitler's unchecked aggressions in Europe—allegedly took it to be true and panicked. Newspapers may have exaggerated the show's impact in order to sell papers, or to paint the rival medium of radio as irresponsible. Welles likely used this typewriter in the 1930s and '40s, when he contributed to the scripts for *War of the Worlds* and the award-winning film *Citizen Kane*, which explores the dangerous ways that media moguls can undermine democracy.

↙ *HANDMAID'S TALE* COSTUME

In the Hulu streaming series adaptation of Margaret Atwood's dystopian novel *The Handmaid's Tale*, women able to have children are rare. Revered yet enslaved, they are forced to conceal themselves under winged bonnets and red robes that mark them as handmaids—vessels of procreation for the elite in their theocratic state. The show debuted in 2017 and quickly became a platform for conversations about women's political and sexual rights, inspiring protestors to don homemade versions of the costume at the Supreme Court and elsewhere.

↑ Demonstrators from the Center for Popular Democracy Action stand on the US Supreme Court steps dressed in *Handmaid's Tale* costumes to protest Amy Coney Barrett's nomination to the court, September 30, 2020.

TO
GERTRUDE EDERLE
FIRST WOMAN TO SWIM THE ENGLISH CHANNEL
ACCLAIMED BY POPULAR CONSENT
TO BE THE MOST POPULAR PERSONAGE OF HER TIME
THIS TROPHY IS PRESENTED, IN BEHALF OF THE AMERICAN PUBLIC
IN RECOGNITION OF THE GLORIOUS QUALITIES
OF AMERICAN WOMANHOOD
SHE HAS SO NOBLY DEMONSTRATED

GAINING AND LOSING GROUND

GAINING AND
LOSING GROUND

In the same way a football team marches down the field toward a touchdown that can change the outcome of a game, entertainers leaning into the political possibilities of their work hope their performance can gain ground toward desired outcomes, whether by establishing a precedent or shifting public conversation. Musicians, athletes, and actors have used their visibility to challenge harmful stereotypes and to advocate for civil rights, better pay, and institutional change. Yet lasting gains on such issues often take generations to realize and rarely come without setbacks along the way. This chapter focuses on artifacts that tell stories about the long game of effecting change through entertainment.

It is often hard to tell whether recent changes will have a lasting impact, because conversations about pressing issues are influenced by the evolution of broader social, political, economic, and cultural ideas over time, as well as immediate, and unpredictable, audience reactions. Jackie Robinson's 1947 contract with the Brooklyn Dodgers soon led to a significant increase in the number of African American and Afro-Latino players in the major leagues. But after Althea Gibson became the first African American woman to win major tennis titles in the late 1950s, the next forty years witnessed only a handful of African American women in the upper echelons of the pro tour before Venus and Serena Williams began winning Grand Slams in the late 1990s. Conversely, even when expressions of resilience and activism have not brought immediately visible results, they may have planted seeds that bring about longer-term change. Hollywood restricted actors such as Hattie McDaniel and Cantinflas to stereotyped roles, but a generation or two later, actors such as Whoopi Goldberg and John Leguizamo cited their presence onscreen, and the obvious devaluing of their talent, as a motivation for continued efforts to break down those barriers. In this chapter's stories of delayed progress and prolonged conversation, we see that the tension between gaining and losing ground means the game is never over.

↖ LANCE ARMSTRONG BIKE

Lance Armstrong benefited from the light weight and high strength of this Trek 5500 bicycle frame, made of carbon fiber, during the 2000 Tour de France. That was the second of his seven Tour victories, all of which were annulled after Armstrong admitted in 2013 to using illegal performance-enhancing drugs. A US Anti-Doping Agency report—including lab test results and testimony from former teammates—prompted Armstrong's confession after a decade of denials, tarnishing his image as an inspiring cancer survivor and athlete.

PEPE: THE LIMITS OF CANTINFLAS

The Mexican actor Mario Moreno Reyes, better known by the name of his most popular character, Cantinflas, starred in over forty Mexican films in the 1940s and '50s. Often compared to Charlie Chaplin or Groucho Marx, Cantinflas outwits those with more money and power through quick wordplay or physical comedy. Playing a humble rural bumpkin, Cantinflas challenges the status quo and comes out on top, critiquing social hierarchies even if he doesn't change them. Appealing to working- and middle-class audiences as well as film critics, Cantinflas became the face of Mexican cinema and a projection of national identity, delivering political commentary through victories over a wide range of people and institutions with authority—including the United States.

His use of wit to outflank elites did not, however, translate effectively to Hollywood, where film studios preferred to continue capitalizing on racial stereotypes of Mexicans. Despite his huge following across Latin America and Latino communities in the United States, it was only after his 1957 Golden Globe–winning performance in *Around the World in Eighty Days* that he was offered a title role in the 1960 English-language Hollywood film called *Pepe*. The plot follows Pepe, a ranch hand from Mexico, as he searches for his beloved horse after it was sold without his knowledge. Along the way, he helps rescue the careers of a jaded actor and the struggling Hollywood director who bought the animal. He even meets a host of stars, from Frank Sinatra and Sammy Davis Jr. to Cesar Romero, Zsa Zsa Gabor, and Judy Garland. With all these heavy hitters, the film seemed guaranteed to become a hit. But while Cantinflas often had a hand in developing his Mexican scripts and films, and at least had been given space for his talents in *Around the World*, he had little involvement with the script for *Pepe*. The result blunted his edge. *Pepe* ended up critically panned and failed to break even. It also cost Cantinflas his chance to take on the powerful stereotypes that disempowered Mexicans and other Latin Americans in the United States.

As Pepe, Cantinflas is out of his element. Although he comes out on top, the film credits the character's success to luck rather than to his typical clever undermining of social hierarchy. His misadventures, including betting his piggy bank to win big in Las Vegas, being confused by a cross-dressed Jack Lemmon, interrupting a choreographed fight scene thinking that Shirley Jones's character is in actual danger, getting his tortilla autographed by Bing Crosby, and being amazed by automatic doors, all reinforced stereotypes of lazy, dim, or drunken Mexicans.

Instead of letting Cantinflas challenge these stereotypes, the movie industry ignored the very real discrimination such representations supported, including segregation and other civil rights abuses, mass deportation, and dangerous, exploitative working conditions. Big American studios preferred to present Mexicans and other Latin Americans one-dimensionally: in the role of the Latin spitfire and musician, exotic and seductive; the menacing bandido; or the helpless victim who needs saving by white characters.

To introduce white US audiences to Cantinflas, Columbia Pictures used promotional items like this mechanical figure and booklet. Both present him in a pose and style that were longtime Cantinflas trademarks. To Mexican audiences familiar

↑ Cantinflas as Pepe, meeting Bing Crosby as he searches for the Hollywood director who has his horse, in a scene from the film *Pepe*, 1960.

with Cantinflas, the image signaled a parody of the rural, uneducated *pelado* character. But in the US, and in the role of Pepe, it simply reinforced the stereotype. Hollywood was not ready for a true Cantinflas character. So, as Cantinflas scholars have noted, Moreno acquiesced in the creation of a safer version, one that lacked the charm and wit required for either a big Hollywood break or, more importantly, a meaningful assault on anti-Mexican prejudice.

L. Stephen Velasquez

↑ A souvenir program from the film *Pepe*, 1960.

→ Wind-up mechanical figure of Cantinflas as Pepe, distributed in 1960 to promote the film.

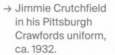

→ Jimmie Crutchfield in his Pittsburgh Crawfords uniform, ca. 1932.

← JIMMIE CRUTCHFIELD SHOES AND WILLIE MAYS SHOES

The shoes above, worn by Negro League all-star Jimmie Crutchfield during the 1930s and 1940s, show signs of long-term wear, including cracked leather and the sole splitting from the toe of the left shoe. After major league baseball desegregated, African American Hall of Famer Willie Mays, near the end of his career in 1971, sported little-worn shoes with the branding of the well-equipped San Francisco Giants.

↑ Outfielder Willie Mays of the San Francisco Giants at bat, ca. 1970.

JACK CALVO BAT AND MARIANO RIVERA GLOVE

In the late 1800s, US businesses and international tours brought baseball to Latin America, where local players made the game their own. But those interested in playing in the United States could reach the major leagues only if they could pass as white. Afro-Cuban outfielder Jacinto "Jack" Calvo was one of a handful of Latino players who moved back and forth between the Negro leagues, major leagues, and white minor leagues in the 1910s and 1920s. Some seventy-five years later, Panama-born relief pitcher Mariano Rivera was a thirteen-time all-star, five-time World Series champion, and part of a wave of Latino players who made up nearly 30 percent of major leaguers by the time Rivera retired in 2013.

↑ Baseball card depicting Jack Calvo playing for the Los Angeles Angels, ca. 1914.

↓ Mariano Rivera of the New York Yankees throws a pitch against the Boston Red Sox at Fenway Park in Boston, Massachusetts, April 13, 2002.

HOLLYWOOD'S RED SCARE, ON GELATIN SILVER

The iconic Cold War question "Are you now or have you ever been a member of the Communist Party?," intoned by Wisconsin senator Joseph McCarthy, has come to symbolize the tension between authoritarianism and freedom of thought and expression in the United States. After World War II, a fear of communist power and infiltration boosted McCarthy's influence in the Senate and expanded the scope of the House Committee on Un-American Activities (more popularly known as HUAC, the House Un-American Activities Committee). Because McCarthy and other members of HUAC believed the entertainment industry was using its popularity and distribution networks to disseminate communist propaganda, McCarthy's invasive question is perhaps best remembered for leading to the blacklisting of star entertainers and the creative writers who drafted their material.

Starting in 1947, HUAC called actors, directors, screenwriters and playwrights, singers, radio commentators, and others (including the sports hero Jackie Robinson) to the Capitol to defend themselves against accusations of disloyalty to the United States and to testify about colleagues also suspected of being communists. Ten of the first eleven witnesses cited the First Amendment and refused to speak (the exception was the German-born playwright Bertolt Brecht, who testified but then left the country for East Germany). When courts found the unwilling witnesses guilty of contempt, producers and their sponsors refused to hire them or anyone suspected of communist leanings—a suspicion that extended to almost any critic of the

→ John Huston, photographed by
Richard Avedon, 1956.

hearings. Over the next decade, the growing blacklist cost more than three hundred entertainers their livelihoods and dampened creative expression.

Plenty of texts cover these events, but the toll this process took on targeted entertainers becomes uniquely clear in the photographs Richard Avedon made of them. A New York–based fashion photographer, Avedon had many well-known friends and acquaintances who were affected or threatened by the committee's overreach. He began making a name for himself in the pages of *Harper's Bazaar* just as HUAC was ramping up its interrogations. Although professional photographers were not investigated to the same degree as Hollywood or other sectors of the entertainment industry, Avedon was socially aware and a close friend of the writer and HUAC critic James Baldwin. He used his friendships, his magazine assignments, and his status as an influential photographer to document the personalities of several of HUAC's victims in Hollywood.

Avedon's most distinctive photographs depict his sitters against white backgrounds, catching them in mid-sentence, holding a musical note, or engaged in conversation. Although the portraits are not always conventionally flattering, they illuminate his sitters' humanity by foregrounding their emotion, energy, and life experience.

Avedon's portrait of John Huston is a case in point. Huston was an Oscar-winning screenwriter and filmmaker. He was also among the founding members of the Committee for the First

Amendment, a network of stars who criticized HUAC and defended those first ten witnesses. Other members included Lucille Ball, Groucho Marx, Judy Garland, and Humphrey Bogart. But after a star-studded protest in Washington, DC, in the fall of 1947, and two radio broadcasts titled *Hollywood Fights Back*, HUAC painted the new committee as communist sympathizers and dug up evidence that at least one had briefly joined the Communist Party. The group disbanded with little effect. Huston grew increasingly disgusted by McCarthyism and moved to Ireland in 1952. Four years later, Avedon took this photograph on page 172, an outtake from a *Harper's Bazaar* photo session that captures Huston's animation as he tells a fish story. The session was timed to promote Huston's version of *Moby Dick*, the ultimate fish story. In its portrayal of a vengeful Captain Ahab relentlessly chasing the white whale—to the point that he destroys lives, including his own—the film offers a subversive commentary on the obsessiveness of McCarthyism.

Avedon photographed Humphrey Bogart when he was starring in Huston's 1953 film *Beat the Devil*, cowritten by Avedon's friend, the author Truman Capote. The aging actor's diffident gaze and his old-fashioned bow tie invite viewers to see him as an ordinary middle-aged man rather than a movie star. Bogart distanced himself from the Committee for the First Amendment by claiming he had been hoodwinked into joining. After he issued statements asserting, "I am no communist," his career suffered only a modest backlash, and he followed up *Beat the Devil*—his last Huston film—

← Humphrey Bogart, photographed by Richard Avedon, 1953.

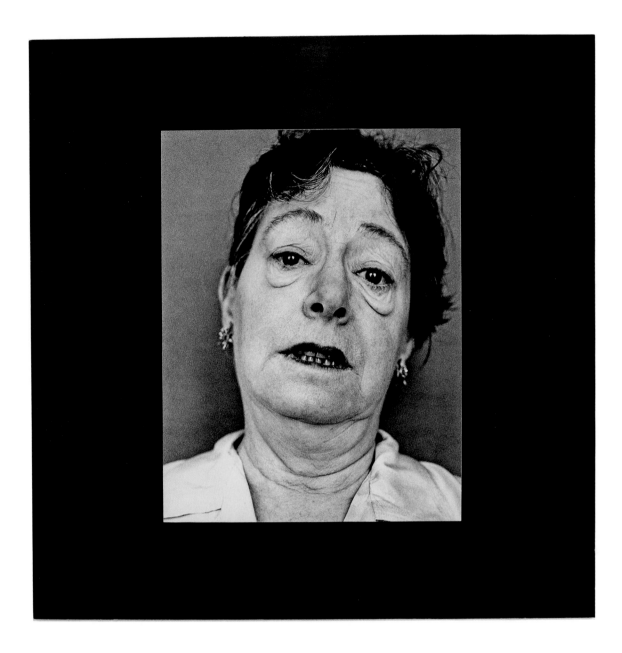

with *The Caine Mutiny* in 1954, which latently supported the HUAC hearings by ultimately prizing loyalty over a justified mutiny.

Others were less fortunate. The sharp-tongued and sharp-witted writer Dorothy Parker helped found and chair antifascist organizations the FBI labeled as "communist fronts" and was active in a variety of liberal causes with Jewish and LGBTQ friends, whose identities alone aroused HUAC's suspicion. She left the *New Yorker* to write screenplays in Hollywood in the 1930s, but she was blacklisted by 1949, and her screenwriting career never recovered. When Avedon photographed Parker in 1958, she was writing book reviews for *Esquire* magazine. His stark portrait of her invites viewers to see her strength tinged with sadness.

Like Parker, the English silent-film star Charlie Chaplin had long been harassed by the US government, including by HUAC. The morning of September 18, 1952, before sailing to Britain for a film premiere, Chaplin visited Avedon's studio. In a last-minute gesture before leaving the studio, Chaplin posed with his fingers at the side of his head like devil's horns, referencing the way he was depicted by McCarthy and Hollywood gossip. The next day, the US attorney general announced an inquiry into Chaplin's political beliefs that kept him from returning to the United States for two decades.

HUAC's investigations into suspected communist sympathizers began to subside in the late 1950s, after McCarthy was censured for targeting US Army generals and the Supreme Court ruled that motion pictures were a form of free speech protected by the First Amendment. But painting liberal entertainers as enemies of the nation is a practice that has persisted. Avedon's photographs, reflecting the toll McCarthyism took on individuals and creativity, serve as a cautionary tale for our currently divided country.

Shannon Perich

Avedon used his friendships, his magazine assignments, and his status as an influential photographer to document the personalities of several of the House Un-American Committee's victims in Hollywood.

↑ Jackie Robinson testifies before the House Committee on Un-American Activities (HUAC), Washington, DC, July 18, 1949.

→ Album cover for *Hazel Scott: A Piano Recital*, 1946.

← JACKIE ROBINSON SIGNED BASEBALL AND HAZEL SCOTT RECORD COVER

In 1949, when the House Committee on Un-American Activities (HUAC) accused Black activist, singer, and former all-American football star Paul Robeson of communist sympathies, the committee called on Jackie Robinson—famous for desegregating major league baseball—to testify against him. But when Robinson appeared, he denounced "injustice in the courts, police brutality, and lynching," and declared segregation a greater threat to American democracy than communism. Undeterred, the committee continued to brand civil rights activists as "reds" and damaged their careers. One victim of this campaign was the Trinidadian-born piano virtuoso and groundbreaking television host Hazel Scott.

→ MICHAEL JORDAN JERSEY

During the 1990s, as racial tensions erupted in the United States in the wake of the videotaped police beating of Rodney King and the O. J. Simpson murder trial, the world's most popular athlete was African American basketball star Michael Jordan. The Chicago Bulls shooting guard was a five-time NBA MVP and won six championships over the course of the decade. "Air" Jordan's competitiveness and flair made him a superstar on and off the court and one of the most successfully marketed individuals in history. Though he was criticized for not being politically engaged as a player, his on-court and commercial success led him to a groundbreaking role as owner of the Charlotte Hornets franchise. Since then, he has been a vocal supporter of Black businesses and Black Lives Matter.

← A pair of Nike brand red, white, and black Air Jordan 1 high-top sneakers signed by Michael Jordan, ca. 1984–85.

↓ **BABE RUTH SIGNED BASEBALL AND STREET BALL FROM HAVANA, CUBA**

These two baseballs illustrate different ways the game has enthralled young people for generations. For Thomas J. Jones, growing up in Scranton, Pennsylvania, it was the thrill of a lifetime to have a baseball signed by major league home-run king Babe Ruth when he visited the town on a barnstorming tour around 1920. And the lower ball, made of adhesive tape by kids growing up in Havana, Cuba, during the 1990s, represents the kind of make-do equipment that kids in urban neighborhoods have devised since the early twentieth century.

↑ **NYU "BATES MUST PLAY" BUTTONS**

These buttons were created in 1940 by students at New York University who protested the school's decision to follow the widespread practice of excluding Black athletes from their teams when traveling to compete at segregated universities. NYU administrators reacted forcefully to the protest, sending the university's football team to play the University of Missouri without its star fullback Leonard Bates and suspending seven students for leading the public effort to change university policy.

→ Australian volume of sheet music for Frank Sinatra hits, ca. 1944.

↓ FRANK SINATRA BOW TIE

Frank Sinatra wore this bow tie in 1942, the year he left Tommy Dorsey's band to pursue a solo career. Cash-strapped but ambitious, Sinatra performed in ties that his wife, Nancy, made from her old dresses. The son of a working-class Democratic Party ward captain, Sinatra campaigned for Franklin D. Roosevelt in 1944 and was for decades an outspoken advocate for labor and civil rights, until a falling-out with the Kennedys and opposition to Vietnam War protests shifted his allegiance in 1970, and he became a vocal supporter of Ronald Reagan and Richard Nixon. By then, he had also moved on from Nancy and her bow ties.

Farrah Fawcett became the pinup girl of the 1970s in this iconic swimsuit, enshrined in the best-selling poster of all time. Yet Fawcett's success as a sex symbol kept her from getting the more serious acting roles she wanted. Only in the last years of her life did she finally win critical acclaim, for a documentary about her battle with cancer.

↑ Poster of Farrah Fawcett wearing a red swimsuit, 1976.

→ COSTUME FROM *A CHORUS LINE*

In the mid-1970s, declining attendance suggested that the Broadway musical had lost its cultural relevance. Vietnam, Watergate, and the movements for civil and human rights all belied the homogeneous and happy tales of the shows that made the "Great White Way" a reference to more than just the bright lights of theater marquees. Into these headwinds sailed *A Chorus Line*, a gritty psychological "antimusical" that debuted in 1975 and became a Pulitzer Prize–winning sensation, the longest-running production in the history of Broadway. The plot introduces a diverse array of hungry, ambitious, and traumatized supporting dancers, both men and women, who ultimately blend into a single anonymous chorus line wearing matching shimmering costumes.

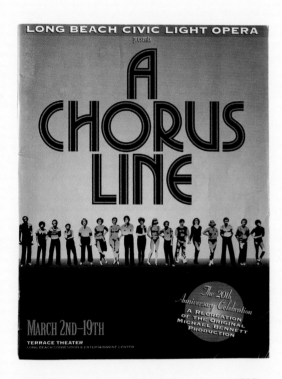

↑ Playbill for a production of *A Chorus Line*, ca. 1995.

PERFORMING FREEDOM, ENACTING SLAVERY

By the time this collectible photograph of Chang and Eng Bunker was being sold, around 1860, the conjoined twins had become more than famous. They had both defied and defined the limits of freedom in the United States.

The fine suits and posh furnishings in the photograph demonstrate the brothers' rise in status. They had arrived in America in 1829 as Chinese-speaking teenagers from Thailand (then known to Americans as Siam). A contract they signed paid their mother $500 and promised them a shared payment of $2.50 per week working for the ship captain who had brought them over— "wherever he chooses." That phrase, present in the brothers' contract, was intentionally vague. It gave the captain the power to determine how they would be toured as "curiosities," a term that soon gave way to the even more derogatory word *freaks*.

Widely described in newspapers and medical reports as having been "purchased" or "bought," Chang and Eng fought notions that they were enslaved by taking control of their own shows, offering some of the captain's take to the man the captain had paid to manage them. The relatively small number of Asian people in the United States at this time were not clearly categorized as "white" or "Black," but race defined who could be enslaved, and running a commercial performance tour required rights to mobility and property that were largely restricted to white people. Thus, the brothers' entrepreneurship helped them win recognition as free men.

Chang and Eng exhibited themselves for several years, coining the term *Siamese twins* to advertise their exotic foreignness as much as their conjoinment. But steadily their performances shifted from staged acts to witty, unscripted conversation, and their advertisements stopped referencing large commercial "audiences." A broadside from the around 1840 shows them in the midst of this transition, still trading on their Asian heritage even as they declare their intention to "receive visitors" like refined American elites.

Profits from running their own tours allowed Chang and Eng to strengthen their claims to elite status. They took the Anglo surname Bunker and became US citizens at a time when naturalized citizenship was restricted to white people. They bought a plantation in the North Carolina foothills, married sisters from a locally prominent family, and had twenty-one children between them. They also purchased and sold enslaved people.

Newspapers from all over the country frequently reported on the Bunkers' improbable ascent up the social and economic ladder. Several correspondents paid them a visit, remarking on the enslaved people they saw and wondering "how slavery works with the Siamese Twins"—not least because the brothers once had to resist the perception that they were enslaved.

In the years after this photo was taken, Chang and Eng sided with the Confederacy in the Civil War. Their eldest sons were wounded in its service. They also invested heavily in Confederate war bonds, money they lost—along with their enslaved workforce— when the Union won. They had largely retired from touring as their family and plantation grew, but they returned to exhibitions after the war to make money in their late fifties. Fatigue from travel contributed to their death in 1874. By then, increased immigration from East Asia was already generating a backlash that made it harder for later Asian immigrants to claim the rights accorded to white people.

Kenneth Cohen

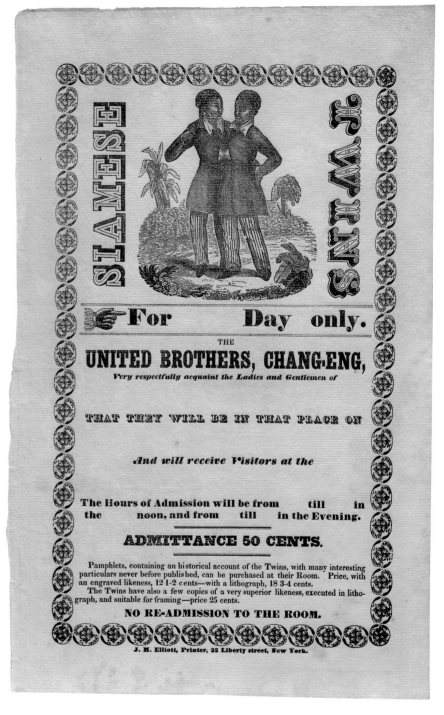

↑ Collectible cabinet card of
 Chang and Eng Bunker, ca. 1860.

↑ Blank broadside advertisement,
 printed in 1834, that could be
 filled out with local details as the
 Bunker brothers toured.

↑ William Sidney Mount, *The Banjo Player*, 1856.

← WILLIAM BOUCHER JR. BANJO

Banjos are West African in origin, but by the early 1800s both Black and white musicians were creating versions of the increasingly popular instrument, incorporating new designs and materials. This early mass-produced example, manufactured in 1845 in Baltimore by a white drum maker named William Boucher Jr., appears in an 1856 portrait of George Freeman, an African American coachman and musician on Long Island. The painting notably depicts Freeman without the effect of minstrelsy that was sweeping the nation at the time.

GRACIELA MICROPHONE

Afro-Cuban singer Felipa Graciela Pérez y Gutiérrez, popularly known as Graciela, broke down racial and gender barriers in the 1940s and 1950s. Her risqué shouts and double entendres got her songs banned from Spanish-language radio but earned her wide popularity. Upscale New York City nightclubs broke their prohibitions against hiring bands mostly made up of musicians of color in order to book the "First Lady of Latin Jazz," while her performances of *son* music defied its categorization as masculine among Latina/o audiences.

→ Portrait of Graciela and her brother, Francisco Raúl "Machito" Gutiérrez Grillo, at Glen Island Casino in New York City, July 1947.

CULTURAL RESILIENCE: LYDIA MENDOZA AND SELENA

From the 1920s through the 1980s, Lydia Mendoza's evocative and empowering lyrics, soulful voice, and colorful traditional Mexican performance costumes—like this iconic and colorful traditional Jalisco dress—embodied the shared cultural heritage and experience of working-class Tejanos (Texas Mexicans) and Mexican refugees and migrants. Mendoza was one of the first superstars of the Tejano music world, a world Selena Quintanilla-Pérez expanded at the end of the century by crossing over to the US English-language music scene. Through her powerhouse vocals, signature dance moves, and edgy fashion—exemplified by the leather outfit on page 188, which she wore to perform at the 1994 Tejano Music Awards—Selena fused traditional Mexican and Latin American music with the contemporary beats and sexy looks of the 1990s. With their different styles, Lydia Mendoza and Selena gave voice and visibility to Tejana women in a male-dominated world, and their syntheses of sounds reflect the resilience and contributions of Latina/o communities in a country where they face discrimination, marginalization, and violence.

Lydia Mendoza was born in Houston, Texas, to musically inclined, working-class parents. She spent part of her early childhood in Monterrey, Mexico, where her mother nurtured her musical talent. First performing with her family's band in 1928 at age twelve, Lydia went on to record over fifty Spanish-language albums and earned numerous awards, including the National Heritage Award from the National Endowment of the Arts in 1982. She was also the first Tejana inducted into the Conjunto Music Hall of Fame in 1991. Considered the voice of the laboring ethnic Mexican community, Mendoza is fondly remembered as *la alondra de le frontera* (the lark of the border) and *la cancionera de los pobres* (songstress of the poor). She earned these titles because her music reflected her firsthand experience with poverty as well as with the rampant discrimination and violence directed against Mexicans and Mexican Americans in the United States during the first half of the twentieth century.

The Mendozas resettled in South Texas from Mexico in the 1920s, joining many political asylum seekers and laborers who fled the violence of the Mexican Revolution. Fearing that the influx of Spanish-speaking peoples across the Southwest would threaten their political and cultural dominance, US public health officials and nativist groups portrayed Mexicans, regardless of their citizenship status, as disease-ridden and racially inferior, and thus both exploitable and unfit for full citizenship. At four years old Mendoza was deloused with gasoline at the border crossing in Laredo, Texas, a common and intentionally dehumanizing practice.

In Texas, the Mendozas initially worked on farms, but they found greater success and satisfaction as a family musical act, El Cuarteto Carta Blanca (the Carta Blanca Quartet). Lydia played the mandolin and sang lead vocals, performing mostly traditional Mexican folk songs for Mexican and Mexican American audiences along agricultural migrant-labor routes extending from Texas to Michigan to California.

By 1934, the seventeen-year-old Lydia had recorded her first solo album, and her 1937 single "Mal hombre" (Evil Man) became a hit on the Spanish-language radio airwaves in the United States and Latin America. The song, ahead of its time for its feminist undertones, emblematized the affirmation of Tejana women's

↓ Cover of program from 1978 American Old Time Music Festival, featuring images of Lydia Mendoza and Sweet Honey in the Rock.

← Jalisco dress worn by
Lydia Mendoza, ca. 1980.

↓ Autographed photo of Lydia
Mendoza with the inscription
"Para Marie Cariñosamente.
Lydia Mendoza. 1–19–48."

← Leather outfit worn by Selena Quintanilla-Pérez at the 1994 Latino Music Awards.

↓ Selena Quintanilla-Pérez wearing the leather outfit during the 1994 Latino Music Awards, photographed by Al Rendon.

voices and experiences that became a hallmark of Lydia's music. Continuing to tour with her family, Lydia performed in vaudeville acts for Spanish-speaking audiences. Some of her performances were sponsored by the League of United Latin American Citizens (the oldest Latino civil rights organization in the United States) and radio stations alike, to promote pride in their Mexican heritage and culture and raise funds to address the needs of the Mexican American community.

At a time when Mexican communities were fighting to claim their humanity and civil rights, and faced segregation in schools, theatres, and restaurants, Mendoza's performances and vibrant stage costumes invoked ethnic and cultural pride while signifying the important role Tejanas played in forging both Tejano identity and dynamic cultural expressions that resisted injustice. As "the first Queen of Tejano," Mendoza paved the way for future artists like Selena, who would take Tejano music mainstream without forgetting the stories and people it centered.

Selena Quintanilla-Pérez's natural talent and charisma transformed the Tejano music industry just as Lydia Mendoza's career was winding down in the 1990s. That decade was marked by a resurgence of anti-immigrant policies and rhetoric, including militarization of the US-Mexico border and the mass deportation and criminalization of undocumented immigrants. At the age of twenty-three, in 1994, Selena became the first Tejana artist to win the Grammy award for best Mexican American album, with *Live!*, and the first Latina artist to have an album to debut at No. 1 on the Billboard 200, with *Dreaming of You*. The next Queen of Tejano

← Selena Quintanilla-Pérez,
photographed by Al Rendon, 1993.

was on her way to a major crossover into the US English-language music market when she was tragically murdered in 1995 by an enamored fan-club president. Selena's death was deeply and intimately mourned by the Latina/o community, which saw her as a symbol of resilience and pride, just as Mexican Americans had treasured Lydia Mendoza.

Selena, like Lydia, was born in Texas to a working-class family with rich musical roots. She spent her life in the Black and brown working-class barrio of Molina, in Corpus Christi, Texas. Influenced by her father's experience in a doo-wop group that blended musical styles and played to Anglo and Mexican audiences, Selena's music crossed cultural, language, generational, and physical borders.

Just like Lydia, Selena was twelve when she recorded her first album with the family band, Selena y Los Dinos (Selena and the Guys), formed by her father in the early 1980s. And the Quintanilla family, like the Cuarteto Carta Blanca, performed Spanish-language songs for Mexican and Mexican American audiences at family celebrations, restaurants, and county fairs. They also performed on *The Johnny Canales Show*, a popular Tejano television program.

Like Lydia and other female artists, Selena faced discrimination in the male-dominated Tejano music industry. But Selena's response was to transcend and transform the genre. Her powerful vocals, her distinctive fusion of cumbia, hip-hop, pop, and R&B, her charismatic personality, and her unapologetic celebration of her Tejana working-class roots and aesthetics brought her transnational popularity and commercial success. These achievements in turn encouraged the reconstruction of a pan-ethnic Latina/o identity that emphasized shared experiences and culture over significant differences within the community. Young Latinas, especially, saw themselves in Selena's brown skin, black hair, curvaceous body, fierce fashion, and transgressive use of Spanglish (a mixture of English and Spanish). Her success challenged the negative and politicized media portrayals of Latina/o youth as criminals, instilling hope, self-love, and a sense of shared identity and belonging to an entire generation.

Twenty-six years after Selena's death, her legacy lives on in her music, biopics, makeup collections, and limited-edition collectibles, as well as her depiction in vibrant murals around the United States. Linked in so many ways, Lydia Mendoza and Selena represent the diversity and evolution of Latina/o identity and culture. They remain a source of pride and inspiration for new generations, who see in them the spirit of perseverance and synthesis through which Latinas have reimagined greater possibilities and shaped their communities and world.

Verónica A. Méndez

LATIN BOIZ JACKET

The Dominican American group Proyecto Uno was founded in New York in 1989. Combining musical styles such as Caribbean merengue, hip-hop, and house, and singing in both Spanish and English, Proyecto Uno helped define Latin urban music in the 1990s. The group's custom-decorated jacket, proclaiming that "Latin boiz do it mejor" (Latin boiz do it better) draws on street art and a mixture of Spanish and English to project a multicultural Afro-Latino identity.

→ FAB 5 FREDDY'S BOOMBOX

Boomboxes became the emblematic portable sound systems of hip-hop. This Sharp HK-9000 from the mid-1980s was used by graffiti artist, rapper, and filmmaker Fred Braithwaite, known as Fab 5 Freddy. He was the original host of the groundbreaking show *Yo! MTV Raps*, which brought hip-hop into the mainstream in the US and globally.

GRANDMASTER FLASH'S TURNTABLE AND MIXER

Hip-hop music was invented in the 1970s by African American, Caribbean, and Latinx youth in the Bronx. Joseph Saddler, known as Grandmaster Flash, was a leading hip-hop DJ. He pioneered new techniques for creating music and beats by manipulating sounds on vinyl records using his Technics turntable and Rane mixer. In 1982, he collaborated with rap group the Furious Five on "The Message," a song that addressed systemic inner-city poverty and contributed to making hip-hop a platform for social commentary and activism.

→ ALTHEA THOMAS ORGAN SHOES

From 1955 through 1960, Althea Thomas served as organist at Dexter Avenue Baptist Church in Montgomery, Alabama, where Martin Luther King Jr. was pastor. In 1955 and 1956, community activists met at the church to organize the landmark Montgomery bus boycott, which resulted in the desegregation of local public transportation. Using these modified tap shoes to operate the organ's pedals, Thomas uplifted listeners with gospel music that is inextricably linked to the long, ongoing fight for civil rights.

↓ JENI LEGON TAP SHOES

Multitalented performer Jeni LeGon was best known for athletic tap dancing that had been associated with men and often led her to break convention by wearing pants. LeGon's manager predicted that as the first woman of color to be paid a salary by a major Hollywood studio, she would "bridge the gap between the distinctly white and distinctly Black in films." But Hollywood confined LeGon to demeaning stereotyped roles, like the one she played wearing these tap shoes alongside actors in blackface in the 1937 film *Ali Baba Goes to Town*.

↑ Jeni LeGon dancing with Bill "Bojangles" Robinson in *Hooray for Love*, 1935.

↗ **JACKET WORN BY ANGEL IN *RENT***

The musical *Rent* translates Giacomo Puccini's opera *La Bohème*, about young bohemians in nineteenth-century Paris, to New York City in the 1990s. In the original 1994 Broadway production of *Rent*, the character Angel, an HIV-positive transgender woman played by Wilson Jermaine Heredia, wore this collage jacket on her last New Year's Eve. As her lover Collins says, above all else, "Angel believed in love," and a fuchsia strip on the jacket issues the challenge to *be* what you believe, not just say it. Angel lived up to her ideals by fabricating this jacket. Made from a shower curtain and covered with pictures of the fashion and friends she treasured, it countered narratives of lonely AIDS sufferers with Angel's resilient love of life.

BREAKING THROUGH, AGAIN AND AGAIN

American identity has long been defined through sport. Values learned in competition—persistence, endurance, and self-improvement—are often portrayed as intrinsic to the character of the nation. Competition on the playing field is reflected in US economic, academic, and political systems. Given the role of sport in American life, it is no wonder that women, historically dismissed as the "weaker sex," have employed it to challenge stereotypes, change opinions, and fight for greater participation in public life. Each generation of women athletes has carried on that fight over the past century.

Women's efforts to participate in athletics gained ground in the 1920s, a period recognized by sportswriters and scholars as America's "Golden Age of Sport." As sports competitions became an essential product of a burgeoning entertainment marketplace, sporting success led some women to be ranked among the era's greatest celebrities. In the wake of the long and bitter struggle for women's enfranchisement, these groundbreaking performers inspired vigorous debate about the defiance of traditional constraints by "modern girls."

Gertrude Ederle was one such competitor. The daughter of German immigrants, she won three gold medals in swimming at the 1924 Olympic Games in Paris. Two years later, at the age of twenty, Ederle was crowned the "Queen of the Waves" and became the first woman honored with her own ticker tape parade in New York City. Later that year, she received an ornate silver trophy from the publishing giant William Randolph Hearst after she beat out Babe Ruth in a newspaper poll for the title of the nation's most popular athlete.

Ederle earned these accolades for becoming the fastest person to swim the English Channel. On August 6, 1926, dressed

→ Gertrude Ederle, covered in grease, on the beach at Cap Gris-Nez, France, before beginning her historic swim across the English Channel, 1926.

in a custom two-piece bathing suit emblazoned with a small American flag, wearing homemade goggles, and slathered with grease to insulate herself from the icy waters, Ederle swam the Channel in fourteen hours and thirty-four minutes, shattering the previous record by nearly two hours. The dangerous undertaking had previously been completed by only five men. Ederle herself had failed the previous year. Supported by newspaper syndicates and a public eager to believe in the triumphant possibilities of modern life, Ederle and a handful of other women participated in a well-publicized competition to be the first woman across. Challenging gender conventions, these athletes provoked discussion not only about whether women were physically capable of the feat but whether it was socially appropriate for them to try.

Trudy, as she was affectionately called, became a worldwide sensation. Her achievement bolstered the shift toward a new concept of womanhood rooted in equality and freedom, as represented by suffrage and the flapper movement of the 1920s. As the inscription on the Hearst trophy read, Ederle's fame was due in part to "the glorious qualities of American womanhood she has so nobly demonstrated."

Unfortunately, although newspapers profited richly from selling her story, professional mismanagement, combined with growing anxiety from her public profile, hearing loss, and an accident that severely damaged her spine prevented Ederle from fully capitalizing on her fame. Yet by beating the male swimmers who preceded her, Ederle quieted many critics who believed that female athletes were inherently inferior to their male counterparts.

But not all critics were silenced. Even as American women increasingly participated in sports, their athletic interests and abilities remained targets for exploitation and criticism, as

↑ William Randolph Hearst trophy awarded to Gertrude Ederle in 1926 by "National Vote of the American People" for most popular athlete.

← Goggles worn by Gertrude Ederle as she swam the English Channel, 1926.

Billie Jean King discovered in the 1970s. Ranked the top player in the world five times, King fought bitter battles with the American Tennis Association over a number of issues, including its promotion and remuneration of female players. These disputes led to her founding the Virginia Slims Circuit in 1970, an organization that evolved into today's Women's Tennis Association.

In 1973, while the women's liberation movement built on the precedent of the 1920s to push more forcefully for gender equality, an event was staged that gave King an opportunity to challenge sexist rhetoric and again prove the ability of female athletes. The "Battle of the Sexes" exhibition tennis match pitted the twenty-nine-year-old King against Bobby Riggs, a fifty-five-year-old retired champion who had made headlines by disparaging the athletic abilities of women. For Riggs, a former Wimbledon and US Open Champion, the match was an opportunity to exploit chauvinism for personal gain. Claiming that he could defeat any female tennis professional, Riggs stated, "Women play about 25 percent as good as men, so they should get about 25 percent of the money men get."

King initially refused to play Riggs, accepting only after the world's number one woman player, Margaret Court, lost to him in straight sets. Featuring high-visibility sponsorships and sensational entrances that outdid even the most outlandish prize fights, the exhibition was held at the Houston Astrodome on September 20, 1973. With 30,472 spectators in attendance and

Set at the height of the women's liberation movement, the "Battle of the Sexes" tennis match drew global attention and provided an unprecedented opportunity to refute long-standing prejudices.

over 90 million television viewers worldwide, it was the most widely viewed tennis match in history.

Wearing a sequined dress designed by Ted Tinling, King embraced the spectacle, despite thinking "it would set us [women] back fifty years if I didn't win that match." After a rough start, King won handily, vanquishing her outspoken male opponent in three straight sets.

Women's sports continue to face significant inequalities in financial compensation and public recognition. However, women's athletic achievements, from Ederle's Channel crossing to the "Battle of the Sexes," along with more recent pushes for equality by professional women soccer and basketball players, remind us of the powers of sport as a forum where biases can be exposed and barriers broken.

Eric Jentsch

← Billie Jean King warming up for the Battle of the Sexes match against Bobby Riggs in the Houston Astrodome, September 20, 1973.

THE LEGACY OF ALTHEA GIBSON

As a trailblazing leader of women's sports, Billie Jean King has often spoken of her admiration for Althea Gibson, who broke color barriers in US and global tennis in the 1950s and became the first African American win a Grand Slam tournament. Gibson generously donated her 1958 Wimbledon championship trophy to the National Museum of American History, along with her tennis dress and rackets.

We all have turning points in our lives, and I had a huge one at the age of thirteen when I had the privilege of seeing Althea Gibson play. She was my first tennis hero. I got to see her play on the grandstand court at the Los Angeles Tennis Club, and got to see what it looked like to be number one, and I've always remembered how inspired I was that day. If you can see it, you can be it. . . . I was able to play tennis because it was free, it was accessible, and the Parks and Recreation of Long Beach provided free instruction, but African Americans weren't allowed to play in any [US Lawn Tennis Association-] sanctioned tournaments until 1950. So it was so hard for me to imagine how hard life had to be for her, and yet there she was in 1957, the number one player. She

← Althea Gibson in her opening-round match at Wimbledon, 1957.

↓ Venus Rosewater Dish awarded to the ladies' singles champion at Wimbledon, won by Althea Gibson in 1958.

was beautiful and graceful and intimidating all at the same time on the court. She was so inspiring. Her road to success was a challenging one, but I never saw her back down. She's really the person who showed me what it took to be number one.

Althea faced her challenges differently than Arthur Ashe and I. We used tennis as a platform. That's not what Althea wanted. She just wanted to play. She was saying, "Just let me be one of you." But unfortunately in the 1950s it just wasn't that easy. But you have to remember that if it hadn't been for her, it would have been even harder for Arthur, for Venus and Serena Williams and the ones that followed. So she is the Jackie Robinson of tennis, but didn't have the chance to make a living like he did. She once said that "being champion is all well and good, but you can't eat a crown." People don't remember today that she went on to break the color barrier in the LPGA, too, and was a great bowler, but in addition to the barriers she faced because of racism, people also didn't appreciate her in her own time because she was a girl. If she had been a boy, she'd have had a lot more attention and opportunity.

Billie Jean King

← Tennis blouse and skirt worn by Althea Gibson at Wimbledon, 1957.

↑ Cover of *Time* magazine featuring Althea Gibson, August 26, 1957.

→ Harry C. Lee tennis racket used by Althea Gibson at Wimbledon, 1958.

→ SAMANTHA MEWIS AND MIA HAMM JERSEYS

Samantha Mewis, rated by the soccer statistics firm GoalPoint as the best US soccer player in the 2019 Women's World Cup, wore the #3 jersey seen here in the final match against the Netherlands, a 2–0 victory for the US. Mewis and her teammates used that championship to fuel their argument that the US national women's team should be paid commensurately with the men's team—a fight that began around the time of the 1996 Atlanta Olympics, when superstar Mia Hamm had to wear this oversized (men's cut) #9 jersey. From better-fitting uniforms to equal travel and training conditions, and finally to equal pay (promised by the US Soccer Federation in 2022), the US women's national soccer team has played a prominent role in continuing to press for the equal treatment of women athletes that was spearheaded by Billie Jean King.

↑ Fans supporting the US women's national soccer team's demands for equal pay as the team takes the field in a friendly match in Philadelphia, August 2019.

↗ DISNEY ANIMATOR'S DESK

This wooden desk with a lightbox was used by Andy Engman, an animator for the Walt Disney Studios during the production of Disney's first animated feature film, *Snow White*, released in 1937. Sometimes artifacts say more about who didn't use them than who did. Engman's desk reflects the gender-segregated work environment at Disney, where women developed storylines and filled in animations made by men but were not credited as animators until 1942. Even in 2019, women made up 70 percent of students at the animation school Disney founded but held fewer than 25 percent of unionized animation jobs.

← Sheet music for "One Song," from the Disney movie *Snow White*, 1937.

RAY CHARLES CHESS SET

Ray Charles was one of the most celebrated American vocalists, composers, and musicians of the twentieth century. He also loved chess. Charles's chess set was designed to accommodate his blindness: the dark squares are slightly indented into the board, and all the squares have holes to anchor the chess pieces. The dark pieces have metal tips that enabled Charles to identify which side each piece belonged to. With this set Charles defeated many opponents, including his friend and musical collaborator Willie Nelson.

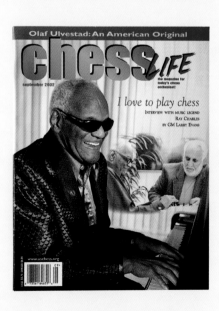

← Ray Charles on the cover of *Chess Life*, September 2002.

← Mary Wilson, Diana Ross, and Florence Ballard (left to right) performing on the NBC musical variety show *Hullabaloo*, 1965

↓ DIANA ROSS & THE SUPREMES DRESSES

A glamorous musical trio from Detroit's segregated public housing projects, the Supremes sang of love, heartbreak, and, occasionally, social issues. In 1961 they signed with Black-owned Motown Records and built a crossover audience with their exquisite vocals and elegant styling, as exemplified by these dresses from 1967. Scoring twelve chart-topping hits, including five in a row in 1965, their music resonated with teens across America's racial divide.

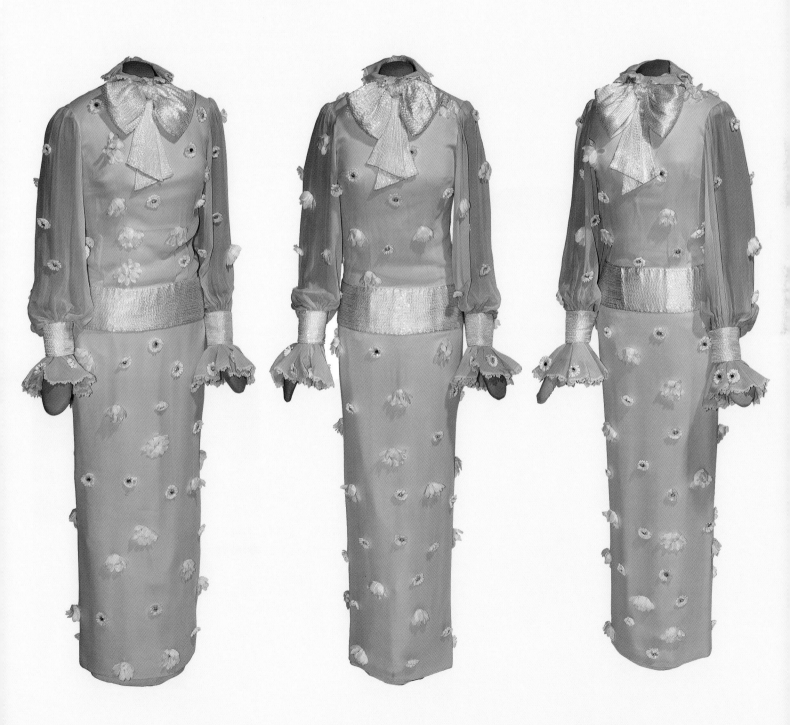

THIS-ABILITY

Loretta Claiborne speaks four languages. She holds a fourth-degree black belt in karate, has completed twenty-six marathons, and has won the inaugural White Rose open five-mile road race in her native York, Pennsylvania. She was born in 1953, partially blind, with an intellectual disability. She did not walk or talk until she was four.

Too often, stereotypes and assumptions limit how people with disabilities are perceived. Those notions can also shape the ideas that people with disabilities have of themselves. Claiborne recalls coming home from school after another day of bullying, telling her mother, "I'm a nobody. Nobody cares about me." But when Claiborne found opportunities to develop her athleticism, her confidence grew. She began to focus on her abilities rather than her disabilities and realized that her many talents could be used to effect change. "If I could just make this world better by doing just one little thing for somebody else, it is worth it," she told ESPN's *The Undefeated* in 2019. "I use my voice because senior citizens with intellectual disabilities today still need rights to be fought for: the right to better health care, the right to live in an apartment, the right to be able to work." Claiborne's efforts have made her the subject of a Disney movie and the recipient of the 1996 Arthur Ashe ESPY Award for Courage. She has met with US presidents, the pope, and thousands of schoolchildren, all with the goal of creating a society that treats people with intellectual disabilities as equal citizens and recognizes their contributions to the nation's growth and well-being.

← Pennsylvania Special Olympics T-shirt worn by Loretta Claiborne, 1972.

↓ Loretta Claiborne carries the torch in the Unified Relay Across America that brought the flame to the 2015 Special Olympics World Summer Games in Los Angeles.

Claiborne wore this T-shirt when competing in Special Olympics track events in Pennsylvania in the early 1970s, just as she was discovering her talents and her voice. Her longtime coach and friend Roxanne Dubbs says her accomplishments are due not just to her sporting ability but also to her will to discover new ideas, new talents, and new possibilities. "She's constantly evolving," Dubbs said. "She's constantly finding new things that will help her." For instance, over the past few years, Claiborne has drawn attention to the United Arab Emirates' 2017 decision to start referring to people with disabilities as "people of determination," saying, "We can all be people of determination, and that doesn't separate anyone."

Such adaptability and inventiveness are often overlooked in people with disabilities. In the 1800s and 1900s, being "handicapped" or "crippled"—and the focus on "treating" disability—became so defining and stigmatizing as to overshadow the capabilities, creativity, and ingenuity of disabled people. More recently, however, entertainment has become a crucial arena for resisting misconceptions and advocating for the rights and opportunities of people previously characterized by disability.

Buddy Elias is not as famous as Loretta Claiborne, but his homemade adaptive snowboarding rig demonstrates similar powers of ingenuity and advocacy. Elias lost his right leg at age twenty-nine to Buerger's disease, which causes severe inflammation of blood vessels and reduces circulation in the extremities. An avid snowboarder, he found shredding with his prosthetic leg

uncomfortable. So he secured a crutch into a snowboard boot, in effect making the crutch operate as his right leg. Constructed with everyday materials like foam and a nylon packing strap that he found in his house or at a local hardware store, Elias's rig quickly gained acclaim in the action-sports community for allowing him to continue snowboarding.

Elias now coaches other adaptive-action athletes and works with organizations that provide prosthetic equipment for adults and kids. In 2016 he lost his left leg, but he continues to do tricks on curbs and other street obstacles in a WCMX (wheelchair motocross)–style wheelchair. His innovative efforts to pursue the sports he loves is highlighted in an interview from 2017, in which he said, "Every obstacle is a barrier, but there are always ways to get past barriers." In the end, he said, the key has been to remember that "I determine what mobility I would have, not anybody else."

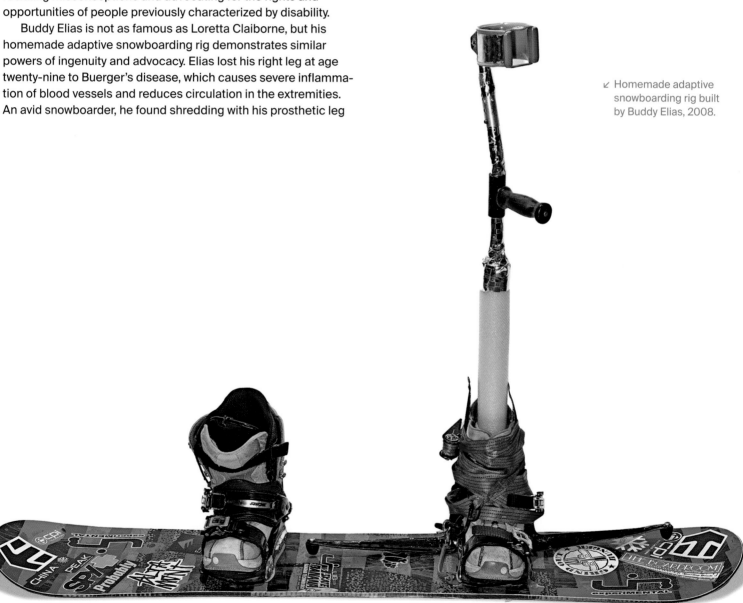

↙ Homemade adaptive snowboarding rig built by Buddy Elias, 2008.

If Claiborne and Elias have applied their talents to develop greater visibility, respect, and opportunities for people with disabilities, Marvel's globally popular X-Men movie and comics franchise does similar work beyond the realm of sports. Each X-Men character is born with a superpower and also experiences mental or physical disabilities. The characters use their powers to defend a world in which they are frequently ostracized and discriminated against as "mutants." The group's leader, Professor X, lives with paraplegia and uses a wheelchair, but his telepathic abilities and strategic thinking make him a commanding figure. Wolverine, famous for his retractable claws, suffers from post-traumatic stress disorder. The character Storm endures debilitating panic attacks stemming from severe anxiety and emotional challenges, but—as the cape on this costume from 2013's *X-Men: Days of Future Past* suggests—has the power to fly by controlling wind and weather.

X-Men storylines show each character managing both their disabilities and their powers while struggling with judgment from "normals." The comics and movies make clear that people with disabilities do not all agree about the best ways to combat the destructive preconceptions that generate those judgments. Characters disagree about whether or how much they should try to integrate into nonmutant society or "cure" what makes them different. On these points, Storm is an outspoken advocate who sounds a lot like Claiborne and Elias. In the second X-Men film, *X2* (2003), Berry's Storm despises people who pity her, and in a 2009 issue of the comic book the character asserts that "for me, there are no such things as limits."

Kenneth Cohen, Katherine Ott, and Jane Rogers

← Members of the X-Men cast during filming for *X2*, 2003.

RAY WERNER WHEELCHAIR NUMBER AND JACKET

Wheelchair basketball was invented by staff at Veterans Administration hospitals seeking to develop sports that wounded World War II veterans could enjoy. The sport quickly gained popularity, and a nationwide competition among VA hospitals led to the creation of "civilian" teams. Ray Werner, who was wounded in the battle of Guadalcanal in 1943, started playing at Oak Knoll Naval Hospital in Oakland, California. He later hung this number on the back of his wheelchair as he captained the Jersey Wheelers to the 1954 national championship.

← Ray Werner and the Jersey Wheelers competing at the 1954 National Wheelchair Basketball Association Championships.

JERSEY WHEELERS 4 RAY WERNER

↘ Basketball jacket worn by Ray Werner as a member of the Jersey Wheelers, 1954 National Wheelchair Basketball Association champions.

HEROES AND VILLAINS

HEROES AND VILLAINS

What distinguishes a hero from a villain? It's often a matter of perspective. Whether you think someone is heroic depends on whether you think they have done right. Sometimes there is broad consensus on that question, but it can be hotly debated. This final chapter of the catalog examines entertainers and characters whose lives have encouraged national conversations about broader values—the definition of good and evil, heroism, and progress.

In nineteenth-century America, audiences came to the play *Mazeppa* in droves, but they had sharply divided opinions about Adah Isaacs Menken, who played the male lead role and rode off apparently nude at the end of the performance. Some applauded Menken for her liberated portrayal of the play's Ukrainian self-sacrificing hero; others saw only the actor and perceived a lewd, villainous harlot who was a danger to public morality. Similar examples in this chapter show the ways that many performers and characters have been judged as talismans of cultural values. Generations of Indigenous performers in Hollywood have been locked into roles as "good" or "bad" Indians, defined by whether they accepted or resisted the Euro-American conquest of the West. During World War II, *the Los Angeles Times* called the baggy zoot suit, popularized by African American and Latino jazz and swing musicians, "a badge of delinquency," while African American musician Cab Calloway called it "the only totally and truly American civilian suit." Considering entertainers' and fans' clothing as markers of their character continues today, of course, in discourses about hip-hop. Recent popular dramas have also complicated our notions of heroism with the introduction of morally ambiguous protagonists. Characters such as Walter White in *Breaking Bad* and Tony Soprano in *The Sopranos* do horrible things for sometimes noble reasons.

Exploring conversations about heroism and villainy in entertainment requires tracing how opinions about these concepts not only differ at any given moment but also change over time. Such change makes this topic an ideal one for concluding the catalog, because it highlights the ongoing nature of the provocative and essential conversations that continue to shape our entertainment nation.

↓ CIGARETTE CARD FEATURING JACK JOHNSON

This 1910 Hassan cigarette card features Jack Johnson, the reigning heavyweight boxing champion. Johnson had gained the title in 1908 by defeating Canadian Tommy Burns in Australia, after decades during which white American champions had refused to fight Black contenders. Johnson then defended his title in 1910 by defeating American Jim Jeffries, whom white opponents of Johnson had called "the Great White Hope." Johnson's victory sparked attacks by white mobs on African American communities across the country. Johnson himself was vilified and persecuted, arrested twice within the next three years for driving across state lines with white girlfriends whom authorities wrongly claimed he was transporting as prostitutes. He served a year in prison in 1920. Decades later, recognition of the racism behind his conviction led to high-profile campaigns for posthumous clemency, culminating in a pardon from President Donald Trump in 2018.

↑ JUDY GARLAND COSTUME FROM *THE HARVEY GIRLS*

The 1946 MGM musical *The Harvey Girls* offered a morality tale about femininity, based on the story of the women who worked in the Harvey Hotel chain that expanded across the West during the 1890s. The film portrays Harvey waitresses, led by Judy Garland wearing this austere, nun-like costume, as respectable "civilizing forces" who help "win the West" by domesticating it. Besting a brazen group of "dance-hall girls," the film's heroes fit within mainstream entertainment just after World World II, which bombarded women with representations encouraging them to step back from expanded wartime roles and conform to expectations of domesticity.

REPUBLIC OR EMPIRE?

At first glance, the android costumes for C-3PO and R2-D2 from *Star Wars: Episode VI—Return of the Jedi* seem to have little in common with a set of paper cutouts depicting Buffalo Bill's Wild West show, printed more than a century earlier. Although they depict technologies that are light years apart, they both bring audiences into a debate as old as the nation: is the United States a heroic republic or a villainous empire?

Star Wars appears to offer a clear answer. The android duo sports more colorful appearances and personalities than the robots belonging to the Empire they fight. It's no accident that the uniforms worn by the Empire's military officers, and even the name of its "stormtrooper" units, reference the forces of Nazi Germany. Even among the ranks of the Rebel Alliance fighting to restore the Galactic Republic, Threepio and Artoo, as some fans call them, stand out for refusing to resort to coercive power. When Han Solo is captured by Ewoks in *Return of the Jedi*, he asks C-3PO to pretend to be a god and order their release. "It's against my programming to impersonate a deity," replies the hard-wired, if fretful, factotum of freedom.

Yet George Lucas developed the iconic droids' characters specifically to persuade American audiences to be more like the Rebel Alliance at a time when he wasn't sure whether the nation was acting the part. "We are at a turning point: fascism or revolution," he wrote in his early project notebook, three years before the first Star Wars movie was released. On one hand, Lucas believed "the hokey stuff about being a good neighbor, and the American spirit and all that crap. There *is* something in it." As he told *Film Quarterly* in 1974, on the heels of his first successful movie, *American Graffiti*, and with a drafted script for the first Star Wars film already complete, "We've got to regenerate optimism. Maybe kids will walk out of the film and for a second they'll feel, 'We could really make something out of this country.'" Americans' potential to be dutiful, rational, fearful, and comically critical defenders of a free society—in sum, their potential to be like these beloved droids—explains why Lucas has called R2-D2 "the hero of the whole thing." If Threepio and Artoo could help Americans see themselves in the ragtag Alliance, working together across vast differences to fight tyranny as they did during World War II, Lucas could be hopeful about the future.

↘ Hand-cut paper diorama figures representing the buffalo hunt scene from Buffalo Bill's Wild West show, 1884.

↙ C-3PO and R2-D2, from *Star Wars: Return of the Jedi*, 1983.

On the other hand, Lucas also wrote in his project notebook that "the empire is like America ten years from now." He intentionally patterned the Imperial Star Destroyers after the Great White Fleet that Teddy Roosevelt sent sailing around the world in 1907 to demonstrate America's emerging imperial might. He has said he elevated the role of Emperor Palpatine in response to Richard Nixon's presidency. A vocal opponent of the Vietnam War, Lucas once likened the Ewoks to the Vietcong. Ronald Reagan later deployed the rhetoric of the first trilogy, casting the Soviet Union as the "Evil Empire" whose threat necessitated a US "Star Wars Defense Initiative," but the iconic droids in the early movies aimed more to convince Americans to be the good guys than to claim that they already were.

The debate about the United States' future as either a republic or an empire dates back at least to Thomas Jefferson's vision of combining them into an "Empire of Liberty." Could there even be such a thing? Empires are built through conquest that usually costs some people's freedom. Jefferson's question resonated throughout the 1800s, as the United States expanded westward by displacing Native Americans. Only a handful of citizens suggested that "our treatment of the Indians cannot be dignified and made a precedent," but Lucas consciously deployed elements of Westerns that recalled this criticism. Beyond Han Solo's gunslinger look and plenty of frontier saloons, Star Wars tells a story common to many Westerns: greed and abusive power drive technologies that destroy freedom and nature. Nothing makes this point clearer than the number of planets and indigenous populations who face extermination by the Empire.

The collectible cutouts illustrating William F. "Buffalo Bill" Cody's Wild West traveling show cautiously raised some of these same points a century earlier. Printed by McLoughlin Brothers, publishers of children's books and board games, the figures were cut out and mounted on wooden bases. They could be arranged to re-create two well-known acts from Cody's enormously popular production. One group of figures enacts "The Capture of the Deadwood Mail," a gunfight over a stagecoach between mounted Native Americans and cowboys. The other group displays the show's buffalo hunt.

Like Star Wars, the cutouts and the show they represented appear to tell a tale that celebrates the United States. The Deadwood Mail scene inaccurately portrayed Native Americans as savage aggressors when they were defending their lives, cultures, and access to land from invasion by US authorities and settlers. The cutouts also position Indigenous horsemen in technically difficult but sneaky "skulking" riding positions. Yet in the show, they were always bested by the cowboys. The point for audiences was clear: US expansion at the expense of Indigenous people was justified. And since the cutouts (and most of the shows) pictured independent cowboys doing the fighting, rather than the US Army, who really did it, the conquest of the West seemed less imperialist.

But, like Star Wars, the Wild West did not let the country off the hook. At a time when missionaries and many federal officials pushed Indigenous Americans to assimilate, infamously aiming to "kill the Indian and save the Man," Wild West shows became popular in part because they showcased Native American culture and traditions. Even if presentations such as the buffalo hunt were not completely authentic, they offered Indigenous performers more freedom for cultural expression than life on reservations. Wild West shows made stars out of Native Americans who defied efforts by the missionaries and the federal government to erase their cultural heritage. Native performers used this platform to make clear that they would fight American imperialism in any way they could. "We take great pleasure in going up against a fair fight with the American soldiers even with blank cartridges," the Lakota performer Short Bull told the Washington Inquirer in 1911. The outcomes of those fights may have been scripted in the shows, but there was nothing to stop fans from depicting alternatives in their dioramas.

Neither Star Wars nor Buffalo Bill's Wild West came right out and called the United States a republic that had become a heartless empire. But these epics, separated by time and intergalactic space, used memorable characters and scenes to present contradictory conclusions and pose a question that has burdened the nation since its origins.

Kenneth Cohen

Wild West shows made stars out of Native Americans who defied efforts by the missionaries and the federal government to erase their cultural heritage.

↗ Hand-cut paper diorama figures representing the capture of the Deadwood Mail, a scene from Buffalo Bill's Wild West show, 1884.

→ US Olympic gymnast Dominique Dawes practicing on the balance beam during a training session at the Georgia Dome in Atlanta, Georgia, July 16, 1996.

↓ DOMINIQUE DAWES LEOTARD

Dominique Dawes wore this leotard at the 1996 Summer Olympics in Atlanta, where at age twenty-one she became the first Black woman to win a gold medal in gymnastics. The ten-year international career of "Awesome Dawesome," a long run by elite gymnastics standards, inspired later African American gymnasts such as Gabby Douglas and Simone Biles, but Dawes later criticized the sport's culture of abuse, which often left her afraid and hiding in the gym. In 2020 she opened her own gym, aimed at providing gymnasts a place where they can "look at themselves in the mirror and love who they are."

↑ BARNUM ITALY STATUE

Around 1900, some Americans believed the United States should build an empire by annexing territories such as Puerto Rico, Hawai'i, and the Philippines. Others believed that incorporating more nonwhite peoples into the nation would lead to ruin. White supremacy underpinned both arguments, but P. T. Barnum's circus lured spectators by playing on the debate. Parading into towns toting this seven-and-a-half-foot tall, faux-marble wooden statue representing Italy, Barnum heralded the value of worldliness. Meanwhile, the fallen column, lyre, and paintbrushes recalled the decline of expansive classical empires and Renaissance republics alike.

↗ BUCK LEONARD TRAVEL BAG

Walter Fenner "Buck" Leonard was the fearsome cleanup hitter on the Homestead Grays baseball team that won ten Negro League pennants between 1937 and 1948. The segregation of professional baseball kept Leonard from playing in the major leagues in his prime. He carried this bag as he and his Grays teammates faced discrimination while crisscrossing the country to play. But Leonard's travel bag also bears a sticker from a hotel in Mexico, where he concluded his career in the 1950s by playing in a league that had been integrated since the 1930s.

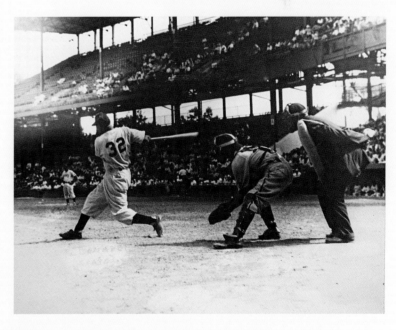

↑ Buck Leonard hitting a home run for the Homestead Grays against the Baltimore Elite Giants, 1945.

WHO GETS TO BE THE HERO?

"Return with us now to those thrilling days of yesteryear!"

This line, accompanied by the galloping strains of Rossini's William Tell Overture, invited radio and television audiences to "return" to the "Old West" of *The Lone Ranger*. It is just one example of how entertainment in the United States offers a romantic mythic past, neglecting uncomfortable historical facts in order to provide nostalgic comfort and certainty to audiences grappling with rapidly changing times.

The Cold War of the mid-twentieth century was an unprecedented battle for the hearts, minds, and economies of the world, inspiring conflict in Korea, fueling Senator Joseph McCarthy's anticommunist hearings, and propelling the space race. Many citizens of the United States believed that communism threatened the basic freedoms that constituted the "American way of life."

During these contentious times, characters such as the Lone Ranger and Indiana Jones celebrated the heroism of earlier eras. As the nation weathered internal and external tensions, they offered retreats to an imagined past whose events justified traditional power structures and identities.

The Lone Ranger first appeared on Detroit radio station WXYZ in 1931. The program's famous introduction followed the character to television in 1949, with Clayton Moore portraying "the masked rider of the plains." The Ranger defeated evildoers with the help of his "faithful Indian companion," the pidgin-English-spouting sidekick Tonto, played by Jay Silverheels. The program was one of the most popular examples of early television's most successful genre.

Returning to the certainties of the "yesteryear" frontier provided not only an escape from the real-world tensions of the Cold War but also ideas about how that war might be won. The Lone Ranger's enemies were the ruthless and underhanded exploiters at the margins of civilization. Executing their schemes through gangs or as individuals infiltrating local governments, they brought to life widespread descriptions of communist strategies for gaining power. Naive and helpless lawful citizens, as well as innocent Native Americans, appeared easy prey for such villains without the intervention of fearless and decisive men such as the Ranger. As the independent, moral, fearless, masculine white protector of less fortunate members of the community, he was essentially a personification of how TV networks saw the United States.

Over the ensuing decades, as America reeled from violent crackdowns on civil rights protesters, the Vietnam War, and the Watergate scandal, Cold War heroes like the Lone Ranger fell out of favor. Increasingly cynical audiences became drawn to antiheroes and ambiguity, with popular television programs such as *All in the Family* directly acknowledging the nation's internal discord.

However, the archetype of the frontier hero returned with a vengeance during the blockbuster film era of the 1980s and 1990s. But unlike their predecessors from the early days of the Cold War, these epic adventures were set in alternative worlds and on seemingly less complicated "frontiers" that more easily and explicitly aligned with the nostalgic national pride effused by the presidencies of Ronald Reagan and George H. W. Bush.

↑ Mask worn by Clayton Moore in the role of the Lone Ranger and a promotional silver bullet like the ones the character left behind after righting a wrong.

→ Jay Silverheels as Tonto and Clayton Moore as the Lone Ranger, characters they played on the TV series *The Lone Ranger* between 1949 and 1957.

↓ Whip and belt loop used by
Harrison Ford as the title
character in the first three Indiana
Jones movies, 1981–89.

One of the period's most enduring heroes was the whip-toting archaeologist Indiana Jones, portrayed by Harrison Ford. The character was first introduced in the 1981 film *Raiders of the Lost Ark*, an unapologetically nostalgic homage to early cliffhanger movies. While the Lone Ranger harked back to the mythical Western frontier, *Raiders of the Lost Ark* returned viewers to the eve of the Second World War, popularly seen as the "Good War." The setting invited Americans to forget Vietnam and once again feel good about the United States' role in the world.

Pistol at his side, wearing a dusty fedora and brandishing a leather bullwhip, Jones adopted not only the look but also the persona of the traditional cinematic Western hero. Independent, noble, and decisive, Jones was another in a long line of movie-dom's masculine white adventurers.

In *Raiders* and its sequels, *Indiana Jones and the Temple of Doom* and *Indiana Jones and the Last Crusade*, the globetrotting professor bypassed inefficient government and academic bureaucracies to rescue other cultures' precious cultural artifacts from ignoble treasure seekers and power-hungry nations. Just like the mythical heroes of the Western frontier, Jones was presented as an essential force for good, protecting the world from the nefarious plans of bullies and outlaws. Aided by subordinate women and infantilized men of color (sidekicks who often found themselves in need of rescuing), Jones reaffirmed the role of the white cowboy hero in the age of the blockbuster.

Coming from different eras and media, the Lone Ranger and Indiana Jones present complementary visions of the United States and its role in the world. As bookends of the Cold War, both ignore the messy contradictions of US history to offer messages of American righteousness, embodied in the form of independent, heroic, gun-wielding white men. Despite the collapse of the Soviet Union and slowly multiplying alternatives, this vision of American identity and the nation's role in the world remains all too present today.

Eric Jentsch

→ Harrison Ford on the set of
Raiders of the Lost Ark, 1981.

↙ Hat and jacket worn by Harrison Ford as Indiana Jones in *Indiana Jones and the Last Crusade*, 1989.

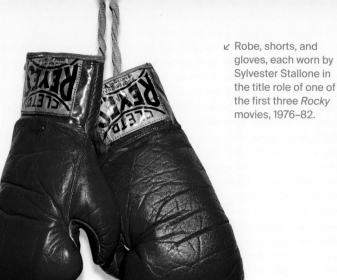

↙ Robe, shorts, and gloves, each worn by Sylvester Stallone in the title role of one of the first three *Rocky* movies, 1976–82.

↖ SYLVESTER STALLONE COSTUME ELEMENTS FROM *ROCKY I* AND *III*

The boxing hero Rocky Balboa (Sylvester Stallone) started out in 1976 as a small-time underdog who finds purpose and passion through a rare opportunity. *Rocky*'s popularity spawned a multimedia franchise, and by 1984, with *Rocky IV*, the character had transformed into an icon of American virtue, challenging a Soviet boxer at the height of the Cold War.

↓ BRUCE WILLIS SHIRT FROM *DIE HARD*

In the 1988 film *Die Hard*, sarcastic police officer John McClain, played by Bruce Willis, battles international terrorists in an undershirt and bare feet. Like many action films of the 1980s and 1990s, the film reinvented the Western hero for the modern age, emphasizing the genre's archetypal qualities of independence, fortitude, and masculinity.

↑ Bruce Willis wears a similar shirt in this still from the third installment of the series, *Die Hard: With a Vengeance*, 1995.

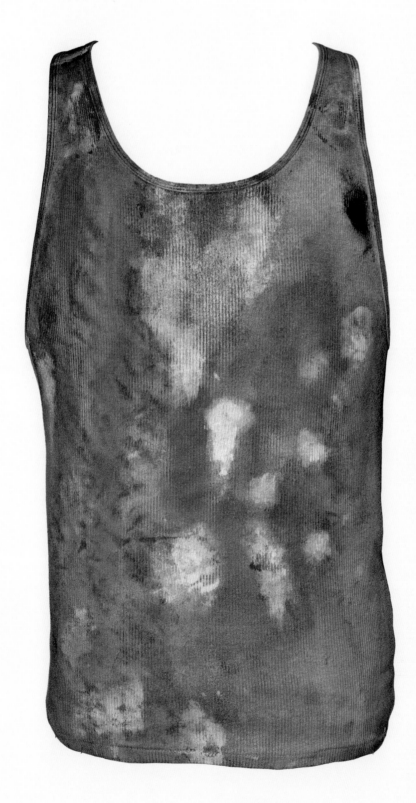

→ JANET GUTHRIE HELMET

Pilot, flight instructor, aerospace engineer, race-car driver—Janet Guthrie was a trailblazer for women in all these fields. In 1978 Guthrie wore this helmet when she became the first woman to qualify for and race in the Indianapolis 500. Facing reluctance from sponsors and open hostility from male drivers, notably Richard Petty, Guthrie emphasized her achievement as the culmination of efforts by generations of heroic women who worked in racing but whose "history gets lost."

← DANA SCULLY PROP CREDENTIALS FROM *THE X-FILES*

On the 1990s smash hit TV series *The X-Files*, Gillian Anderson plays Dana Scully, an FBI agent assigned to investigate unsolved cases involving paranormal activity and aliens. Her partner, Fox Mulder, is a believer. Scully, a doctor and a skeptic, finds truth through science. The character inspired a generation of young women to pursue the sciences, a phenomenon dubbed "the Scully effect."

↑ Felicia Day with the cast of *The Guild*, 2009.

↖ **FELICIA DAY COSTUME FROM *THE GUILD***

In the show *The Guild*, which follows a team of online gamers enacting a medieval fantasy, timid Cyd Sherman's avatar is a powerful priestess who wears this costume. Felicia Day, who created the show, plays the role of Sherman. *The Guild* launched on YouTube in 2007, and Day has been a visionary leader of web television and an advocate for greater diversity in the gaming community.

KRISTI YAMAGUCHI SKATES AND DRESS

Kristi Yamaguchi wore these skates and this dress for performances after she became the first Asian American woman to win an Olympic gold medal in figure skating in 1992. Her victory was a matter of special pride for the Japanese American community. Like tens of thousands of Japanese Americans, Yamaguchi's grandparents had known the indignity and injustice of being incarcerated by the US government during World War II. She has said, "The gold meant so much more than I ever thought it would to other people."

↑ Kristi Yamaguchi skating to a gold medal at the 1992 Winter Olympics in Albertville, France.

JIM THORPE TROPHY

Jim Thorpe won this cup in one of his last amateur running races. After winning the pentathlon and decathlon at the 1912 Olympics, Thorpe was stripped of his medals for violating the period's strict and elitist code for amateur athletes by having played minor league baseball for between $2 and $12 per game. A member of the Sac and Fox Nation who grew up in the oppressive environments of Indian boarding schools, Thorpe became a hero in Indigenous communities for his performances in track, major league baseball, and professional football and basketball. Today he is widely regarded as the greatest all-around athlete of the twentieth century.

BRONXDALE A C

5 MILE HANDICAP ROAD RUN
· MAR 22 ND · 1914 ·

FIRST PRIZE
· WON BY ·
JIM THORPE

→ Jim Thorpe in the uniform of the Canton Bulldogs, an early professional football team for which he played between 1915 and 1920.

"I AM WHO I AM, THAT'S IT"

Elaborately embellished capes like the one at right were the costumes of choice for the TV astrologer and psychic Walter Mercado during his daily broadcasts—programs that reached millions of viewers and broke down barriers to queer representation on Latin American television despite homophobic attacks and Mercado's own silence about his gender identity and sexuality.

Born in Ponce, Puerto Rico, in 1932, from a young age Mercado was interested in music, dance, and theater. He began his career as an actor in the 1960s, starring in both stage productions and Latin American soap operas called *telenovelas*. His true break came in 1969, when he filled an empty time slot on *El Show del Mediodía* (The Midday Show) with an improvised astrological segment. Viewers were hooked, and Mercado was allotted his own weekly segment.

Within months, he was hosting his own astrology show, titled *Walter, Las Estrellas y Usted* (Walter, the Stars and You) and beginning his rise to international stardom. By the 1980s, Mercado's program was airing throughout Latin America and the United States, and his predictions and horoscopes appeared in multiple publications and languages. In the 1990s, his move to the Univision television network—starring in both his own show and a segment on the news program *Primer impacto* (First Impact)—expanded his visibility and popularity among Latinx communities across the country.

Mercado captured viewers' attention with horoscopes, predictions, *consejos* (advice), and spiritual readings delivered in his dreamy, lilting voice, with dynamic hand gestures accentuating his message. In a culture known for traditional masculine gender roles, Mercado performed a unique, camp fusion of feminine and masculine aesthetics. He adorned himself in beaded capes and abundant jewelry, with voluminously teased hair and heavy makeup. His sets added to this theatrical flair with heavy curtains, beaded and embroidered cushions, crystal balls, elaborate floral arrangements, and pan-religious icons. Mercado drew inspiration for his costumes and sets from Moroccan, Persian, and Indian fashions, as well as the pope. This synthesis of cultural and religious references enhanced the universality of his astrological predictions and promoted his core message of peace and love.

For his fans, Mercado's extravagant persona and multicultural performances enhanced the spiritual aspects of this spectacle. But they also helped him deflect questions about his own identity by shrouding it in stereotyped symbols of Eastern mysticism that had long defied European and Latin definitions of masculinity. Walter explained his merging of feminine and masculine aesthetics as a result of his exposure to cosmic mysteries and refused to publicly discuss his gender and sexuality. Once, pressed by the famous Mexican American journalist Jorge Ramos, Mercado said that he didn't care about rumors of his sexuality circulating. He simply responded, "Here I am, I am who I am, that's it."

Immense popularity and deflection did not keep Walter Mercado from being ridiculed and mocked for his gender non-conformity. His onscreen persona was so iconic that homophobic detractors could mock him simply by donning a cape and making effeminate gestures. Despite these attacks, Mercado became an inspirational figure to queer youth in the Latinx community for making gender nonconformity visible on Spanish-language television. He remains a cultural touchstone and beloved figure in the Latinx community even after his death in 2019. As the comedian and writer Gabe González tweeted, "He never identified as queer, but it felt like he refused to be constrained by gender norms and antiquated ideas of masculinity. . . . He was weird and beautiful and eccentric [and] brought a sense of camp and magic to TV that felt lacking in my life as a young queer person."

Ashley Oliva Mayor

↘ Costume worn by Walter Mercado,
early 2019.

↑ Crystal ball used
by Walter Mercado,
1970s–2010.

"I'M FREE TO BE WHAT I WANT"

Muhammad Ali was one of the most controversial athletes of the twentieth century. Even his name stirred controversy. Born Cassius M. Clay, he was renamed Muhammad Ali at the age of twenty-two by Elijah Muhammad, the African American leader of the Nation of Islam. By the late 1960s, fans, reporters, and activists often revealed their political leanings by the name they used to refer to him. Yet by the 1990s, the three-time heavyweight champion had been celebrated as a national hero, then considered a villain by many, only to regain widespread veneration.

Ali, then known as Clay, first emerged as a hero after winning a gold medal in boxing at the 1960 Olympic Games in Rome. Charismatic, witty, and sharp-tongued, he cemented his status with a pointed reply to a Soviet reporter who asked him about racism in the United States. With a Cold War battle under way for influence over seventeen newly independent African nations, American leaders feared how African American athletes would respond to such propagandistic questions. Clay told the reporter, "Tell your readers we've got qualified people working on that problem. . . . To me, the USA is still the best country in the world, counting yours." This retort positioned Clay as a champion of American democratic and capitalist ideals and signaled his adherence to the rules of racial discourse for African American athletes, established by prominent figures such as Joe Louis and Jesse Owens: be deferential, be sensitive to white sensibilities, and stay out of racial protests.

Clay remained a national hero until his stunning upset victory over Sonny Liston to take the world heavyweight championship on February 26, 1964. One day after the fight, a reporter asked Clay about rumors that he was a member of the Nation of Islam. He responded, "I believe in Allah and in peace. I don't try to move into white neighborhoods. . . . I don't have to be who you want me to be. I'm free to be what I want." The Nation of Islam differed from other Black freedom organizations by refusing to appeal to the conscience of white America and by rejecting integration. Both white and Black Americans were highly critical of his affiliation with the group. White Americans were upset that he joined an institution that labeled white people as "devils." Many African Americans were uncomfortable with his rejection of Christianity and feared that the Nation of Islam's growing influence would hinder integration efforts.

Ali cemented his new status as a villain when he refused induction into the US military after being drafted during the Vietnam War. At a 1966 rally with Martin Luther King Jr., Ali defended his position by stating, "No, I am not going ten thousand miles from home to help murder and burn another poor nation simply to continue the domination of white slave masters of the darker people the world over." At a time when a majority of Americans still supported the war, his use of the words *murder* and *burn* and his invocation of the legacies of slavery and colonialism undermined the rhetoric of freedom with which the United States justified its involvement in Vietnam. His denunciation of the war caused Americans to question his patriotism, and he was stripped of his heavyweight title for "conduct detrimental to the spirit of boxing." Ali was not permitted to fight for three years because promoters feared that fans would not attend his boxing matches.

Yet Ali's denunciation of the Vietnam War also led to his reemergence as a hero. As a convicted draft dodger, Ali was positioned as a spokesperson against American imperialism. "My conscience won't let me go shoot my brother, or some darker people, or some poor hungry people in the mud for big powerful America," he said. After his conviction was overturned by the US Supreme Court, and white Americans began to turn against the war, Ali's reputation rebounded. His 1974 bout against George Foreman in the Democratic Republic of the Congo (then called Zaire), a fight held in a newly independent country featuring two African American boxers and an African American promoter, underscored his opposition to colonialism. Ali wore this terry-cloth robe while training in Zaire for months before the bout, when he frequently met with local communities and secured his international legacy as "The People's Champion."

Damion Thomas

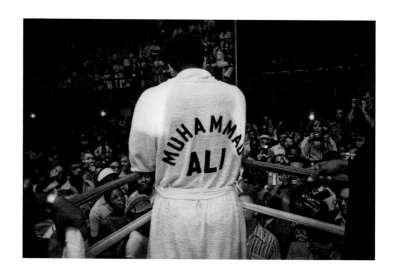

Ali's denunciation of the war caused Americans to question his patriotism, and he was stripped of his heavyweight title for "conduct detrimental to the spirit of boxing."

← Muhammad Ali speaks to fans and the press before his championship fight against Leon Spinks at the New Orleans Superdome, September 1978.

↗ Terry-cloth training robe worn by Muhammad Ali while preparing to fight George Foreman in Zaire, 1974.

ROBERTO CLEMENTE JERSEY

Afro-Puerto Rican outfielder Roberto Clemente, the first Latino player inducted into baseball's Hall of Fame, welcomed the opportunity to put on a major league uniform. But he defiantly spoke out against the discrimination Black and Latino players continued to face even as baseball officially desegregated. Off the field, his free camps for at-risk youth taught baseball and life skills, and his humanitarianism assisted families in need across Latin America. In 1972 he died in a plane crash while delivering aid to earthquake survivors in Nicaragua.

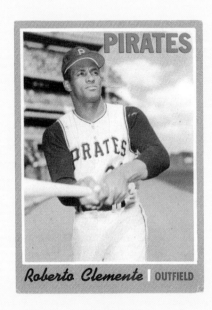

↑ Baseball card depicting Roberto Clemente, ca. 1970.

→ Dizzy Gillespie plays his trumpet during a jazz concert at the Natrona County High School Auditorium in Casper, Wyoming, February 10, 1989.

↓ DIZZY GILLESPIE TRUMPET

In the 1950s, the United States' dismal civil rights record fueled the Soviet Union's global anti-American propaganda campaign. In response, the US State Department asked jazz virtuosos such as Dizzy Gillespie to tour the world to assert racial harmony and the superiority of American democracy. Although Gillespie agreed, he wielded his signature "bent" trumpets to battle not only communism abroad but also racism in the US, by using the media attention to challenge his government for not doing more.

ROGER STAUBACH JERSEY

Six years after winning the 1963 Heisman Trophy as the quarterback for the US Naval Academy, Roger Staubach began his NFL career as a twenty-seven-year-old-rookie. Drafted by the Dallas Cowboys, Staubach could not play until he had completed his required military service. He chose to serve one of those years in Vietnam, before leading "America's Team" to two Super Bowl wins and five NFC titles, earning the nickname "Captain America."

TOBY KEITH GUITAR

Country music hitmaker Toby Keith penned "Courtesy of the Red, White and Blue (the Angry American)" soon after the terrorist attacks of September 11, 2001, to honor his veteran father and inspire US troops fighting the Taliban in Afghanistan. Performing the song on custom, flag-emblazoned guitars, he tirelessly toured military bases throughout the Middle East with his "Shock 'n Y'all" performances. When some criticized his blunt lyrics and hawkish sentiments, Keith responded, "Never apologize for being patriotic."

THE FIGMENT OF THE FONZ

Happy Days *was a sitcom that aired on ABC from 1974 to 1984. Spanning 254 episodes, and still running in syndication, it ranks among the most popular television programs in history. For most viewers, the show's idealized version of the 1950s was best symbolized not by the lead character, a prudish teenager named Richie Cunningham (played by a twenty-something Ron Howard), but by the Fonz (played by Henry Winkler), a greaser who rode a motorcycle, had perfect hair, and wore this leather jacket. As comedian Aasif Mandvi tells us, the Fonz offered a powerful and complicated statement about what an American man was supposed to be.*

→ Jacket worn by
Henry Winkler playing
Arthur Fonzarelli on
Happy Days, ca. 1979.

Arthur Fonzarelli, which was the character's full name, was the epitome of cool, but he was also completely approachable. So here you have the coolest guy in town, and all his friends are dorks, which gave dorks like me hope that we could be cool—or maybe have friends that were. At thirteen, I had a poster of him wearing the jacket and striking his famous pose with his thumbs up, delivering his tagline, "Hey," which Henry Winkler always delivered in a dragged-out baritone voice. I grew up in the north of England, with bullies and racism, and trying to live up to this American symbol of masculinity defined a lot of my childhood. I just remember me and my friend, both of us little Indian kids in this school in the north of England, walking around doing the thumbs and going, "Hey," to each other because it reinforced something for us.

We weren't really aware of why this version of masculinity was so magnetic. It's only later that I put the pieces together. I mean, *Happy Days* came out right after Watergate, and it was also right after the Vietnam War, and after the '60s and the upheaval created by all that stuff, and so this throwback to the '50s was supposed to be comforting. *Happy Days* was a show about how pleasant it was to be a young man maturing into a moral and yet still manly man. Except, of course, the 1950s weren't equally pleasant for everyone. But if you were a white guy, it was a more comforting era than the '60s or '70s. The problem is that the show was airing in the '70s and '80s, and America was basically exporting this chauvinistic idea of sexuality and coolness that didn't age super well. Case in point, the Fonz had an almost superhuman ability to summon girls just by snapping his fingers.

The funny thing about this jacket, it's the center of gravity for Fonzie's coolness, you know, but when you see it up close it's got these soft cloth cuffs, which aren't quite as rough and tough as the Fonz seems. The jacket actually looks like a very sensible winter garment for Wisconsin, where the show was set. It's also very small, because Henry Winkler wasn't the biggest guy. In fact, Winkler once told me that people who saw him in public, after they put their thumb up and went, "Hey," they would go, "Wow, you're a lot shorter than I thought." Which gets to the point that the Fonz was always more a figment of our imaginations than something real. He didn't have a family, and he was kind of adopted by Richie's, and whenever there was a scene of him at home where he had nobody to be cool for, there was an emotional side. Most importantly, in real life, Winkler wisely instructs men to "never snap your fingers at a woman. She will break them."

Aasif Mandvi

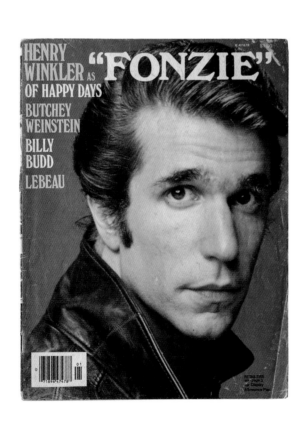

↑ Henry Winkler fan magazine, 1976.

↑ Henry Winkler as Arthur Fonzarelli on *Happy Days*, 1977.

THE SECRET HISTORY OF WONDER WOMAN

"Noted Psychologist Revealed as Author of Best-Selling 'Wonder Woman,'" read the astonishing headline. The identity of Wonder Woman's creator had been "at first kept secret," the ensuing story said, but in the summer of 1942, the comic's publisher announced that "the author of 'Wonder Woman' is Dr. William Moulton Marston, internationally famous psychologist."

But, really, the name of Wonder Woman's creator was the least of her secrets. The veil that has shrouded Wonder Woman's past for seven decades hides a crucial story about comic books, superheroes, censorship, and feminism. As Marston once put it, "Frankly, Wonder Woman is psychological propaganda for the new type of woman who, I believe, should rule the world."

Wonder Woman is the most popular female comic-book superhero of all time. Aside from Superman and Batman, no other

↑ Wonder Woman lunchbox, 1977.

comic-book character has lasted as long. Generations of girls have carried their sandwiches to school in Wonder Woman lunchboxes. But in the 1930s, when comic books first became widely popular, it would have been difficult to imagine this heroine or her staying power. Newspapers called for banning comics, calling them a "national disgrace" that celebrated violence, even sexual violence.

Leading comics publisher Maxwell Charles Gaines, a former elementary school principal, responded to this criticism in 1940 by hiring Marston as a consultant. He did so after reading a *Family Circle* magazine story in which the Harvard-educated psychologist espoused the morality of comics and their readers.

That story is a portal into Wonder Woman's secret history. It was written by a woman named Olive Byrne. In the piece, she of course did not reveal that she was Marston's former undergraduate student, that she was living with him and his legal wife, or that each woman had borne two of his children. That Byrne's mother was Margaret Sanger's sister, and had helped Sanger open the first birth-control clinic in the United States in 1916, perhaps explains something about why Marston proposed Wonder Woman to Gaines as a way of silencing the criticism of comics' "blood-curdling masculinity."

Wonder Woman made her debut at the end of 1941. Drawn by an artist named Harry G. Peter, she wore a golden tiara, a red bustier, blue briefs, and knee-high red leather boots. She was a little slinky; she was very kinky. She'd left Paradise to fight fascism with feminism in "America, the last citadel of democracy, and of equal rights for women!"

↑ Panels from *Wonder Woman* #4,
April–May 1943.

As Marston once put it, "Frankly, Wonder Woman is psychological propaganda for the new type of woman who, I believe, should rule the world."

↑ Margaret Sanger covers her mouth in protest after being denied the right to talk about birth control, April 17, 1929.

It seemed to Gaines like so much good, clean, patriotic fun. But in March 1942, the National Organization for Decent Literature blacklisted the comic for one reason: "Wonder Woman is not sufficiently dressed." A year later came a less prudish and more prudent critique from an expert in children's literature named Josette Frank, who expressed concern about "sadistic bits showing women chained, tortured, etc." She had a point. In story after story, Wonder Woman is chained, bound, gagged, lassoed, tied, fettered, and manacled. "Great girdle of Aphrodite!" she cries at one point. "Am I tired of being tied up!"

Gaines and others within his burgeoning DC Comics business wanted the chains cut, but Marston resisted. He, his wife, Byrne, and even Peter had all been powerfully influenced by the suffrage, feminism, and birth control movements. Each of those movements had used chains as a centerpiece of its iconography. American and British suffragists had chained themselves to gates outside elected leaders' houses. Sanger's petition against charges of obscenity for explaining birth control described "the shackles on every limb—on every thought—on the very soul of an unwilling pregnant woman." Peter had previously worked on the art for the suffrage page of the popular weekly illustrated magazine *Judge*, where chained and roped women featured regularly.

Wonder Woman, like other comics, eventually succumbed and changed its imagery when the Comics Magazine Association of America basically banned depictions of cruelty in 1954. But an argument can be made that Wonder Woman lasted that long only because Marston based her on the legacies and inspiration of Sanger and suffrage. Yet Marston was determined to keep those influences on Wonder Woman a secret, and he took that secret to his grave in 1947.

During the years when Olive Byrne lived with Marston and his wife, Elizabeth Holloway Marston, Byrne wore a pair of bracelets instead of a wedding ring. Wonder Woman wears those same cuffs. When Byrne died in 1990, at the age of eighty-six, no newspaper ran an obituary. She and Holloway had been living together in an apartment in Tampa. When Holloway passed away in 1993, an obituary ran in the *New York Times* with the header "Elizabeth H. Marston, Inspiration for Wonder Woman, 100." This was, at best, a half-truth.

Jill Lepore

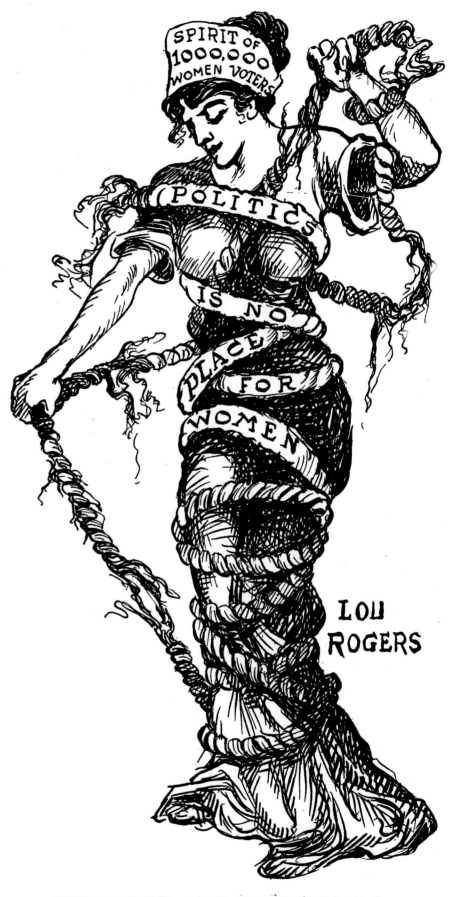

SPIRIT OF 1,000,000 WOMEN VOTERS

POLITICS IS NO PLACE FOR WOMEN

LOU ROGERS

TEARING OFF THE BONDS.

→ Lou Rogers, "Tearing off the
  Bonds," *Judge*, October 19, 1912.

DORA THE EXPLORER ANIMATION SKETCH

For nearly twenty years, from 2000 until 2019, Dora and her friend Boots—the monkey seen on the phone with her in this 2003 sketch—reached their destination on every episode of the animated show *Dora the Explorer* by solving puzzles and overcoming obstacles. The show's creators invented the character of Dora explicitly to counter anti-immigrant rhetoric, and they listened to Latinx consultants such as historian Carlos Cortés, who urged them not to identify her with a single ethnic nationality because lead characters from Latin America were so rare: "It's important that kids of different Latino backgrounds be able to identify with Dora," Cortés said.

LUCY LAWLESS COSTUME FROM
XENA: WARRIOR PRINCESS

Every episode told the backstory: in ancient times, when "a land in turmoil cried out for a hero," it was a woman, not a man, who answered the call. For six hit seasons, from 1995 to 2001, Lucy Lawless portrayed the warrior princess Xena, who outwitted and outfought forces of evil. Her relationship with her companion, Gabrielle, vaulted Xena to iconic status for the show's LGBTQ+ fans.

↑ Lucy Lawless in the *Xena: Warrior Princess* season 4 episode "Endgame," aired May 3, 1999.

← Danai Gurira as Michonne Hawthorne in season 4 of *The Walking Dead*, 2014.

↙ Katana wielded primarily by Danai Gurira as Michonne Hawthorne and costume worn by Steven Yeun as Glenn Rhee during the early seasons of *The Walking Dead*, 2010–15.

↑ **DANAI GURIRA KATANA AND STEVEN YEUN COSTUME FROM *THE WALKING DEAD***

Originating from enslaved Haitians' fears of being forever trapped in bondage, zombie stories in which the dead come back to life have become staples of American horror entertainment. In programs such as *The Walking Dead*, zombies (in this case called *walkers*) personify anxieties over globalization, pandemics, and violence. Fighting the existential threat posed by undead foes demonstrates how social turmoil can be survived by working together.

← Ric Flair wearing an entrance robe, 2008.

→ RIC FLAIR ROBE

This entrance robe was worn by professional wrestler Ric "Nature Boy" Flair before his final match, at WrestleMania 24 in 2008. During his forty-year career, Flair won dozens of championship belts and was known as "the Dirtiest Player in the Game." Wrestling's unique form of "sports entertainment" relies on creating drama, in part by exposing how heroes can become villains and vice versa. So, while many fans loved to hate Flair's self-characterization as a "limousine-riding, Learjet-flying, wheeling-dealing, kiss-stealing, love-making, heart-breaking son-of-a-gun," he also stood for individualism against more conformist and corporatist opponents, like the dauntingly named New World Order.

→ CAPTAIN AMERICA SHIELD

Strengthened by an experimental serum and armed with a star-spangled shield, Captain America first emerged in comic books battling Nazis and reveling in the unambiguous patriotism of World War II. But in the superhero movies of the 2010s, he wrestles with a United States government so obsessed with terrorism that it compromises civil liberties. Played by Chris Evans, who carries this version of the famous shield in the 2013 movie *Captain America: The Winter Soldier*, Captain America must choose between allegiance to the nation's government and devotion to its ideals.

↘ EUGEN SANDOW DUMBBELL

Eugen Sandow became the first celebrity bodybuilder in the 1890s, performing his nearly nude strongman act before titillated throngs. While critics fretted about declining virility in a world of convenient machinery and staid white-collar work, Sandow offered a solution to modern men: you too could have bulging muscles, if you read his *Magazine of Physical Culture*, followed his instructions in *Physical Strength and How to Obtain It*, and trained with this licensed dumbbell.

↑ Eugen Sandow, ca. 1894.

→ GEORGE REEVES COSTUME FROM
THE ADVENTURES OF SUPERMAN

When George Reeves wore this costume in 1952 and became television's first superhero, the United States was deeply invested in a cold war of ideas against the Soviet Union's communism. Television and radio programs highlighted American individualism, innocence, and resolve—attributes embodied by both Superman and his bespectacled alter ego, Clark Kent. Although Superman spent his time fighting crooks, not communists, the show's telling tagline celebrated the "never-ending battle for truth, justice, and the American Way."

"YOU'VE ALWAYS HAD THE POWER, MY DEAR"

In 1979 the National Museum of American History received two red-sequined pumps worn by Judy Garland in the role of Dorothy in the 1939 film *The Wizard of Oz*. Since their arrival at the museum, the magical shoes, clicked together at the heels three times by Dorothy to transport herself home near the end of the film, had been on constant public view. In 2016 I was part of a team asked to study them in order to ensure that they could continue to be displayed. Every sequin, stitch, and bead was examined and cleaned under magnification, using a range of scientific techniques and tools—a task that took hundreds of hours.

We quickly learned that the museum's shoes were not a matching pair. The right shoe was labeled inside with "Judy Garland #1" and the left with "Judy Garland #6." Their silhouettes and heel shapes differed because they were different sizes and models of the Innes Shoe Company's standard white faille pump, which had been dyed red by costumers for the movie and then overlaid with a fine red mesh onto which thousands of red sequins were sewn. The bows on the slippers were also dissimilar in shape, and the left shoe had cylindrical bugle beads, while the right featured hexagonal ones. The right bow also had several clear beads that stood out during examination. They were attached with a different thread from the rest and coated in

↑ Sequins attached to the left ruby slipper belonging to the Smithsonian, photographed at 60x magnification that shows their aged condition.

red cellulose nitrate paint, suggesting repairs made by the costumers.

Fans and collectors have long known that there were several pairs of ruby slippers: some are in private hands; one is held by the Academy Museum of Motion Pictures; and another pair was brazenly stolen from the Judy Garland Museum in Grand Rapids, Minnesota, one night in 2005. The theft remained unsolved and often came up in conversation as our team conserved the Smithsonian's slippers.

Then one day in the summer of 2018 I received an unexpected phone call—from the FBI. The agent said they had recovered a pair of ruby slippers. Knowing we had been working on a similar pair, he offered to bring them to the museum to be examined.

When we opened the box he had brought to the museum, the silhouette of the shoes, the color of the sequins, and the felt on the soles (applied to dampen the sound of dancing on the wooden stage sets) were all immediately familiar. A silent excitement filled the room as we examined the shoes under microscopes, noting the similarities to the museum's pair. The sequins, with layers of gelatin, silver, and red cellulose nitrate, showed the same deterioration from use and age. And when I moved the microscope over the bow, a clear bead with red paint jumped out at me. The left shoe on the recovered pair had the same replacement beads in the bow as our right shoe. The examination revealed other similarities, too, in construction and materials. It was clear that the museum's slippers had found their original partners, even though the interior number labels had been removed from the recovered pair.

For a moment, we rematched the slippers and photographed them together for the first time in decades. Then the recovered pair went back to the FBI, where they remain as evidence: the thief still has not been caught. But just as the Good Witch of the North reminded Dorothy that she had always possessed the power to use the slippers, so the power of conservation science has identified one pair and safeguarded another, which visitors may again see on display in *Entertainment Nation*.

Dawn Wallace

← Ruby slippers worn by Judy Garland as Dorothy Gale in *The Wizard of Oz*, 1939.

→ Poster advertising MGM's 1955 re-release of *The Wizard of Oz*.

TO BE SPOCK

"Live long and prosper."

When *Star Trek* first aired on NBC in the fall television season of 1966, Mr. Spock, the half-human, half-Vulcan science officer, inspired strong public reactions. Appearing devilish to some and heroic to others, Leonard Nimoy's depiction of the character, with his logical demeanor and quizzical visage, got people's attention. Ultimately, the character's distinctive pointed ears came to symbolize not only Spock but *Star Trek* in general.

The Smithsonian collection includes five Spock ear tips, curated by two different museums. The National Museum of American History holds a pair worn by Nimoy during *Star Trek II: The Wrath of Khan* (1982). In addition, the National Air and Space Museum accessioned a single ear tip in 1977, handmade by a fan named Doug Drexler as one of a pair to be worn while dressing up as the character at conventions. Drexler and his business partner sold handmade memorabilia of this kind at the Federation Trading Post, a Star Trek–themed retail store in New York City. (There was also a counterpart in Berkeley, California.) Then, Air and Space received an additional set of ear tips that had been Leonard Nimoy's own keepsakes from the original *Star Trek* television program. During filming in the late 1960s, Nimoy brought the pair home from the set and encased them in a display box. His son Adam offered them to the Smithsonian on behalf of his family in 2021.

These different appendages tells different stories, ranging from movie makeup techniques to fans cosplaying the role of Spock to Nimoy's own connection to the character. But all of them reveal the resonance of the character, which was originally rooted in debates over contemporary social and political issues. In fact,

↓ Multiple participants dressed as Spock at NyCon3, the World Science Fiction Convention in New York City, 1967.

↘ Homemade ear tip fabricated by *Star Trek* fan Doug Drexler in the 1970s, before Drexler went on to produce make-up and visual effects for the franchise.

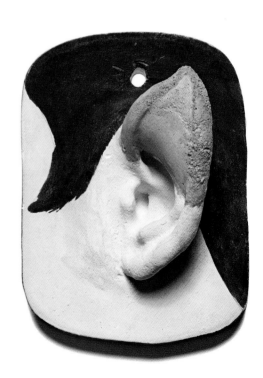

Star Trek's creator, Gene Roddenberry, deliberately positioned the program to engage in those debates.

Roddenberry and Star Trek's other writers often used aliens, whether Spock or the monster-of-the-week variety, to introduce pressing topics, from race relations to law enforcement, the war in Vietnam, gender identity, and sexuality. Extraterrestrial characters enabled audiences to view these issues from a different and more impartial perspective, a technique called defamiliarization.

The half-alien Spock was central to Roddenberry's vision. After NBC initially rejected the original pilot episode of Star Trek as too cerebral (it was a bit dull), Roddenberry rethought and recast almost the entire program, except for the role of Spock. The second pilot had more action and bright uniforms that took advantage of the fairly recent shift to color TV broadcasting. More important, the final crew of the USS Enterprise placed Spock alongside human men and women of different races and nationalities, signaling that the show depicted a future in which the contemporary civil rights and women's movements had secured greater equality on Earth. Nimoy thought "science fiction has a great opportunity to be socially conscious" and frequently encouraged his colleagues in the cast and on the show's writing team to "make a point of it." Roddenberry called Nimoy the "conscience" of the show.

Not everyone embraced that vision. Initially worried that Bible Belt stations might interpret Spock's appearance as demonic, some early NBC publicity photos rounded off Spock's ears. These concerns seemingly abated when bags of fan mail began arriving for Nimoy from across the country. Spock's cool logic offered a new kind of heroic figure.

In 1967, at the twenty-fifth World Science Fiction Convention in New York City, multiple fans, both men and women, dressed as Spock for the masquerade parade. That same year, at NASA's Jet Propulsion Laboratory, managers for the Mariner 5 Venus probe wore paper Vulcan ears while at their consoles. A Boston Globe article dubbed fans' affection for the character Spockmania. Nimoy began to be mobbed at public appearances, even though the program overall was locked into a bad time slot and never enjoyed dominant TV ratings.

During his lifetime, Nimoy's reactions to being cast as the logical alien also evolved. Although the original television program ended in 1969 after just three seasons, its success in syndication—along with fans' passionate dedication—inspired new Star Trek television series, films, conventions, and merchandise for more than fifty years. Yet Nimoy titled his first autobiography I Am Not Spock (1975). He agreed to appear in Star Trek II only if the plot included a death scene for Spock. After a good experience on set, however, he agreed to return for the next film. Over time, he accepted his outsized role in the franchise's popularity. In the end, the character became a through line for Star Trek. Spock appeared in the original and the animated television series, all of the original-cast movies, the series Star Trek: The Next Generation (1987–94), and two of the three reboot movies reimagined by J. J. Abrams. Nimoy titled his autobiography's second volume I Am Spock (1995).

Given Nimoy's personal interest in using his art to highlight social issues, it is perhaps only logical that the Nimoy family's donation of ear tips was made in honor of two organizations addressing public health: the Leonard Nimoy COPD Research Fund at UCLA, and Beit T'Shuvah, a residential addiction-treatment center in Los Angeles.

Margaret A. Weitekamp

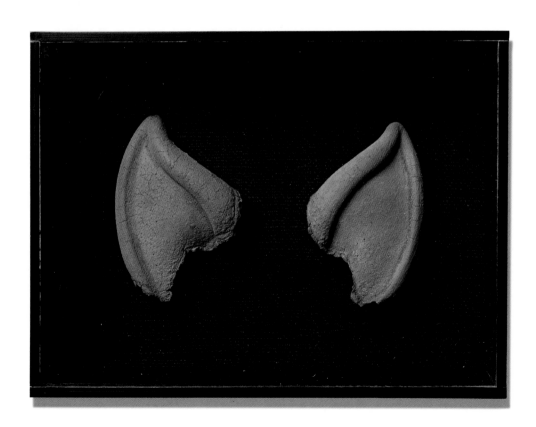

→ Leonard Nimoy saved these ear tips from the original Star Trek television show, keeping them in a box that he built.

MICHELLE YEOH COSTUME FROM STAR TREK: DISCOVERY

In the streaming *Star Trek* series *Discovery*, Sonequa Martin-Green assumes the lead role as parallel-universe-hopping Michael Burnham. Michelle Yeoh plays Philippa Georgiou, who is both a Federation captain and a powerful empress in a mirror universe. *Discovery*'s richly diverse cast epitomizes the franchise's long-held vision of a post-racial society, while its advocacy for gender equity boldly goes where no *Star Trek* series had gone before.

↑ Michelle Yeoh as Philippa Georgiou in *Star Trek: Discovery* in the episode "Terra Firma, Part 1," aired December 10, 2020.

RUTH BADER GINSBURG MTV AWARD

US Supreme Court Justice Ruth Bader Ginsburg's famous dissents made her a feminist icon, and, by the 2010s, a popular-culture celebrity too. First nicknamed "Notorious RBG" after her 2013 dissent in a decision eroding the Voting Rights Act, the moniker linked her to socially conscious rapper and fellow Brooklynite Biggie Smalls, known as the Notorious B.I.G. When the 2019 documentary *RBG* chronicled Ginsberg's sixty-year career, which inspired many Americans—and particularly young women and girls—to fight for equality, MTV viewers responded by voting her "Best Real-Life Hero."

DR. ANTHONY FAUCI MASK

As the deadly COVID-19 pandemic ravaged the nation, major sports leagues stood at the center of a debate over "reopening" the country. Dr. Anthony Fauci, the epidemiologist directing the National Institute of Allergy and Infectious Disease, countered a torrent of misinformation and denial by urging decision-making "based on scientific evidence and public health judgment." Fauci became a hero to those fighting the pandemic and a villain to people ignoring it. But when baseball became the first major sport to resume competition in late July 2020, Fauci threw the ceremonial opening pitch in a stadium empty of fans, wearing a face mask like this one—and then signed this one that he hadn't breathed into.

← Portrait of Ruth Bader Ginsburg by Nelson Shanks, 2012.

→ MORGAN FREEMAN CAP FROM *GLORY*

Hat worn by Morgan Freeman in the role of Sergeant Major John Rawlins in the 1989 Oscar-winning film *Glory*. The movie, which tells the story of the 54th Massachusetts Regiment, the first African American regiment in the Union Army during the US Civil War, was the first major motion picture to highlight the service of the nearly two hundred thousand Black Americans who helped win the war and end slavery despite facing racism and segregation within the military.

← Sketch by artist Kelly Farrah of Black US soldiers on guard duty, used in *The True Story of* Glory *Continues*, a 1991 documentary narrated by Morgan Freeman that continues the history of the 54th Massachusetts Regiment from *Glory*'s end in 1863 to the conclusion of the Civil War in 1865.

ACKNOWLEDGMENTS

Entertainment is like an iceberg. Most of us can only see the gleaming tip that is the performance on stage, on screen, or on the field. But the show requires a massive base of support behind the scenes, from lighting and sound to the ushers who help us find our seats. If all that work is not well orchestrated, the audience will feel like they've run aground instead of admiring the majestic view.

This catalog has been as much a production as any of the performances it documents. Every one of the objects in this volume has been researched, treated by conservators, photographed, and rendered with great care, both in their presentation in these pages and in their daily oversight at the Smithsonian's National Museum of American History.

Hanna BredenbeckCorp and Janet Rockenbaugh are the collections managers who made the magic happen. Designing a process that protected the collection as they prepared objects for the catalog and exhibition has ensured that future generations will be able to enjoy and learn from it.

The *Entertainment Nation* conservation team, led by Dawn Wallace, Janice Ellis, and Sunae Park Evans, and including Philip DePaola, Steph Guidera, Samantha Lee, Tamsin McDonagh, Tia Polidori, Christy Sweet, and Cathy Valentour, surveyed and treated hundreds of artifacts, facilitating the selection of objects for the exhibit and this book. The conservators' work allows you to see the details that reveal the objects' historic significance.

In the end, a catalog is only as powerful as the images of the objects it presents. Staff photographer Jaclyn Nash devised a dramatic, vibrant, and dynamic visual style that animates the collection and illuminates its meanings.

The depth of the collections makes it impossible for just one or two curators to grasp the rich and complicated histories within them, and so contributions from colleagues across the National Museum of American History, National Museum of African American History and Culture, and National Air and Space Museum have enabled this volume to showcase a broad and inclusive range of stories. Among the curatorial team, Eric Jentsch and Ryan Lintelman provided numerous research updates and object descriptions that strengthened this catalog's point: that entertainment has both reflected and shaped the history of the United States. Howard Morrison played a central role in drafting exhibition labels and language that translated to many entries in this catalog. Rebecca Kokinda provided critical support as the museum's Chief of Project Management and Editorial Services. Anthea Hartig, Elizabeth MacMillan Director of the National Museum of American History, has been a steadfast advocate for both the catalog and the exhibit during the turbulent times of the COVID-19 pandemic.

Finally, the team at Smithsonian Books embraced the challenge of working with our cast of dozens and our desire to share as much of the collections as possible. Carolyn Gleason, Jaime Schwender, Julie Huggins, Erika Bűky, Miko McGinty, and the rest of the publication crew developed a layout to match the energy of the photography and scoured vast repositories for images that showed the collections in action, while also scouring our prose to make it clearer and more purposeful.

Both the *Entertainment Nation* exhibition and this catalog were supported by the generosity of Dagmar Dolby, the Tom and Karen Rutledge Family Foundation, A+E Networks, American Cruise Lines, Linda and Mike Curb, the Hollywood Foreign Press Association, Andry and Anya Shiva, and Barry and Wendy Meyer. Additional support was provided by Dolby Laboratories, Inc., the William Randolph Hearst Foundation, the Jane Henson Foundation, Don and Maggie Buchwald, Vin and Erica Di Bona, Kiki Ramos Gindler and David Gindler, Google Arts and Culture, and Enrique and Alejandra Segura.

Unlike the credits in a movie, the names on this page will stay up. Deservedly so, because without them this exhibit and catalog would never have emerged.

YANKEE STADIUM TICKET BOOTH

In 1923, the New York Yankees built a grand new ballpark in the Bronx, made possible by the popularity and success that followed the club's 1919 acquisition of Babe Ruth, whose home-run hitting forever changed the game. Like other urban stadiums built during this era, the "House that Ruth Built" was also an important public venue. Visitors passed by this ticket booth to attend concerts, rallies, and religious services as well as sporting events.

REFERENCES

Introduction

Bernard, C. T. Letter to Smithsonian Institution. October 17, 1986. *A Nation of Nations* Exhibition Records, Smithsonian Institution Archives 17-063.

Clague, Mark. *O Say Can You Hear? A Cultural Biography of the Star-Spangled Banner.* New York: Norton, 2022.

Cohen, Kenneth. *They Will Have Their Game: Sporting Culture and the Making of the Early American Republic.* Ithaca, NY: Cornell University Press, 2017.

Collier, Hatty. "This is Why NFL Players are Kneeling." *Evening Standard* (UK), September 25, 2017.

Cross, Gary. *Consumed Nostalgia: Memory in the Age of Fast Capitalism.* New York: Columbia University Press, 2015.

Curran, Kathleen. "Displaying Cultural History: The Smithsonian Institution and the World's Fairs." In *Meet Me at the Fair: A World's Fair Reader*, ed. Laura Hollengreen, 31–37. Pittsburgh: ETC Press, 2015.

Curti, Merle. Letter to Harold K. Skramstad. September 3, 1972. Smithsonian Institution Archives 17-063.

Feagler, Dick. *Cleveland Press* clipping, February 16, 1980.

Ferris, Marc. *Star-Spangled Banner: The Unlikely Story of America's National Anthem.* Baltimore: Johns Hopkins University Press, 2014.

Galindo, Brian. "Exclusive Photos from Cyndi Lauper's 'She's So Unusual' Cover Shoot." Buzzfeed, April 15, 2004.

Green, Emma. "The Feisty Feminism of 'Girls Just Want to Have Fun,' 30 Years Later." *The Atlantic*, April 1, 2014.

Hughes, Ellen Roney. Memorandum on closing *A Nation of Nations.* September 5, 1991. Smithsonian Institution Archives 17-063.

Hughes, Ellen Roney. "The Unstifled Muse: The *All in the Family* Exhibit and Popular Culture at the National Museum of American History." In *Exhibiting Dilemmas: Issues of Representation at the Smithsonian*, ed. Amy Henderson and Adrienne Kaeppler, 157–75. Washington, DC: Smithsonian, 1997.

Hunt, Darnell, Ana-Christina Ramón, Michael Tran, et. al. "Hollywood Diversity Report 2021." Los Angeles: UCLA College of Social Sciences, 2021. https://socialsciences.ucla.edu/hollywood-diversity-report-2021/.

Koski, Genevieve. "In Times Like These, It Can Feel Like Entertainment Doesn't Matter. It Does." *Vox*, November 10, 2016.

McCausland, Phil. "Farm Aid Was Inspired by a Farm Crisis. Now in Its 34th Year, It Faces Another One." *NBC News*, September 21, 2019.

McKelway, John. "A Suggestion or Two for Smithsonian." *Washington Times*, January 25, 1984.

McLellan, Frances E. Letter to Smithsonian Institution. September 20, 1978. Smithsonian Institution Archives 17-063.

Molotsky, Irvin. "Smithsonian Offers Offbeat with a Purpose." *New York Times*, October 19, 1984.

Moyer, Justin W., and Sarah Kaplan. "Cyndi Lauper and the Secret Feminist History of 'Girls Just Want to Have Fun.'" *Washington Post*, April 30, 2015.

"Red Sox Beat Cubs in Initial Battle of World Series." *New York Times,* September 6, 1918.

Shaw, Maureen. "Debra Messing's 2018 Golden Globes Red Carpet Speech Sets Powerful New Precedent." *NBC News*, January 7, 2018.

Smith, James T. III. Letter to Senator John P. Tower, forwarded to Smithsonian Institution. April 12, 1976. Smithsonian Institution Archives 17-063.

Troutman, John W. "Musician José Feliciano Shook Up a Baseball Tradition at Age 23." O Say Can You See, National Museum of American History blog, October 9, 2018. https://americanhistory.si.edu/blog/feliciano.

Yahr, Emily. "In Defense of Escapism." *Washington Post*, July 26, 2017.

Harmony and Discord: Introduction

Rosenberg, Michael. "Ibtihaj Muhammad Didn't Need a Medal to Leave Her Mark on U.S., Olympics." *Sports Illustrated*, August 8, 2016.

Aloha Blues

"Elizabeth Cotten: Master of American Folk Music." Smithsonian Folkways Recordings. https://folkways.si.edu/elizabeth-cotten-master-american-folk/music/article/smithsonian, accessed April 26, 2022.

Imada, Adria L. "'Aloha 'Oe': Settler Colonial Nostalgia and the Genealogy of a Love Song." *American Indian Culture and Research Journal* 37, no. 2 (June 2013): 35–52.

Ratcliffe, Philip R. *Mississippi John Hurt: His Life, His Times, His Blues.* Jackson: University Press of Mississippi, 2011.

Seeger, Mike. "A 'Freight Train' Picker: Elizabeth Cotten." Folklife, September 20, 2016. https://folkways.si.edu/elizabeth-cotten-master-american-folk/music/article/smithsonian.

Stillman, Amy K. "History Reinterpreted in Song: The Case of the Hawaiian Counterrevolution." *Hawaiian Journal of History* 23 (1989): 1–30.

Troutman, John W. *Kīkā Kila: How the Hawaiian Steel Guitar Changed the Sound of Modern Music.* Chapel Hill: University of North Carolina Press, 2016.

Brass Band *Sonido*

Alamillo, Jose. *Making Lemonade out of Lemons: Mexican American Labor and Leisure in a California Town, 1880–1960.* Chicago: University of Illinois Press, 2006.

Gonzalez, Gilbert G. "Labor and Community: The Camps of Mexican Citrus Pickers in Southern California." *Western Historical Quarterly* 22, no. 3, (August 1991): 289–312.

McBane, Margo. "Whitening a California Citrus Company Town: Racial Segregation at the Limoneira Company and Santa Paula, 1893–1919." *Race/Ethnicity: Multidisciplinary Global Contexts* 4, no. 2 (Winter 2010): 211–33.

Pena, Manuel. *The Mexican American Orquesta: Music, Culture, and the Dialect of Conflict.* Austin: University of Texas Press, 1999.

Pena, Manuel. *Musica Tejana: The Cultural Economy of Artistic Transformations.* College Station: Texas A&M University Press, 1999.

Costume for Tevye from *Fiddler on the Roof*

Solomon, Alisa. *Wonder of Wonders: A Cultural History of* Fiddler on the Roof. New York: Picador, 2013.

Incarceration Camp Baseball and Mitt

Staples, Bill. *Kenichi Zenimura: Japanese American Baseball Pioneer.* Jefferson, NC: McFarland, 2011.

Basketball Awarded to Bill Russell

Russell, Bill. "Bill Russell's Hope for America: That This Time Will Be Different." *Boston Globe Magazine*, June 16, 2020.

"We Just Have to Come Together"

Moss, Randy. Artifact donation interview with Kenneth Cohen, 8 June 2019.

Reid, Jason. "Randy Moss: 'We've Got to Put the Attention on the Right Things.'" *The Undefeated*, August 9, 2018.

Schad, Tom. "Randy Moss Describes Hate Mail He Received after Wearing Controversial Tie at HOF Induction." *USA Today*, August 9, 2018.

The Meaning of Making Everyone Dance

Henry, Zoe. "How Tragedy Inspired Entrepreneur and DJ Steve Aoki to Innovate." Inc., November 11, 2015. www.inc.com/zoe-henry/tragedy-inspired-steve-aoki.html.

Loza, Steven. *Tito Puente and the Making of Latin Music*. Urbana: University of Illinois Press, 1999.

"Steve Aoki." The American Scene, National Museum of American History, February 10, 2018, updated August 2018. https://americanhistory.si.edu/american-scene/steve-aoki.

Broadcasting Remaps Boundaries

Acosta, Teresa Palomo. "KCOR." Texas State Historical Association, Handbook of Texas, updated July 15, 2020. www.tshaonline.org/handbook/entries/kcor.

Allen, Craig. *Univision, Telemundo and the Rise of Spanish-Language Television in the United States.* Gainesville: University of Florida Press, 2020.

Léon, Arnoldo de. *They Called Them Greasers: Anglo Attitudes toward Mexicans in Texas, 1821–1900*. Austin: University of Texas Press, 2010.

Martinez, Monica Muñoz. *Injustice Never Leaves You: Anti-Mexican Violence in Texas.* Cambridge, MA: Harvard University Press, 2018.

"Mex-Slanted San Antone Station Readying Bow," *Variety*, May 25, 1955.

"San Antone Preps 1st Spanish-Language TV." *Variety*, May 26, 1954.

Wilkinson, Kenton T. *Spanish-Language Television in the United States: Fifty Years of Development.* New York: Routledge, 2016.

Los Suns Jersey

Witz, Billy. "'Los Suns' Join Protest, Then Stop Spurs." *New York Times*, May 5, 2010.

Miss Representation

Rivas, Mekita. "Ha Truong on the 'Crazy Rich Asians' Inspired Dress She Made for Her Daughter." *Teen Vogue*, August 18, 2018.

Yamato, Jen. "Constance Wu's 'Crazy Rich Asians' Dress Heads to Smithsonian Museum." *Los Angeles Times*, May 15, 2019.

Prince's Guitar

Murphy, Bill. "Dave Rusan: Building Prince's Cloud Guitar." Premier Guitar, June 10, 2016. www.premierguitar.com/articles/24199-dave-rusan-building-princes-cloud-guitar.

Petrusich. Amanda. "Here's the Guitar That Prince Revolutionized Music With in 'Purple Rain.'" *Smithsonian*, October 2019.

Woodland, John, and Gerald Ronning. "The Origin of Prince's Cloud Guitar." *Fretboard Journal*, May 2020.

Widening One's Scope

Landsberg, Alison. *The Transformation of American Remembrance in the Age of Mass Culture.* New York: Columbia University Press, 2004.

Merritt, Russell. "Nickelodeon Theaters, 1905–1914: Building an Audience for the Movies." In *The American Film Industry*, ed. Tino Balio, 59–82. Madison: University of Wisconsin Press, 1976.

Musser, Charles. *The Emergence of Cinema: The American Screen to 1907.* Berkeley: University of California Press, 1990.

Comedy Is Tragedy Reversed

Frick, John W. *Uncle Tom's Cabin on the American Stage and Screen.* New York: Palgrave Macmillan, 2012.

Lear, Norman. "As I Read How Laura Saw Archie." *New York Times*, October 10, 1971.

Tan, Eduard Sioe-Hao. "Entertainment is Emotion: The Functional Architecture of the Entertainment Experience." *Media Psychology* 11, no. 1 (Spring 2008): 28–51.

"Uncle Tom's Cabin," *Barre Evening Telegram* (VT), August 21, 1900.

Vidmar, Neil, and Milton Rokeach. "Archie Bunker's Bigotry: A Study in Selective Perception and Exposure." *Journal of Communication* 24, no. 1 (Winter 1974): 36–47.

Mae West Figurine

Anthony, Carl Sferrazza. "She Was No Angel, Thank Goodness." *Washington Post*, August 17, 1993.

Charlie McCarthy Ventriloquist Dummy

Craig, Steve. "Out of Eden: The Legion of Decency, the FCC, and Mae West's 1937 Appearance on *The Chase & Sanborn Hour*." *Journal of Radio Studies* 13, no. 2 (2006): 232–48.

Harlem Globetrotters Uniform

Thomas, Damion. "Around the World: Problematizing the Harlem Globetrotters as Cold War Warriors." In *Sport: Race, Ethnicity, Identity*, ed. Daryl Adair, 42–55. London: Routledge, 2012.

Thomas, Damion. *Globetrotting: African American Athletes and Cold War Politics.* Urbana: University of Illinois Press, 2012.

Nick Yemana Police Badge, Nameplate, and Coffee Mug

You Don't Know Jack: The Jack Soo Story. Directed by Jeff Adachi. San Francisco: Center for Asian American Media, 2009.

Misty Copeland "Pancaked" Ballet Shoes

Harlow, Poppy, and Dalila-Johari Paul. "Misty Copeland Says the Ballet World Still Has a Race Problem and She Wants to Help Fix That." *CNN*, May 21, 2018.

M*A*S*H Sign

Bruton, Elsa M., Michael R. Harris, Bernice Johnson Reagon, and Carl H. Scheele. M*A*S*H: *Binding Up the Wounds.* Washington, DC: Smithsonian Institution Press, 1983.

Tom Thumb Hat

Lehman, Eric D. *Becoming Tom Thumb: Charles Stratton, P. T. Barnum, and the Dawn of American Celebrity*. Middletown, CT: Wesleyan University Press, 2013.

Singing for Justice, Draped in Courage

Catlin, Roger. "Sweet Honey in the Rock Has Been Making Music, and Taking a Stand, for 43 Years." *Washington Post*, May 13, 2016.

Reagon, Bernice Johnson. Interview conducted by Blackside, Inc., January 23, 1986, for *Eyes on the Prize: America's Civil Rights Years (1954–1965)*. Washington University Libraries, Film and Media Archive, Henry Hampton Collection.

Reagon, Bernice Johnson. "Message from the Founder." https://sweethoneyintherock.org/about/bjr, accessed October 29, 2021.

An Emotional History of Circus Elephants

Angers, Angie. "Ringling Bros. Circus to Return, but Animal-Free." Spectrum News, October 27, 2021. www.baynews9.com/fl/tampa/news/2021/10/27/ringling-bros--circus-returns--but-animal-free.

Animal Defenders International. "Federal Circus Bill: Worldwide Summary." www.federalcircusbill.org/briefings/worldwide-summary, accessed April 26, 2022.

Free, Cathy. "Former Circus Elephants Just Arrived at a New Sanctuary." *Washington Post,* May 13, 2021.

Nance, Susan. *Entertaining Elephants: Animal Agency and the Business of the American Circus* Baltimore: Johns Hopkins University Press, 2013.

Rothfels, Nigel. "Why Look at Elephants?," *Worldviews* 9, no. 2 (July 2005): 166–83.

Veronese, Keith. "The Circus Elephant Retirement Home." Gizmodo, January 20, 2012. https://gizmodo.com/the-circus-elephant-retirement-home-5877226.

Wood, Amy Louise. "'Killing the Elephant': Murderous Beasts and the Thrill of Retribution, 1885–1930." *Journal of the Gilded Age and Progressive Era* 11, no. 3 (July 2012): 405–44.

Ivory Billiard Balls

Elephants and U.S. Exhibition at Smithsonian National Museum of American History, 2019–20. https://americanhistory.si.edu /elephants-and-us.

Early Boxing Belt

Adelman, Melvin. *A Sporting Time: New York City and the Rise of Modern Athletics, 1820–1870.* Urbana: University of Illinois Press, 1990.

Pepe: The Limits of Cantinflas

Berg, Charles Ramirez. *Latino Images in Film: Stereotypes, Subversion, Resistance.* Austin: University of Texas Press, 2002.
Pilcher, Jeffery M. *Cantinflas and the Chaos of Mexican Modernity.* Wilmington, DE: Scholarly Resources, 2001.

Jack Calvo Bat and Mariano Rivera Glove

Armour, Mark, and Daniel R. Levitt. *Baseball Demographics, 1947–2016.* Society for American Baseball Research. https://sabr .org/bioproj/topic/baseball-demographics -1947-2016.

Jackie Robinson Signed Baseball and Hazel Scott Record Cover

Lanning, Michael Lee. *The Court-Martial of Jackie Robinson: The Baseball Legend's Battle for Civil Rights during World War II.* Lanham, MD: Stackpole, 2020.

Performing Freedom, Enacting Slavery

Huang, Yunte. *Inseparable: The Original Siamese Twins and Their Rendezvous with American History.* New York: Liverlight, 2018.

William Boucher Jr. Banjo

Smith, Christopher J. *The Creolization of American Culture: William Sidney Mount and the Roots of Blackface Minstrelsy.* Urbana: University of Illinois Press, 2017.

Cultural Resilience: Lydia Mendoza and Selena

Mendoza, Lydia, Chris Strachwitz, and James Nicolopulos. *Lydia Mendoza: A Family Autobiography.* Houston, TX: Arte Público, 1993.
Paredez, Deborah. *Selenidad: Selena, Latinos, and the Performance of Memory.* Durham, NC: Duke University Press, 2009.
Valdivia, Angharad N. *Latinas/os and the Media.* Malden, MA: Polity, 2014.

Jeni LeGon Tap Shoes

Hutchinson, Pamela. "Hooray for Jeni LeGon: The Hollywood Pioneer Who 'Danced Like a Boy.'" *Sight and Sound,* March 8, 2017.

Disney Animator's Desk

Holt, Nathalia. *The Queens of Animation: The Untold Story of the Women Who Transformed the World of Disney and Made Cinematic History.* New York: Back Bay, 2019.
Ito, Roberto. "These Female Animators are Redrawing an Industry's Gender Lines." *Los Angeles Magazine,* August 18, 2017.

This-Ability

Chemers, Michael M. "Mutatis Mutandis: An Emergent Disability Aesthetic in *X-2: X-Men United.*" *Disability Studies Quarterly* 24, no. 1 (Winter 2004).
Jones, Maya A. "The Power of Being Loretta Claiborne." *The Undefeated,* January 2, 2019.
"Loretta Claiborne, Chief Inspiration Officer, Special Olympics." That Made All the Difference podcast. September 30, 2019. https://thatmadeallthedifference.podbean .com/e/loretta-claiborne-chief-inspiration -officer-special-olympics.
Solimando, Jessic. "Buddy Elias: Adaptive Athlete and Mentor." 101Mobility blog. July 22, 2016. https://www.101mobility.com /blog/2016/july/buddy-b1l-elias-adaptive -athlete-and-mentor.

Judy Garland Costume from *The Harvey Girls*

Robinson, Mark A., *The World of Musicals: An Encyclopedia of Stage, Screen, and Song.* Santa Barbara, CA: Greenwood, 2014.

Republic or Empire?

"Declaration of the Anti-Imperialist League." *Anti-Imperialist,* August 20, 1899.
Farber, Stephen. "George Lucas: The Stinky Kid Hits the Big Time." *Film Quarterly* 27, no. 3 (Spring 1974): 2–9.
Kornhaber, Spencer. "Star Wars: A New Droid." *The Atlantic,* August 17, 2016.
McDowell, John C. *Identity Politics in George Lucas' Star Wars.* Jefferson, NC: McFarland, 2016.
"Small Boys Happy; Wild West Here," *Washington Intelligencer,* April 19, 1911.

Dominique Dawes Leotard

Unger, Mike. "Olympian Dominique Dawes Won Gold. Now, She's Giving Back." *Bethesda Magazine,* March 14, 2022.

Janet Guthrie

Martinelli, Michelle R. "Racing Trailblazer Janet Guthrie on Indy 500 and Sexism in Motor Sports." For the Win, May 24, 2019. https:// ftw.usatoday.com/2019/05/indy-500-janet -guthrie-sexism-nascar-motor-sports -espn-qualified.

Kristi Yamaguchi Skates and Dress

Chung, Nicole. "Kristi Yamaguchi, Unlaced." *Shondaland,* January 3, 2018. www .shondaland.com/inspire/a14436692/kristi -yamaguchi-interview.

The Figment of the Fonz

"Fonzie's Jacket." *Lost at the Smithsonian with Aasif Mandvi.* Midroll Media. Podcast. September 26, 2019.

The Secret History of Wonder Woman

Lepore, Jill. *The Secret History of Wonder Woman.* New York: Vintage, 2015.

Dora the Explorer Animation Sketch

Pfeiffer, Sacha. "The Lasting Impact of 'Dora The Explorer.'" *NPR Weekend Edition,* August 10, 2019.

VITASCOPE PROJECTOR

Unlike mutoscopes and kinetoscopes that only one person could peer into, vitascope projectors cast movie images on a screen for audiences to enjoy together. The vitascope's debut in 1896 led to thousands of movie theaters opening across the United States, from small nickelodeons to grander palaces. Battles over censorship and control ensued as cinema provoked tensions between advocacy for social change and resistance to it.

→ Strip of 35mm motion picture negative film showing a sailboat, ca. 1900.

CONTRIBUTORS

SMITHSONIAN CONTRIBUTORS

Center for Folklife and Cultural Heritage

Jeff Place, Archivist

National Air and Space Museum

Margaret A. Weitekamp, Curator and Chair, Space History Department

National Museum of African American History and Culture

Damion Thomas, Sports Curator

National Museum of American History

Hanna BredenbeckCorp, Project Assistant, Division of Cultural and Community Life

Kenneth Cohen, Edward and Helen Hintz Secretarial Scholar and Curator, Divisions of Cultural and Community Life and Political and Military History

Kathleen Franz, Curator, Division of Work and Industry

Theodore S. Gonzalves, Curator, Division of Cultural and Community Life

Lisa Kathleen Graddy, Curator, Division of Political and Military History

Andrea M. Hartig, Elizabeth MacMillan Director

Eric Jentsch, Curator, Division of Cultural and Community Life

Ryan Lintelman, Curator, Division of Cultural and Community life

Melinda Machado, Director, Office of Communications and Marketing

Ashley Olivia Mayor, Curatorial Assistant

Howard Morrison, Director of Education and Interpretation

Crystal Moten, Curator, Division of Work and Industry

Jaclyn Nash, Photographer

Katherine Ott, Curator, Division of Medicine and Science

Shannon Perich, Curator, Division of Work and Industry

Jane Rogers, Curator, Division of Cultural and Community Life

John W. Troutman, Curator, Division of Cultural and Community Life

L. Stephen Velasquez, Curator, Division of Cultural and Community Life

Dawn Wallace, Objects Conservator

Tsione Wolde-Michael, Curator, Division of Political and Military History

OTHER CONTRIBUTORS

Kareem Abdul-Jabbar is an NBA all-time leading scorer, author, and US Cultural Ambassador.

Billie Jean King is a tennis champion and social activist.

Alison Landsberg is a professor in the history and art history department and director of the Center for Humanities Research at George Mason University.

John Legend is a singer, songwriter, actor, and producer.

Jill Lepore is a journalist and the David Woods Kemper '41 Professor of American History at Harvard University.

Aasif Mandvi is an actor, comedian, and writer.

Kathy Peiss is the Roy F. and Jeannette P. Nichols Professor of American History at the University of Pennsylvania.

Ali Wong is a stand-up comedian, writer, and actor.

ILLUSTRATION CREDITS

Unless otherwise noted below, images are from the collections of the Smithsonian's National Museum of American History.

7: Bob Willoughby/Redferns; 9*tr*: Chris Graythen/Getty Images; 12*t*: Steve Granitz/WireImage; 15*l*: *She's So Unusual* album by Cyndi Lauper/Alamy; 16*t*: Michael Ochs Archives/Getty Images; 16*b*: SAUL LOEB/AFP via Getty Images; 17: Library of Congress Prints and Photographs Division; 18: Aaron Sechrist; 19*t*: © HBO/Courtesy: Everett; 23*t*: Vaughn Ridley/Getty Images; 26*t*: The Archambault Family; 27*tl*: © Family of Charmian Reading; 27*tr*: © John Cohen, courtesy L. Parker Stephenson; 29: Museum of Ventura County Research Library and Archives; 30*t*: National Portrait Gallery, Smithsonian Institution, c. 1925; 32*r*: Folger Shakespeare Library; 34: Billy Rose Theatre Division, The New York Public Library. "Bessie Bonehill" New York Public Library Digital Collections; 36*b*: Deborah Feingold/Corbis via Getty Images; 42*l*: Smithsonian Folkways; 42*r*: National Portrait Gallery, Smithsonian Institution, c. 1946–48; 43: Smithsonian Folkways; 45*b*: GAB Archive/Redferns; 46*tr*: © Herman Leonard Photography, LLC; 47*b*: Library of Congress Prints and Photographs Division; 48*b*: National Portrait Gallery, Smithsonian Institution, 1942; 50: National Portrait Gallery, Smithsonian Institution, acquired through the generosity of David C. Ward, 1968; 51: Collection of the Smithsonian National Museum of African American History and Culture; 52*t*: Hal Sweeney/The Boston Globe via Getty Images; 55: Chris Haston/NBC/NBCU Photo Bank via Getty Images; 60*l*: University of Washington Libraries, Special Collections, JWS12918; 62: Chris Graythen/Getty Images; 65*t*: National Portrait Gallery, Smithsonian Institution; acquisition made possible through the Smithsonian Latino Initiatives Pool, administered by the Smithsonian Latino Center, 1984 (printed 2014); 66*t*: Taylor Hill/Getty Images; 71*t*: ROOTS, Levar Burton, 1977, Everett Collection; 72*b*: © Disney+/Courtesy Everett Collection; 78*t*: Library of Congress Prints and Photographs Division; 81*l*: Acey Harper/Getty Images; 82–83: © Sesame Workshop; 83*t*: © Sesame Workshop/Courtesy: Everett Collection; 86: © 1993 Sesame Workshop; 88*r*: Jerry Cooke/Sports Illustrated via Getty Images; 89*r*: AP Photo/Matt York; 90: Billy Rose Theatre Division, The New York Public Library. "Diosa Costello (Bloody Mary replacement) in South Pacific" New York Public Library Digital Collections; 92*b*: Sanja Bucko/© Warner Bros. Pictures/Courtesy Everett Collection; 94*b*: © Newmarket/courtesy Everett Collection; 95*t*: Photograph by Leigh Weiner. National Portrait Gallery, Smithsonian Institution, 1963; 96*t*: Photograph by Ian Logan, 2020; 98: Alex Wong/Getty Images; 103*b*: Michael Ochs Archives/Getty Images; 107*r*: Tim Mosenfelder/Getty Images; 110*t*: Collection of the Smithsonian National Museum of African American History and Culture, gift of Robert and Greta Houston, © Robert Houston; 111*l*: Annie Leibovitz/Trunk Archive; 112: National Portrait Gallery, Smithsonian Institution, January 5, 1861 (date of publication); 116*t*: Tim Mosenfelder/Getty Images; 121*t*: National Portrait Gallery, Smithsonian Institution, gift of Paula Scher/PENTAGRAM, 1995; 112*br*: © Castle Rock Entertainment/courtesy: Everett Collection; 124: CBS via Getty Images; 131: Gary Null/NBCU Photo Bank/NBCUniversal via Getty Images; 132: © Disney; 133*r*: Focus on Sport via Getty Images; 134*t*: ABC Photo Archives/Disney General Entertainment Content via Getty Images; 135*tr*: Patrick Fraser/Contour by Getty Images; 136: Alex Crick/© Netflix/Courtesy: Everett Collection; 140*r*: Getty images; 141*r*: TM and © 20th Century Fox Film Corp; 142: Silver Screen Collection/Getty Images; 146-7: Gift of the Celia Cruz Estate, courtesy of the Celia Cruz Legacy Project; 148: Courtesy Sing It Online; 150*l*: Michael Ochs Archives/Getty Images; 151*r*: Michael Ochs Archives/Getty Images; 156*l*: Gift from the family of Jim Henson; 156*r*: © Disney; 158: National Portrait Gallery, Smithsonian Institution, c. 1915; 163*r*: Caroline Brehman/CQ-Roll Call, Inc via Getty Images;

↑ Bill Nye in costume for *Bill Nye the Science Guy*.

→ BILL NYE COSTUME

During the 1990s, new laws and regulations required television stations to offer a minimum number of hours of weekly programming to meet the "intellectual/cognitive and social/emotional needs" of children. A wave of new shows surfaced in response, including one fast-paced science-education program that drew on comedy sketches and music videos to capture kids' interest. Wearing this lab coat and bow tie from 1993 to 1998, engineer and comedian Bill Nye became Bill Nye the Science Guy in the show of the same name, declaring, "Science rules!"

INDEX

Published by Smithsonian Books

Director: Carolyn Gleason
Senior Editor: Jaime Schwender
Assistant Editor: Julie Huggins
Edited by Erika Bűky
Photo research by Julie Huggins and Amy Pastan

Designed by Rebecca Sylvers, Miko McGinty Inc.
Typeset in ITC Neon, GT America, and Suisse Int'l by Tina Henderson

ITC Neon was designed by Ronné Bonder and Tom Carnase in 1970 and digitized by Julia Ma in 2022 for this catalog.

National Museum of American History

Elizabeth MacMillan Director: Anthea M. Hartig

Publications Team: Kenneth Cohen, John W. Troutman, Jaclyn Nash, and Hanna BredenbeckCorp

Captions: Kenneth Cohen, Lisa Kathleen Graddy, Eric Jentsch, Ryan Lintelman, Ashley Oliva Mayor, Howard Morrison, Emma O'Neill-Dietel, Jane Rogers, John W. Troutman, L. Stephen Velasquez, Margaret A. Weitekamp, Brooke Yung

Smithsonian Contributors: Hanna BredenbeckCorp, Kenneth Cohen, Kathleen Franz, Theodore S. Gonzalves, Lisa Kathleen Graddy, Eric Jentsch, Ryan Lintelman, Melinda Machado, Ashley Oliva Mayor, Howard Morrison, Crystal Moten, Katherine Ott, Shannon Perich, Jeff Place, Jane Rogers, Damion Thomas, John W. Troutman, L. Stephen Velasquez, Dawn Wallace, Margaret A. Weitekamp, Tsione Wolde-Michael

Contributors: Billie Jean King, Alison Landsberg, John Legend, Jill Lepore, Aasif Mandvi, Kathy Peiss, Ali Wong

This book may be purchased for educational, business, or sales promotional use. For information, please write:

Special Markets Department, Smithsonian Books, P.O. Box 37012, MRC 513, Washington, DC 20013

Library of Congress Cataloging-in-Publication Data

Names: National Museum of American History, author. | Cohen, Kenneth, editor. | Troutman, John William, editor.
Title: Entertainment nation : how music, television, film, sports, and theater shaped the United States / edited by Kenneth Cohen and John W. Troutman.
Other titles: How music, television, film, sports, and theater shaped the United States
Description: Washington, DC : Smithsonian Books, [2022] | Catalog of an ever-changing selection from its collection of theater, music, sports, movie and television objects held by the National Museum of American History under the banner of "Entertainment Nation" exhibited since December 2022. | Includes bibliographical references and index. | Summary: "U.S. history gets the star treatment with this essential guide to the Smithsonian's first permanent exhibition on pop culture"—Provided by publisher.
Identifiers: LCCN 2022019744 | ISBN 9781588347244 (hardcover)
Subjects: LCSH: Popular culture—United States—History—Catalogs. | Americana—Catalogs. | Arts and society—United States—Catalogs. | National Museum of American History (U.S.)—Catalogs.
Classification: LCC E169.12 .E58 2022 | DDC 306.0973/074—dc23/eng/20220518
LC record available at https://lccn.loc.gov/2022019744

Printed in China, not at government expense

26 25 24 23 22   1 2 3 4 5

For permission to reproduce illustrations appearing in this book, please correspond directly with the owners of the works, as seen on pages 264–65. Smithsonian Books does not retain reproduction rights for these images individually or maintain a file of addresses for sources.

p. 2: This poster promotes the Woodstock Music and Art Fair, a countercultural festival attended by roughly four hundred thousand people between August 15 and 18, 1969. Some praised the festival as the embodiment of a utopian movement advocating for much-needed "peace and love" as the Vietnam War raged on. Others criticized it as an embrace of antiauthoritarian, hedonistic self-indulgence by out-of-touch, and mostly white, middle-class attendees.